Modern Irish and Scottish Literature

Modern Irish and Scottish Literature

Connections, Contrasts, Celticisms

RICHARD ALAN BARLOW

OXFORD
UNIVERSITY PRESS

Great Clarendon Street, Oxford, OX2 6DP,
United Kingdom

Oxford University Press is a department of the University of Oxford.
It furthers the University's objective of excellence in research, scholarship,
and education by publishing worldwide. Oxford is a registered trade mark of
Oxford University Press in the UK and in certain other countries

First Edition published in 2023

Impression: 1

Published in the United States of America by Oxford University Press
198 Madison Avenue, New York, NY 10016, United States of America

British Library Cataloguing in Publication Data
Data available

Library of Congress Control Number: 2022939690

ISBN 978-0-19-285918-1

DOI: 10.1093/oso/9780192859181.001.0001

Printed and bound by
CPI Group (UK) Ltd, Croydon, CR0 4YY

To Guinevere, Niamh, Clodagh, and Séamus

Acknowledgements

Many thanks to Jacqueline Norton, Karen Raith, Ellie Collins, Emma Varley, Rob Wilkinson, and the rest of the team at Oxford University Press for all their hard work. I would also like to thank the three anonymous scholars who read this for OUP. Taing mhòr to Kate Mathis for reading and commenting on Chapter 2. Go raibh míle maith agaibh to Anne Marie D'Arcy and Nicholas Allen for reading the manuscript at different stages and for providing valuable advice and suggestions. I would like to thank my friends and colleagues, particularly John McCourt, Willy Maley, Niall Whelehan, Shane Darcy (and the rest of the Darcy family in Limerick and Galway), Katherine Ebury, Paul Fagan, Euan Bain, Steven Archibald, Paul Fraser, Laura Pelaschiar, Michelle Witen, Maria-Daniella Dick, Ronan Crowley, Brian Caraher, Lynne and Rob Taplin, Edel Hughes, Javier Santoyo, Chris Trigg, Kate Wakely-Mulroney, Barrie Sherwood, and Tamara Radak. Thanks also to my parents Harry and Judi and my sister Lucy. Thanks to the School of Humanities at Nanyang Technological University for allowing me to take a sabbatical to finish writing this and to Ng Kai for help with the bibliography. My biggest thanks go to my wife Guinevere and my children Séamus, Clodagh, and Niamh.

An early version of Chapter 1 appeared as 'Celticism, ballad transmission, and the schizoid voice: Ossianic fragments in Owenson, Yeats, Joyce, and Beckett' in *Irish Studies Review* 27.4 (2019). A version of Chapter 3 appeared as 'James Joyce and Walter Scott: Incest, Rivers of History, and "old useless papers"' in *Scottish Literary Review* 12.1 (2020). Part of Chapter 4 appeared in Willy Maley and Kirsty Lusk, eds., *Scotland and the Easter Rising* (Edinburgh: Luath Press, 2016). I am grateful to the editors of these publications for permission to reproduce these sections here.

The cover image of this book is reproduced by kind permission of the National Library of Scotland.

Thanks to the University of Strathclyde Archives and Special Collections for permission to quote from the Patrick Geddes Papers.

An excerpt from John Hewitt's 'To a Modern Irish Poet' is reproduced by kind permission of The John Hewitt Society.

Extracts from Hugh MacDiarmid's *Complete Poems Vol. I* are reprinted by kind permission of Carcanet Press, Manchester.

Sorley MacLean's 'Àrd-Mhusaeum na h-Èireann' is reproduced with permission of Birlinn Limited through PLSclear.

Excerpt/s from FINDERS KEEPERS: SELECTED PROSE 1971–2001 by Seamus Heaney. Copyright © 2002 by Seamus Heaney. Reprinted by permission of Farrar, Straus and Giroux. All Rights Reserved.

Excerpts from OPENED GROUND: SELECTED POEMS 1966–1996 by Seamus Heaney. Copyright © 1998 by Seamus Heaney. Reprinted by permission of Farrar, Straus and Giroux. All Rights Reserved.

Excerpts from SWEENEY ASTRAY by Seamus Heaney. Copyright © 1984 by Seamus Heaney. Reprinted by permission of Farrar, Straus and Giroux. All Rights Reserved.

Excerpts from *Sweeney Astray* by Seamus Heaney are also reprinted by permission of Faber and Faber Ltd.

Every reasonable effort has been made to secure permissions for the quotation of literary works. The author will gladly rectify matters if anything has been inadvertently overlooked.

Contents

Abbreviations   xi

   Introduction: Ireland, Scotland, and Celticism   1

1. *Ossian* and Irish literature: Owenson, Yeats, Joyce, Beckett   21

2. Gender, nationality, and Celticism in Gregory and Macleod   43

3. Joyce and Scott: Sex, history, and Celticism   75

4. Scottish Modernism and the Celtic world: MacDiarmid
   and MacLean   93

5. Heaney, the North, and Scotland   120

   Conclusion: Early Celticism/Late Celticism   139

Bibliography   151
Index   169

Abbreviations

CL I   Yeats, W.B. *The Collected Letters of W.B. Yeats Volume I: 1865–1895* edited by John Kelly. Oxford: Clarendon Press, 1986.

CL II   Yeats, W.B. *The Collected Letters of W.B. Yeats Volume II: 1896–1900* edited by Warwick Gould, John Kelly, and Dierdre Toomey. Oxford: Clarendon Press, 1997.

CP   MacDiarmid, Hugh. *Complete Poems Vol. I* edited by Michael Grieve and W.R. Aitken. Manchester: Carcanet, 2017.

D   Joyce, James. *Dubliners*. New York: Viking Press, 1967.

FK   Heaney, Seamus. *Finders Keepers: Selected Prose, 1971–2001*. London: Faber and Faber, 2002.

FW   Joyce, James. *Finnegans Wake*. New York: Viking Press, 1939. Citations for *Finnegans Wake* are made in the standard fashion, i.e. page number followed by line number.

IMJJ   MacDiarmid, Hugh. *In Memoriam James Joyce: A Vision of World Language*. Glasgow: William Maclellan, 1955.

JJ   Ellmann, Richard. *James Joyce*. Rev. ed. New York: Oxford University Press, 1982.

OCPW   Joyce, James. *Occasional, Critical, and Political Writings*, edited by Kevin Barry. Oxford: Oxford University Press, 2000.

P   Joyce, James. *A Portrait of the Artist as a Young Man*. New York: The Viking Press, 1964.

RT I   MacDiarmid, Hugh. *The Raucle Tongue: Hitherto Uncollected Prose Vol. I* edited by Angus Calder, Glen Murray, and Alan Riach. Manchester: Carcanet, 1996.

RT II   MacDiarmid, Hugh. *The Raucle Tongue: Hitherto Uncollected Prose Vol. II* edited by Angus Calder, Glen Murray, and Alan Riach. Manchester: Carcanet, 1997.

RT III   MacDiarmid, Hugh. *The Raucle Tongue: Hitherto Uncollected Prose Vol. III* edited by Angus Calder, Glen Murray, and Alan Riach. Manchester: Carcanet, 1998.

SA   Heaney, Seamus. *Sweeney Astray: A Version from the Irish*. Derry: Field Day, 1983.

U   Joyce, James. *Ulysses*. The corrected text, edited by Hans Walter Gabler. New York: Random House, 1986. Citations for *Ulysses* are made in the usual way: episode number followed by line number.

Introduction

Ireland, Scotland, and Celticism

In *The Trembling of the Veil* (1922), W.B. Yeats tells of his encounters with the occultist and self-styled Scotsman Samuel Liddell MacGregor Mathers.[1] Aside from his apparent gifts for prophecy and clairvoyance, Mathers was also an enthusiast for Scottish Highland culture, or certain visions of it. Mathers seems to have been a slightly prickly individual and on one occasion Yeats drew his ire by doubting the authenticity of James Macpherson's *Ossian* poems:

> Once when I questioned [the authenticity of] Ossian, he got into a rage—what right had I to take sides with the English enemy?—and I found that for him the eighteenth-century controversy still raged. At night he would dress himself in Highland dress, and dance the sword dance, and his mind brooded upon the ramifications of clans and tartans. Yet I have at moments doubted whether he had seen the Highlands....[2]

Macpherson's *Ossian*, the subject of the disagreement between the two men, is the basis of literary Celticism. *Ossian* is also a hugely important set of texts in the overall development of Irish and Scottish literature. The publication of Macpherson's *Ossian*, beginning with *Fragments of Ancient Poetry, Collected in the Highlands of Scotland, and Translated from the Galic or Erse Language* in 1760, was a pivotal event in the development of the English-language literatures of Scotland and Ireland. In addition to being the work that

---

[1] Mathers, a founder member of the Hermetic Order of the Golden Dawn, was from London and was assigned the name Samuel Liddell at birth. However, he identified as Scottish and claimed, perhaps spuriously, Highland ancestry. According to Foster, Yeats 'probably met Mathers in the Reading Room of the British Library after 1887' (Foster, *Yeats I*, 104). Yeats and Mathers met on a number of occasions in Paris in the mid-1890s. It is not clear from *The Trembling of the Veil* when exactly the meeting described above took place, but it was probably in February 1894. See Finneran, 543.
[2] Yeats, *Collected Works III*, 257. The terms 'Ossian' and 'Macpherson's Ossian' are used here to denote the totality of Macpherson's Ossianic output, including *Fragments of Ancient Poetry, Collected in the Highlands of Scotland and Translated from the Galic or Erse Language* (1760); *Fingal, an Ancient Epic Poem in Six Books, together with Several Other Poems composed by Ossian, the Son of Fingal, translated from the Galic Language* (1761); and *Temora* (1763).

Modern Irish and Scottish Literature: Connections, Contrasts, Celticisms. Richard Alan Barlow, Oxford University Press.
© Richard Alan Barlow 2023. DOI: 10.1093/oso/9780192859181.003.0001

introduced the tone of Romanticism,[3] Macpherson's poems inspired and influenced countless Irish and Scottish texts over the following centuries (including works that were written as a reaction against them). While the *Ossian* controversy had largely died down by the nineteenth century—Mathers notwithstanding—literary Celticism has had a very long and varied existence. Mutated forms of Celticism survived beyond the era of Yeats and Mathers and well into the twentieth century. Varieties of Celticism also attracted key figures of nineteenth- and twentieth-century Irish and Scottish culture such as Sydney Owenson, Walter Scott, Augusta Gregory, Fiona Macleod, James Joyce, Hugh MacDiarmid, and Seamus Heaney. This book traces Irish and Scottish literary engagements with Celticism, from the era of Romanticism, through the Celtic Revival(s) and the Irish and Scottish Revivals more broadly,[4] within Modernism, and into the contemporary era. An analysis of Irish and Scottish Celticisms is carried out here as part of a comparative study of the modern literatures of Ireland and Scotland.

Since Macpherson's *Ossian* poems can be thought of as 'belonging' to both Ireland and Scotland (as Scottish texts but largely based on originally Irish stories), and since they also initiated literary Celticism, it makes sense to think about the development of writing in both countries during the modern period in relation to the central theme of the Celtic, while also considering the processes in which the literature of Scotland has influenced Irish writing and vice versa. This text offers such an examination, within the context of the relatively new field of Irish-Scottish studies. This discipline has developed in recent decades, especially after Scottish devolution and the peace process in the north of Ireland,[5] alongside a devolved approach to the history and culture of the Atlantic archipelago and a movement away from Anglocentrism within historical and cultural studies. The work of historian J.G.A. Pocock, especially his text *The Discovery of Islands*, has been central to this new approach.

In *The Discovery of Islands*, Pocock suggests that 'British history' 'has in the past denoted nothing much more than "English history" with occasional transitory additions,'[6] adding that 'there was, and still is, no "British history" in the sense of the self-authenticated history of a self-perpetuating polity or

---

[3] See Crawford, 'Post-Cullodenism', 18, Mercier, 230, and Stafford, 'Romantic', 27.

[4] NB: This text refers to the Celtic Revivals of Ireland and Scotland (and hence uses the terms 'Irish Celtic Revival' and 'Scottish Celtic Revival' to differentiate between these two phenomena) as well as to the broader cultural revivals of the two nations (i.e. the Irish Revival and the Scottish Revival, with the latter including the 'Scottish Literary Renaissance'). In both Ireland and Scotland, a Celtic-focused revival formed an initial stage of a larger cultural revival.

[5] See Longley, 8.   [6] Pocock, 77.

culture. The term must be used to denote a multiplicity of histories, written by or (more probably) written about a multiplicity of kingdoms and other provinces.[7] Part of Pocock's multiplicity of histories is his awareness of a 'Celtic, oceanic and extra-European world' to the west of England during the period of the consolidation of the Scottish kingdom.[8] Within this Celtic world, there are particularly strong similarities between Scotland and Ireland, in the present day as in the ancient past. As Ray Ryan has noted,

> Scotland and Ireland both have a Gaelic and English linguistic tradition (with Scots a third dimension in Scotland), a Catholic and Protestant sectarian conflict, urbanized centres, and benighted rural hinterlands; and linked to this last point, the creation of a mystique of Irishness and Scottishness traceable to these depopulated zones. In both countries, an Act of Union with the British state still remains contested.[9]

Following the Roman era of European history, important links between Ireland and Scotland continued to develop in the Medieval period. As Murray Pittock reminds us, 'until at least the twelfth century, "Scotus" was a term indicative of either Scots or Irish nationality'.[10] The formation of the Scottish nation began with the crossing of an Irish group known to the Romans as the 'Scoti' and their gradual amalgamation with the indigenous Picts. During the Middle Ages, areas of Ireland and Scotland spoke closely related languages (Scottish Gaelic developed out of Old Irish and both are part of the Q-Celtic or Goidelic group of Celtic languages) and shared what we now refer to as early Irish literature, including the Fenian and Ulster Cycles. According to Edna Longley, 'during the high bardic period (c. 1200–1600), literary

---

[7] Ibid., 75.

[8] Ibid., 31. This Celtic world is 'extra-European' since the Roman empire did not 'effectively penetrate to all the oceanic or Atlantic regions of the archipelago, and the second-largest island [was] not directly affected by Roman government' (Ibid., 30).

[9] Ryan, 10. See also: 'Even on the most superficial examination, it [is] clear that both countries have been profoundly affected by a similar geography, by a Celtic heritage, and by a history of close political and economic links with England' (Cullen and Smout, v). However, as Ryan notes, the Republic of Ireland is 'a state that does not correspond with the historically defined nation' while Scotland is currently a 'stateless nation' (Ryan, 12).

[10] Pittock, *Celtic Identity*, 15. See also: 'in 1004…the Irish hero Brian Boru was described as "imperator Scotorum". The Scots repaid this compliment by deriving their royal line from Irish roots: the Scottish crown's descent from Irish kings, though less emphasized as the Middle Ages progressed, was an important indicator of difference from England and Wales, and indeed betokened a continuing consciousness of cultural alliance with Ireland: the Scottish kingdom was born of Irish immigration. When Bruce appealed to Irish leaders as representatives of "our common people", "*nostro nacio*", he was simply recognizing the continuing political and cultural significance of this fact' (Pittock, *Celtic Identity*, 15).

connection was constant: a "supra-national" learned class shared a common literary language and trained in the same schools. By the same token, the collapse of the Irish bardic order "deeply splintered" the Gaelic world.[11] In the early modern period, Irish troops served in Scottish armies, powerful families held land in both countries, and large numbers of Irish students attended university at Glasgow and Edinburgh.[12] Later, the plantation of Lowland Scots (and English people) into the north of Ireland in the seventeenth century created what Pocock has called a 'settler nation' and an 'anti-nation' within Ireland.[13] In the post-Famine period, large-scale emigration went in the opposite direction, with Irish labourers seeking work in industrial centres such as Glasgow. As R.F. Foster has noted, 'By 1851, 6.7 per cent of the entire Scottish population was Irish-born, a percentage that rose to over 18 per cent in Dundee and Glasgow.'[14] In addition to mass emigration from Ireland, the Great Famine of 1845 to 1852 caused a steep decline in the Irish language. Gaelic faced similar deterioration in the Highlands and Islands of Scotland, especially after the clearances of the eighteenth and nineteenth centuries.

Given the close historical and cultural links between Ireland and Scotland, it is unsurprising that the literatures of the two nations should be intertwined. As Ryan notes, Ireland and Scotland 'share an oppressive relation to the English literary tradition which was at least partly responsible for the ideological conviction held by Pearse and Yeats, MacDiarmid and Scott, that a community existed that had to be recovered and restored.'[15] Irish-Scottish literary connections have been studied in texts such as Ryan's *Ireland and Scotland: Literature and Culture, State and Nation, 1966–2000* (2002), McIlvanney and Ryan's edited collection *Ireland and Scotland: Culture and Society, 1700-2000* (2005), Murray Pittock's *Scottish and Irish Romanticism* (2008), and Peter Mackay, Edna Longley, and Fran Brearton's volume *Modern Irish and Scottish Poetry* (2011). As McIlvanney and Ryan comment in the introduction to their text,

> Scotland – subject to so many of the same linguistic, religious, political and cultural pressures as Ireland, caught up in its own obsessive engagement with England and Britain, and marked both by a breach with its Gaelic past and a philosophical and economic modernization around

---

[11] Longley, 10.
[12] See Pittock, *Scottish and Irish Romanticism*, 15 and Trumpener, 'Ireland, Scotland, and the politics of form', 166.
[13] Pocock, 33.   [14] Foster, *Modern Ireland*, 368.   [15] Ryan, 10.

metropolitan markets – provides a compelling comparative context for Irish culture and society.[16]

The literary links explored in the aforementioned texts, and in Irish-Scottish studies more broadly, are too numerous to be mentioned extensively here. However, some of the most important are the relationship between the traditional cultures of the Irish and Scottish Gaelic languages (the shared Fenian stories, for example),[17] the connections between Irish and Scottish Jacobite poetry, the influence of Maria Edgeworth's regional novels on Walter Scott's historical fiction and national tales, Robert Burns' reception in the north of Ireland, Thomas Carlyle's impact on the development of the Irish Revival, and James Joyce's interest in Scottish history, literature, and philosophy. One of the most important and long-standing interfaces between the literary cultures of Ireland and Scotland is the discourse of Celticism. Since this discourse is important to both literary traditions, this book will study modern Irish and Scottish literature within the context of Celticism.

Within the Atlantic archipelago, there is a persistent idea that Ireland, Scotland, and Wales are qualitatively different to England, that they are inherently and permanently 'Celtic' in spite of modern realities, and that nations of the 'Celtic Fringe' (a term which places England at the centre and places the 'Celtic nations' at the periphery) share some vague spiritual or racial bond.[18] As Barry Cunliffe writes in *The Ancient Celts*, 'The Celt as "other" living in the wild extremities of Atlantic Europe is a metaphor still very much alive today'.[19] The use of this term as a way to draw Ireland, Scotland, and Wales together happens despite a lack of evidence to suggest a racial link between the modern 'Celtic nations'. Furthermore, no modern nation could be considered purely or predominantly Celtic in terms of everyday language, let alone

---

[16] McIlvanney and Ryan, 13.

[17] Fenian literature is 'a versatile and long-lived tradition manifesting in a number of forms over the centuries, from medieval and early modern prose-sagas and poetry down to oral material collected in Ireland and Gaelic Scotland over the last two hundred years' Williams, Mark, 199).

[18] Of the nations of the 'Celtic Fringe' of the Atlantic archipelago, this book focuses on Ireland and Scotland in order to follow the development of a series of literary exchanges and connections that begins with the publication of Macpherson's *Ossian*. Also, many of the texts studied here—or sections of those texts—focus specifically on Irish-Scottish links (such as Sydney Owenson's *The Wild Irish Girl*, Hugh MacDiarmid's *To Circumjack Cencrastus* and *In Memoriam James Joyce*, Seamus Heaney's *Sweeney Astray* and 'Sweeney Redivivus') or were produced within a loose network of Irish and Scottish writers (such as the texts of Augusta Gregory and Fiona Macleod). Some of these texts include references to Wales (such as *In Memoriam James Joyce*) but these are not as obviously foregrounded in the way that Irish-Scottish connections are.

[19] Cunliffe, 22. Indeed, claims to Celtic ethnicity and identity also occur beyond Atlantic Europe in places like Italy and the USA and have, in recent years, been linked to far-right politics. See Hague et al.

through what James Joyce called 'Celtic blood'.[20] Indeed, there was never a single European 'Celtic' race even in ancient times. The notion that Ireland, Scotland, and Wales are essentially Celtic, and that they are part of a racial family, has strong connections with the supranational culture of Celticism, 'a multi-genre, multinational phenomenon' which dates back to the eighteenth century.[21] George Watson has defined Celticism is an 'ideological construction' and 'an attempt to create, re-create or assert a cultural identity for the people of Ireland, Scotland and Wales which will distinguish them from the majority inhabitants of the British Isles [sic], the English'.[22] Celticism 'may be generated internally; or imposed from the centre externally, as may be seen to this day in the common and contentious designation of these three nations as "the Celtic Fringe"'.[23]

In the ancient world, the first reference to the Celts appears in the work of the Greek geographer Hecataeus of Miletus in the sixth century BCE.[24] In the fourth and third centuries BCE,

> the Celtic stereotype was to acquire its familiar form. They were unrestrained, fearless warriors, irrationally brave in the first onslaught but prone to wild despair if the battle turned against them. Unpredictable and unreliable as allies, they could easily be aroused to battle fury but could quickly become too drunk or too paralysed by superstitious fear to fight. And above all they were barbarians: people of alien behaviour, cruel, and prone to such savagery as human sacrifice and even cannibalism.[25]

In the later work of Poseidonius, a slightly different picture emerges. As Cunliffe has noted, in Poseidonius' *Histories* the Celts were warlike and 'impetuous' but they also lived under the wise rule of the Druids who acted as philosophers and men of science.[26] The term 'Celt' has also been used as a blanket term to cover tribes such as the Gauls and Britons mentioned in Roman documents.[27] Eventually the Celts disappear—for a time—from

---

[20] *OCPW*, 115. 'In March 2015, an article titled "The Fine-Scale Genetic Structure of the British Population" [showed that] there was no common genetic link between the supposed Celtic peoples of Britain and Ireland' (De Barra, 13).
[21] Leerssen, 'Celticism', 20.   [22] Watson, George, 'Aspects', 129.   [23] Ibid., 129.
[24] See Cunliffe, 2.   [25] Cunliffe, 6.   [26] Ibid., 11.
[27] See Leerseen, 1. On the subject of the word 'Celt', Cunliffe observes that 'Classical observers refer to the Continental Celts by a variety of names. The Roman historians writing of the migrations from north of the Alps to the Po valley and beyond called them *Galli*, and this tradition was followed by Polybius, to whom they were *Galatae*, a name also commonly used in other Greek sources. Most of the first-century BC writers, however, realized that these names were interchangeable with the Greek *Keltoi* and Latin *Celtae*' (Cunliffe, 3). However, Rachel Pope has argued that 'Archaeologists trained in the 1960s and 1970s [generalized]. Instead of working to understand texts historically/

history. There is a period from the fourth century until the sixteenth century when

> the world cared little for Celts. The classical texts were largely lost or forgotten, and the universal appeal of Christianity, with its own texts, mythologies, and stereotypes, provided all the models that were required to order behaviour and to inspire origin myths and protohistories. Yet it was Christianity that kept alive a knowledge of the Celts in the manuscript copies of the classical sources preserved in monastic libraries. In the sixteenth century many of these texts began to become more widely available in printed form...By the beginning of the eighteenth century the antiquarians concerned with early Europe had access to the principal classical texts, a varied array of ethnological analogies, and a growing knowledge of the prehistoric monuments and artefacts of their own countries.[28]

Perhaps the most important sixteenth-century scholar of Celtic languages was the Scottish historian George Buchanan. According to Eoin MacNeill, Buchanan was 'the pioneer in Celtic philology' and 'the first in modern times who recognised that the Irish, the Scots and the Britons were nations of Celtic origin'.[29]

Within linguistics, the use of the terms 'Celt' and 'Celtic' was firmly established in eighteenth-century works of comparative philology such as Paul-Yves Pezron's *Antiquité de la nation et de la langue des Celtes autrement appelez Gaulois* (1703, translated into English in 1706 as *Antiquities of nations, more particularly of the Celtae or Gauls, Taken to be originally the same people as our ancient Britons*) and Edward Lhuyd's *Archaeologia Britannica* (1707).[30] Beginning with these texts, a field developed that categorized modern languages spoken in parts of the Atlantic archipelago (that 'Celtic, oceanic and extra-European world' mentioned by Pocock) such as Irish, Scottish Gaelic, and Welsh as part of the same linguistic family, along with Breton and some

---

contextually...references to Keltoi, Celtae, Galatai, Galatae, and Galli were all simply conflated. This was the generalizing method of d'Arbois de Jubainville' adding that 'while 20th century archaeologists (Déchelette, Kruta, Cunliffe) used "Celts" as a generic term for Iron Age Europe, this was not the case among early Mediterranean writers' (Pope, 16, 32). For Pope, 'The name "Celt" was, and remains, a categorization by Greeks, Romans, and archaeologists for various small-scale Early Iron Age groups' (Pope, 57).

[28] Cunliffe, 14–15.   [29] MacNeill, 'Re-Discovery', 522.
[30] According to Leerssen, Pezron's text 'seems to have brought the notion "Celt" as an umbrella term for ancient Gauls and modern Cymri/Bretons into general use; at the same time, Edward Lhuyd demonstrated the Celtic co-familiarity between Cymri and Gaels in his *Archaeologia Britannica*' (Leerssen, 'Celticism', 5).

extinct European languages. It should be noted that the ancient peoples now thought of as Celtic did not refer to themselves as Celts (something that was pointed out by prominent figures following the late nineteenth/early twentieth-century Irish Revival).[31]

The origins of Celticism itself are to be found later in the eighteenth century, in the work of the Scottish Highlander James Macpherson.[32] Macpherson claimed to have discovered lost ancient epic poetry of Scotland by the bardic figure Ossian (Oisín). Products of post-Culloden Scotland, Macpherson's English language 'translations'—*Fragments of Ancient Poetry* (1760), *Fingal* (1761), and *Temora* (1763)—sparked a Celticist craze across Europe and had a massive influence on European culture and scholarship.[33] However, Macpherson never produced his source texts and his work is now often regarded as a hoax, a forgery, or as a form of literary fraud. This assessment is unfair to an extent, since Macpherson did work with traditional sources.[34] Macpherson carried out fieldwork in the Highlands and Islands of Scotland in 1760 and 1761, searching for oral and textual examples of ancient Gaelic poetry and gathering together a valuable manuscript collection.[35] However, Macpherson reworked and embellished his source material, making it accessible and palatable for a late eighteenth-century Anglophone audience and adapting it to suit the age of sentiment.[36] As is discussed in Chapter 1, Irish authors and scholars were simultaneously offended by Macpherson's activities and creatively stimulated by them. Furthermore, the scholarly activity that arose in the years following Macpherson's *Ossian*, by figures such as Sylvester

---

[31] For example, see Eoin MacNeill's comments in his 1919 text *Phases of Irish History*: 'The term Celtic is indicative of language, not of race. We give the name Celtic to the Irish and the Britons because we know that the ancient language of each people is a Celtic language. A certain amount of enthusiasm, culminating in what is called Pan-Celticism, has gathered around the recognition of this fact that the Irish, the Gaels of Scotland, the Welsh and the Bretons are Celtic peoples... There is no small amount of pride in the notion of being Celtic. It is somewhat remarkable, then, to find that throughout all their early history and tradition the Irish and the Britons alike show not the slightest atom of recognition that they were Celtic peoples' (MacNeill, *Irish History*, 3–4).

[32] Though they are the most influential texts of early Celticism, they are predated by Thomas Gray's Welsh-themed *The Bard. A Pindaric Ode* from 1757 and Macpherson's own *The Highlander* from 1758.

[33] For an overview of the huge influence of *Ossian* on European culture, see Porter, 'Bring Me the Head of James Macpherson', 396–7.

[34] 'Although the relationship between *The Poems of Ossian* and traditional Gaelic verse has been the subject of major scholarly investigations since the 1760s, and it has long been established that Macpherson drew on traditional sources to produce imaginative texts not modelled closely on any single identifiable original, the idea that he was the author of an elaborate hoax persists' (Stafford, 'Introduction', vii).

[35] 'Macpherson had...in his travels gathered together an important collection of manuscripts which, but for his intervention, might have been entirely lost. Important among them were the early sixteenth-century work now known as *The Book of the Dean of Lismore, An Leabhar Dearg*...and *An Duanaire Ruadh*' (Chapman, 39).

[36] See Pittock, *Celtic Identity*, 35.

O'Halloran, laid some of the foundations for the Irish Revival of the late nine-teenth/early twentieth century.

Despite the rage for all things Celtic that spread across Europe in the wake of Macpherson's *Ossian*, there was also a strong current of anti-Celtic senti-ment in the long eighteenth century, even in the Celtic nations themselves (sometimes involving a fierce reaction against Macpherson's work). This was related to a political discourse in which the population of the archipelago was neatly divided into Celtic and Germanic (or Gothic) components, with Celts imagined to be the racially inferior group. One of the leading figure of this discourse was the notoriously racist Scottish antiquarian John Pinkerton. For Pinkerton, modern Celts were

> mere radical savages, not yet advanced even to a state of barbarism; and if any foreigner doubts this, he has only to step into the Celtic part of Wales, Ireland, or Scotland, and look at them, for they are just as they were, incap-able of industry or civilization, even after half their blood is Gothic, and remain, as marked by the ancients, fond of lyes, and enemies of truth.[37]

Within Scotland, according to Pinkerton, the Gothic/Germanic Lowlanders were 'acute, industrious, sensible, erect, free' while the Celtic Highlanders were 'indolent, slavish' and 'strangers to industry'.[38] As Silke Stroh has shown, anti-Celtic bias in Scotland was linked to anxieties concerning the condition of British rule in Ireland. Furthermore, the

> Gaelic, and thus part-Irish, element in Scottish history had to be played down. To admit that Scotland had developed from a 'Dark Age' Irish colo-nial movement would have meant an uncanny reversal of these regions' modern roles, where Scotland was not only a globally imperialist junior partner but had also played a key role in colonizing Ulster.[39]

Negative attitudes in Scotland towards the Gaelic language increased markedly during this period.[40]

---

[37] Pinkerton, *Dissertation*, 69.

[38] Pinkerton, *Enquiry*, 339. As Michael Shaw has observed, 'various Scottish Enlightenment figures attempted to highlight the supposed Germanic ethnicity of the Scottish Lowlands as a means of inte-grating Scotland into the English "economic and imperialist core" and distancing themselves from dissenting Jacobites' (Shaw, 39).

[39] Stroh, 195.

[40] According to Murray Pittock, 'antipathy to Gaelic Scotland had been around since the fifteenth century and had been deepened by the Reformation; but the eighteenth century moved it on to the level of theory' (Pittock, *Scottish and Irish Romanticism*, 69).

In the nineteenth century, within the work of Matthew Arnold and Ernest Renan, an influential theory developed in which the Saxon and the Celt (i.e. the English and the non-English inhabitants of the Atlantic archipelago, respectively) were diametrically opposed in terms of their essential qualities:

> Renan's Celt...takes much of his shape in opposition to rationality, intellectuality, and a materialist world of scientific and political manipulation. Instead of these the Celt has an artistic capacity beyond the ordinary, a religious instinct of unusual depth, a strength and profundity of thought and feeling but a weakness in the external world of action, a ready emotionality and an easy communion with nature, a strength in domesticity but a weakness in a wider political sphere, and a femininity...Passion, irrationality, obscure consciousness, sensitiveness, affection and nature are opposed to and thus defined by contrast to intellectuality, reasonings, hard scholasticism, merciless dissection and science. The opposition of the Celt to the qualities ascribed to science is made more explicitly by Arnold....[41]

In many of the texts covered in this study, Celtic nature forms one half of a binary structure—it exists against either modernity, Christianity, the 'centre', the Anglo-Saxon world, or Englishness (or the English core *as* modernity), or it is associated with one gender as opposed to another. However, all of the above can be complicated by a number of factors—Celticism is an essentially modern phenomenon, many of its writers were committed Christians, our knowledge of pre-Christian beliefs in Ireland is derived mainly from monastic scriptoria, some the most important branches of Celticism developed in London, and one of its major proponents was a man writing as a woman.

Developing Renan's work, Matthew Arnold wished to find a perfect synthesis of the 'lively' Celt and the 'prosaic, practical Saxon', and called for a 'fusion of all the inhabitants of these islands into one homogenous, English-speaking whole'.[42] As Leith Davis has noted, Arnold wanted to

---

[41] Chapman, 86–7. There are important connections between the development of Celticism and that of Orientalism. As Joseph Lennon has noted: 'Orientalism in Ireland undeniably influenced the coemergence of Celticism, and vice versa' (Lennon, 62). See also: 'Edward Said's statement of the relations of power inscribed in the discourse of Orientalism are equally applicable to Celticism: 'Orientalism [Celticism] depends for its strategy on...flexible positional superiority, which puts the Westerner [Englishman] in a whole series of possible relationships with the Orient [Ireland] without ever losing him the upper hand' (Cairns and Richards, 47–8).

[42] Arnold, 9, 11, 12. For Arnold, an interest in Celtic languages did not equate to a desire to see those languages flourish. Arnold called for the establishment of a chair of Celtic at Oxford while also commenting that 'the sooner the Welsh language disappears as an instrument of the practical, political, social life of Wales, the better' (Arnold, 12).

reduce Celtic languages down into 'products that would be consumed within the English university system'.[43] In Arnold's Celtic/Saxon binary, the Celt is feminine, spiritual, and imaginative but is useless at politics[44] while the Saxon is the rational and scientific masculine master of the material world, but is lacking in soul. So, the partnership of these two races complements and completes both, with obvious political-ideological implications. In *On the Study of Celtic Literature* (1866)

> Celticism is... deployed for assimilative purposes: its subtext is how to bring Ireland more firmly into the Union. Arnold, who knew very little about the philology of the Celtic languages, and not very much even about their literary history... nevertheless presents a sympathetic, even attractive picture of the Celt, as spiritual, melancholy, natural and poetic. The contrast is with the materialist, philistine, utilitarian, excessively rational, artificial, industrialized and urbanized Saxon... Not only is the Celt impractical, he has a fatal 'readiness to revolt against the despotism of fact'... So, Arnold's repressive tolerance suggests that the Celt is lucky to have the dull and muddy-mettled Saxon to run his affairs for him; in return the Celt will serve to leaven the Saxon lump, bringing with him to the heavy imperial dining table his wit and his visionary and spiritual qualities.[45]

Arnold's work has a clear colonial and imperialist mentality. As David Lloyd has pointed out, Arnold 'subordinates a colonized people's culture and literature to the major canon by stereotyping the essential identity of the race concerned'.[46] Arnold's *On The Study of Celtic Literature*

> identified the 'Celtic Irish' in traditionally racist terms as 'undisciplinable, anarchical and turbulent by nature,' 'ineffectual in politics' and 'poor, slovenly and half barbarous,' but... also detected an eloquence and delicacy in Celtic literature indicative of an ardent aspiration 'after life, light and emotion, to be expansive, adventurous and gay.' According to Arnold, this instinct for 'spontaneity' and 'imagination' stood in stark contrast to the materialism of Victorian England....[47]

---

[43] Davis, 176.

[44] For Arnold, 'the skilful and resolute appliance of means to ends which is needed to make progress in material civilization, and also to form powerful states, is just what the Celt has least turn for' (Arnold, 105).

[45] Watson, George, 'Aspects', 136.   [46] Lloyd, *Nationalism and Minor Literature*, 6.

[47] Platt, *Joyce, Race, and Finnegans Wake*, 43.

Arnold's work (and therefore Macpherson's work, which influenced Arnold) is also an important background to the Irish and Scottish Revivals.[48]

A crucial feature in Arnold's presentation of the Celts is that they are an essentially feminine race.[49] Arnold states that 'the Celt is...particularly disposed to feel the spell of the feminine idiosyncrasy'.[50] Similarly, Renan wrote in 1859 that 'If it be permitted to assign sex to nations as to individuals, we should have to say without hesitation that the Celtic race, especially with regard to its Cymric or Breton branch, is an essentially feminine race'.[51] A reaction against this idea is part of the more scientific, text-based scholarship of the late-nineteenth century, especially by 'Celtologist' scholars such as Marie Henri d'Arbois de Jubainville, Whitley Stokes, Henri Gaidoz, Ernst Windisch, Kuno Meyer, and in the pages of the *Revue Celtique*, founded in 1870.[52] For Sínead Garrigan Mattar, the most important feature of the *Revue*'s approach 'was the fastidiousness of its criticism: rigorous attention to textual detail and historical contextualization of all texts and etymologies were deemed essential if Celticism was to redefine itself as a scientific discipline'.[53] This new scientific Celticism developed in line with anthropological research into the cultures of 'primitive' peoples.[54] Research into Irish culture continued during the nineteenth century, a process that would reach a culmination at the end of the century—and the beginning of the following century—with the Irish Revival. A key early figure in this process was the Protestant barrister and antiquarian Samuel Ferguson, whose texts—such as *Congal* (1872)—were part of a Unionist cultural programme in which Ireland's culture is presented as being equal in value to England's.[55] However, there were also nationalist roots to the Revival, such as the United Irishmen movement and the Young Ireland movement.[56] In addition to scholarly and political developments, archaeological events such as the discoveries in Ireland of the eighth-century

---

[48] 'It was Ossian by way of Matthew Arnold who structured the Celtic Twilight in Ireland and Scotland' (Watson, George, 'Aspects', 131).

[49] See Cairns and Richards, 42–57.   [50] Arnold, 108.   [51] Renan, 8.

[52] See Garrigan Mattar, 9. According to Mark Williams, 'the first genuinely authoritative statement on Irish mythology to derive from the comparative method [was] the 1884 *Cycle mythologique irlandais et la mythologie celtique* by the French historian and philologist Marie Henri d'Arbois de Jubainville. This was to become the scholarly handbook on the meaning of Irish myth and its divinities for the Literary Revival...Little in it would pass muster today without modification, and much was simply wrong; but upon publication it laid the foundation for all future scholarship on the subject...The problem, of course, was that the book was written in French, which limited its accessibility in Ireland until a translation was published in 1903. (Yeats, who did not know the language, finally 'read' the book in the late 1890s by having Maud Gonne...translate parts of it out loud.)' (Williams, Mark, 296–7).

[53] Garrigan Mattar, 27.   [54] See Garrigan Mattar, 9.   [55] See Garrigan Mattar, 14–15.

[56] See Castle, 3–4 and McDonald, 52.

Tara Brooch in 1850 and the Ardagh Chalice (also eighth century) in 1868 led to a widespread fashion for 'Celtic' art and design.[57]

In the mid to late nineteenth century, a number of political events cleared the way for the cultural revivals of Ireland and Scotland, including a general reduction in antipathy towards the Celt:

> There were various reasons why, during the second half of the nineteenth century, a more sympathetic outlook on the Celtic Other again appeared more widely tolerable. Several of these reasons resembled the factors which had been responsible for earlier romanticizations of Gaelic noble savagery in the romantic period: capitalism, industrialization, urbanization, rural depopulation, overseas emigration, and mass pauperism not only persisted, but had greatly intensified, and still created longings for actually or supposedly more traditional, rural, slow-paced, socially cohesive, and humane ways of life.[58]

An increased sense of 'Celtic consciousness' during the latter half of the nineteenth century—following or overlapping with the Famine, the rise of Daniel O'Connell, and rural agitation in Ireland and Scotland—can also partly be attributed to a series of important political events (or non-events), including measures regarding the 'Irish question'.[59] In Irish affairs, these events were the disestablishment of the Anglican Church in Ireland in 1869, the Land Act of 1870, failed educational reform in 1873, and Gladstone supporting Home Rule for Ireland in 1886. In Scotland, these were the development of the Highland Land League in the 1880s, the founding of the Crofters' Party in 1885, and the Scottish Liberal Association voting for Home Rule in 1888.[60]

---

[57] Elsewhere in Europe during this period, the discovery of the La Tène archeological site in Switzerland in 1857 led to new understanding of Iron Age material culture.

[58] Stroh, 213. The work of Thomas Carlyle—especially in his emphasis on the horrors of urbanization and industrialization—were influential on the development of Celticism. See Harvie, *Floating*, 119. However, Carlyle also contemplated the extermination of the Irish, as did his contemporary, the Scottish anatomist Robert Knox. See Shaw, 42. With regards to reduced antipathy towards the Celt in Scotland, see Harvie: 'By the 1880s much of the hostility to the Scottish Celt had evaporated, not least because so many had migrated south and intermarried with the lowland population...by the 1920s [Celtic culture in Scotland] was regarded as positive, a culture which distinguished Scotland from England. But the Scottish Celts were a component of nationality, not the whole of it – and the word (with a soft C) meant, for 99 per cent of the male population, Glasgow Celtic Football Club, founded in 1888 and directly identified with Catholic Irish immigrants' (Harvie, *Floating*, 123 and 113).

[59] 'The rise of a Celtic consciousness during the 1890s was partly related to the emergence of Home Rule movements of varying significance in Ireland, Wales and Scotland. If the rise of a Fenian nationalist independence movement in the 1860s stimulated Arnold into writing his Celtic essays, it also led Liberal politicians, especially Gladstone, to consider conciliatory measures on the "Irish question"' (Williams, Daniel G., 134).

[60] Adapted from a list in Williams, Daniel G., 135–6.

The latter part of the nineteenth century saw an explosion in revivalist or Celticist organizations, on both national and international levels. Some of the key groups founded during this upsurge—in Ireland unless otherwise stated—were the Society for the Preservation of the Irish Language (established in 1876), the Gaelic Union (1880), the Young Ireland Society (1881), the Chair of Celtic at the University of Edinburgh (Scotland, 1882), the Gaelic Athletic Association (1884), the Pan-Celtic Society (international, 1888), the Irish Literary Society (1891), An Comunn Gàidhealach (Scotland, 1891), Conradh na Gaeilge (1893), the National Mòd (Scotland, 1892), and the Oireachtas (1897). Marjorie Howes has noted that Irish revivalism 'encompassed a vast range of fields', including 'translation, music, folklore, antiquities, science and art'.[61] These fields were cultivated within a range of institutions such as societies, educational establishments, theatres, and *feiseanna* (festivals) as well as publishing houses, journals and newspapers, libraries, and bookshops.[62] Key texts on Celtic matters from this period include W.F. Skene's *Celtic Scotland: A History of Ancient Alban* (1876–80) and John Stuart Blackie's *The Scottish Highlanders and the Land Laws* (1885), both of which led to reappraisals of Scottish Highland culture and society.[63] In 1895, Patrick Geddes founded his Celtic Revival journal *The Evergreen*.[64] In 1892, Douglas Hyde had called for the 'De-Anglicising' of Ireland in order to protect a Celtic essence: 'In a word, we must strive to cultivate everything that is most racial, most smacking of the soil, most Gaelic, most Irish, because in spite of the little admixture of Saxon blood in the north-east corner, this island *is* and *will* ever remain Celtic at the core.'[65]

For Yeats, Ireland was able to channel ancient 'passions and beliefs' to the modern world as, unlike other European nations, it had stayed close to a 'main river' of primitive culture and an 'ancient worship of Nature':

[61]   Howes, 'Introduction', 8.

[62]   Adapted from a list in Hutton, 118. In Scotland, examples of cultural resurgence beyond the Gaelic world during this period include the foundation of the Scottish National Portrait Gallery (1882), the Scottish Text Society (also 1882), and the Scottish Historical Society (1886).

[63]   Skene's *Celtic Scotland* discusses land issues and tenants rights in the Highlands. Blackie's text was written in the wake of the 1880s Land Wars and contests the marginalization of Highland culture. See Shaw, 46–7.

[64]   '*Evergreen*... which proclaimed a "time of Renascence", largely remained a vehicle for images of "the majesty of Celtic sorrow, the eerie song of northern winds...the chant of Ossian...amid the underlying moan of Merlin for a passing world", including Celticism only in the context of "the larger responsibilities of united [British] nationality and race"' (Pittock, *Celtic Identity*, 72).

[65]   Douglas Hyde, 'The Necessity for De-Anglicising Ireland', qtd in Kiberd and Mathews, 137. As Kiberd and Mathews have discussed, 'For every approved English institution, there [was] an equal but opposite Irish institution–for soccer, Gaelic football; for the wearing of trousers, the donning of kilts. There was a danger in all of this of producing Ireland as a not-England, a zone based on neurotic negation' (Kiberd and Mathews, 272).

...literature dwindles to a mere chronicle of circumstance, or passionless fantasies, and passionless meditations, unless it is constantly flooded with the passions and beliefs of ancient times, and that of all the fountains of the passions and beliefs of ancient times in Europe, the Slavonic, the Finnish, the Scandinavian and the Celtic, the Celtic alone has been for centuries close to the main river of European literature. It has again and again brought 'the vivifying spirit' 'of excess' into the arts of Europe.[66]

In Yeats' view, 'the characteristics [Arnold] has called Celtic, mark all races just in so far as they preserve the qualities of the early races of the world'.[67] Within Ireland, Celticism found expression in texts such as Yeats's 'The Wanderings of Oisin', Augusta Gregory's collections of legend and folklore, and in numerous plays performed at the Irish Literary Theatre. As the literary critic Mary Colum commented many years later, 'at this period the Irish were claiming almost everybody of distinction as Celtic or Gaelic if not Irish'.[68] In the early twentieth century, Celticism was an important 'mode' of the '1916' poets (men such as Patrick Pearse, Thomas MacDonagh, and Joseph Mary Plunkett), alongside 'a cult of primitivism, an ideal of simplicity...and the Roman Catholic religious traditions of saintliness, sacrifice, and martyrdom'.[69] Even the revolutionary socialist James Connolly, another 1916 leader, wrote that 'The chief enemy of a Celtic revival today is the crushing force of capitalism which irresistibly destroys all national or racial characteristics'.[70]

There were many tensions within the extensive network of Irish cultural and nationalist movements, not least regarding attitudes to language. In 1892, Yeats wished to create a national literature that would be Irish in 'spirit' even if it was written in the English language: 'Can we not build up a national tradition, a national literature, which shall be none the less Irish in spirit from being English in Language?'[71] In the opposing camp were figures such as Douglas Hyde and the journalist D.P. Moran. In his 1905 text *The Philosophy of Irish Ireland*, Moran wrote that 'The foundation of Ireland is the Gael, and the Gael must be the element that absorbs'.[72] As such, Moran was opposed to

---

[66] Yeats, *Essays and Introductions*, 185.
[67] Yeats, 'Irish Language and Irish Literature.' In *Uncollected Prose II*, 241.   [68] Colum, 96.
[69] Dawe, 86.
[70] Connolly, James, qtd in Kiberd and Mathews, 317. See also: 'The national and racial characteristics of the English and Irish people are different'. Connolly, James, qtd in Kiberd and Mathews, 388.
[71] Yeats, *Uncollected Prose I*, 255.
[72] Moran, 37. 'Moran is widely regarded as being the leading spokesman for the more reactionary vein of the Irish cultural revival, as one who sought to construct an exclusivist Irish identity based on Roman Catholicism and the Irish language' (Williams, Daniel G., 121–2).

the false nature of 'Celtic' poetry in the English language (such as the work of Yeats). Moran called the 'Celtic note' 'one of the most glaring frauds that the credulous Irish people ever swallowed'.[73] Aside from falsifying Irish culture, Celticist poetry was also charged by poets such as John Hewitt with casting a deceptive, bewildering spell over readers, numbing them to the oppressions of capitalism: 'You came with your strange, wistful, trembling verse, / Beguiled me for a while in quant deceit; / and I forgot th'oppressor's blow and curse, / the muffled tread of workless in the street'.[74] There was a similarly weary response to Celticism in some readers of early twentieth century Scotland. In 1926, Donald MacKenzie wrote a letter to the editor of the *Scottish Educational Journal*, protesting that

> Celtic literature is not 'misty', and it is certainly not 'elusive' and it is less 'dreamy' than many suppose. The old Gaelic bards dearly loved a satire—one that (as they said) 'raised blisters', and many modern Highlanders are very satirical fellows and are not lacking in 'pitiless common sense'... The nineteenth century nonsense about the 'Celtic temperament', the 'Celtic gloom' and 'Celtic dreamers' should be flung into the nearest ashbin with other rubbish.[75]

According to George Watson, 'Celticism, so dominant in Ireland and to a lesser extent in Scotland in the closing decades of the nineteenth century, fades away as a significant cultural movement quite rapidly after the turn of the century'.[76] However, a number of significant texts of Irish and Scottish literature engage with Celticism and/or Celtic matters. This book argues that Celticism continues past the Revival period and demonstrates how it intersects with later cultures and movements.

This book will also suggest that twentieth-century texts are generally more interested in forms of Celtic solidarity and pan-Celticism (sometimes in extreme forms), or in stressing the historical or cultural links between Ireland and Scotland, than previous phases of the phenomenon. Since these instances differ significantly from earlier examples of Celticism—for reasons discussed in the following chapters—these have been categorized here as occurrences of

---

[73] Moran, 22. See also: 'there appear at present quantities of so-called Celtic poems, plays, stories, which, for all their Irish phrases, and indeed because of them, are obvious shams. A writer of these could turn almost any sentence into his "Celtic". Where I have said 'Which are obvious shams' just now, he would say something like this: 'And, Johnny, I give you my hand on it this night, "tis out and out humbugs they are surely"' (MacDonagh, 48).

[74] Hewitt, 'To a Modern Irish Poet' (1928), in *Collected Poems*, 443.

[75] Qtd in McCulloch, *Modernism and Nationalism*, 276.   [76] Watson, George, 'Aspects', 142.

'late Celticism'. The era of the Celtic Revivals is a turning point in the development of Celticism, not its conclusion. Although there is no Celtic movement in literature after the Revivals, there are numerous texts that engage extensively with Celtic subjects and that foreground Irish-Scottish connections. In late Celticism there is a decisive shift in the phenomenon, brought about by political and cultural changes. However, there are certain continuities with the earlier form. Furthermore, late Celticism also features a series of engagements with early Celticism. This text aims to demonstrate that an awareness of the development of early and late Celticisms is essential for an understanding of the links between modern Irish and Scottish literatures.

The present work begins with a study of the influence of Macpherson's *Ossian* on Irish writing—probably *the* most significant connection in Irish and Scottish literature—and then looks at the subsequent phases of literary Celticism and other major links of Irish-Scottish literature in the nineteenth and twentieth centuries. There is a strange balance in terms of the rough equivalence of Scotland's prominence within Romanticism on the one hand and Ireland's importance within Modernism on the other. Within those phenomena, Scottish Romanticism, especially *Ossian*, made an enormous impact on Irish writing while Ireland (in terms of both its politics and culture) is a huge influence on Scottish Modernism. This book studies Romantic and Modernist texts from both countries. In addition to works from Ireland and Scotland, this text examines works by men and women writers. There are sections dedicated to Sydney Owenson and Augusta Gregory in this book (as well as sections on 'Fiona Macleod', the female authorial persona of William Sharp). However, expressions of Celticism by Irish women writers tend to focus specifically on Ireland, with Scotland generally mentioned only in passing.

There is no mention of Scotland in Mary Balfour's Romantic-era Celticist text 'Kathleen O'Neil' (1810), although the 'rocky Hebrides' feature as a setting in Vincentia Rodgers' Ossianic poem 'Cluthan and Malvina' (1823) from the same period.[77] Alice Milligan, an Irish Methodist descended from Scottish settlers who arrived in Ireland in the 1690s,[78] wrote poetry inspired by Loch Fyne[79] and used Scots language in her poem 'The Dauntless Laddie'. Another poem, 'Mountain Shapes' mentions Edinburgh, Jura, and Skye and gestures towards the ancient literary connections of Scotland and Ireland through a

---

[77] Rodgers, 35. Both of these texts 'reassign the traditionally male role of bard to a female figure' (Behrendt, 132).
[78] See Johnston, 13.
[79] See Milligan, 'A Scottish Picture – Inverary on Loch Fyne' in *Poems*, 20–1.

reference to the Red Branch warriors of the Ulster Cycle.[80] Katharine Tynan, on the other hand, is less interested in presenting such links. In *Peeps at Many Lands: Ireland* (1911), Tynan is more concerned with presenting Scotland as the source of an anti-Celtic, unartistic, and overly religious community present in modern-day Ulster,

> that north-east corner of Ireland which no Celt looks upon as Ireland at all. In speech, in character, in looks, the people become Scotch and not Irish... There is nothing Irish about North-East Ulster except the country itself... The Belfast man is very shrewd, but he has a great simplicity withal. He has none of the uppish notions of the Celt... Like his Scottish progenitors, he stands by the Bible. There is as much Bible-reading in the fine red-brick mansions of Belfast as there is in Scotland. He does not produce literature.[81]

Published later in the Revival period, Ella Young's collection *The Tangle-Coated Horse* (1929) stresses that the stories of her book belong to 'Gaelic-speaking Scotland' as well as Ireland[82] and in the foreword to *The Wonder Smith and His Sons: A Tale from the Golden Childhood of the World*, Young introduces

> The Gubbaun Saor, whose other name was Mananaun, whose other name was Cullion the Smith... a great person long, long ago. He was a maker of worlds and a shaper of universes... People have forgotten about these things now, but in the thatched cottages in Gaelic-speaking Ireland and Scotland, they talk about him and his son Lugh and his daughter Aunya. Men cutting turf in the bogs know about him....[83]

The influence of Macpherson can also be detected in Young's work. In her poem 'Twilight' Young uses Macpherson's spelling for Oisín; Ossian.[84] Despite these passing references and connections, Scotland is generally a fairly

---

[80] See Milligan, 'Mountain Shapes', *Hero Lays*, 31. In terms of material with Scottish connections, Milligan also wrote an Ossianic trilogy for the stage; *The Last Feast of the Fianna, Oisín in Tír-Nan-Oig*, and *Oisin and Padraic*, first performed in Belfast, Derry, and Letterkenny in 1898 and published in 1899. See Morris, 158. In 1900, *The Last Feast of the Fianna* was produced by the Irish Literary Theatre.

[81] Tynan, *Peeps*, 44–7. Regarding Tynan's Bible comment, perhaps the secular Scottish Enlightenment had escaped her attention.

[82] Young, *The Tangle-Coated Horse*, foreword.

[83] Young, *The Wonder Smith and His Sons*, 9–10.

[84] 'And all the world is hushed as though [Niamh] called / Ossian again, and no one answered her'. Young, *Poems*, 23.

indistinct, peripheral location in Young's texts. At one point in *The Tangle-Coated Horse* a character says, 'And if there is one who withholds service from you, let him take ship for Alba or for Scotland' as though were two Scotlands available.[85] Fittingly, there *were* two Scotlands in texts of the Irish Celtic Revival and the Irish Revival; the Scotland that is part of the world of ancient 'Sagas' and Celtic wonder, and the Scotland that is a distinctly unCeltic space and the root cause of the supposedly unIrish nature of the north of Ireland.

With the exceptions of Owenson and Gregory, it seems that Irish women writers in the period covered here were not particularly interested in Scottish culture (though they may have been interested in 'Celtic' aspects of Irish history or culture). The same is true with regards to Anglophone Scottish women writers and Irish culture. In the Modernist era, women writers such as Nan Shepherd were 'motivated by the search for self-determination at personal rather than national levels'.[86] As T.J. Boynton has suggested, 'Celticism seems to have held particular appeal for *male* writers'.[87] For Boynton, this is 'most readily explicable as an outgrowth of Arnold's own gendering of the Celt' with male writers in the nineteenth century using 'qualities conceived as female as an oppositional strategy' directed against 'the normative qualities of capitalist modernity'.[88]

Some of the writers covered in this text are major or canonical figures— Scott, Yeats, Joyce, Heaney. However, less prominent writers such as Sydney Owenson, Fiona Macleod, and Sorley MacLean are also studied here. Arguably, Augusta Gregory belongs in the latter category. Although Gregory is a well-known figure of the Irish Revival, her actual work was somewhat overlooked within literary studies for many years, although that has started to change in recent decades. In addition to these writers, Hugh MacDiarmid is a major presence only in Scottish literature—he is seldom mentioned in Modernist studies. The focus is on works in the English language here—since Celticism is largely an Anglophone phenomenon[89]—although texts in Scottish Gaelic and Irish are also engaged with, in addition to the 'Wakese' of Joyce's *Finnegans Wake* and the 'Synthetic English' of MacDiarmid's *In Memoriam James Joyce*. This book studies drama and poetry as well as novels, and attempts to strike a rough balance between Irish and Scottish writers and matters in each chapter. While this text is informed by postcolonial criticism, it does not adopt postcolonialism as the sole approach to these texts and contexts, since the fields of Irish and Scottish studies have moved into productive

---

[85] Young, *The Tangle-Coated Horse*, 59.   [86] Bell, 127.   [87] Boynton, 15.
[88] Ibid., 15.   [89] See Mackay, 'The Gaelic Tradition.'

new forms of discourse in recent years. As Ray Ryan has suggested, 'the need now is for more alternative analyses and comparisons, histories and causalities, than can be produced under a single methodology like postcolonialism or a single notion like identity'.[90] The emergence of eco-criticism and the development of archipelagic studies have led to exciting new ways of approaching and understanding Irish and Scottish writing. This text responds to these critical modes in its analysis of Scottish and Irish literatures, and also works with texts exploring the relationship between those literatures and gender.

[90] Ryan, 10–11.

1

Ossian and Irish literature

Owenson, Yeats, Joyce, Beckett

The Poems of Ossian had an immense effect on European literature.[1] As opposed to a highly enthusiastic reaction across much of Europe, Irish reactions to James Macpherson's work were often hostile. Of course, Ireland is central to the story of the impact of *Ossian*, since it is the home of most of the source material (the Fiannaíocht tales and ballads based on the exploits of Fionn mac Cumhaill and his warrior band the Fianna, often narrated by his son Oisín) and because Macpherson's work provoked a wave of scholarly debate and artistic responses there, including the publication of texts such as Sylvester O'Halloran's *An Introduction to the Study of the History and Antiquities of Ireland* (1772), Joseph Cooper Walker's *Historical Memoirs of the Irish Bards* (1786), Charlotte Brooke's *Reliques of Irish Poetry* (1789) and Edward Bunting's *General Collection of the Ancient Music of Ireland* (1796).[2] Irish scholarly reactions to *Ossian* have been covered extensively in recent decades.[3] However, as Clare O'Halloran has pointed out, less attention has been paid to the influence of *Ossian* on Irish culture.[4] This chapter provides an account of the key responses in Irish literature in order to move towards a broader understanding of the reaction to *Ossian* in Irish writing. Celticist Romantic and Revivalist engagements with *Ossian* should be central to any such account. However, a comprehensive consideration of *Ossian* and Irish literature also needs to consider English-language Irish literary engagements with *Ossian* in Modernism and beyond.

---

[1] 'It is difficult to overstate the impact of *The Poems of Ossian* on the literature of Western Europe' (Moore, 'Introduction', 6). Edna Longley has observed that 'If Colm Cille/Columba is the patron saint of Irish/Scottish poetry, Oisín/Ossian is the equally "ambiguous" patron pagan' (Longley, 10). NB: In this text, '*Ossian*' refers to Macpherson's Ossianic corpus and 'Ossian' refers to the figure from the Fenian cycle/Ossianic cycle.

[2] See Frawley, 40.

[3] For further details on Macpherson's influence on Irish studies, see Clare O'Halloran's 'Irish Re-Creations of the Gaelic Past' and Mac Craith's 'The Irish Response to *Ossian*'.

[4] See O'Halloran, Clare. 'Re-Creations', 70.

Modern Irish and Scottish Literature: Connections, Contrasts, Celticisms. Richard Alan Barlow, Oxford University Press.
© Richard Alan Barlow 2023. DOI: 10.1093/oso/9780192859181.003.0002

Literary Celticism can be separated into two main phases. 'Early Celticism' stretches from the era of the United Irish Rebellion of 1798 and the Act of Union of 1800 up to the delayed Romanticism of the Irish and Scottish Celtic Revivals of the late nineteenth century/early twentieth century. 'Late Celticism' arrives alongside or within literary Modernism and after the decline of the Celtic Revivals. Texts from both of these phases engage with Macpherson's *Ossian*. Despite being key works behind the development of literary Celticism in Ireland, Macpherson's *Ossian* is rejected and sidelined in Irish Romanticism and in the Celtic Revival.[5] *Ossian* is either considered threatening, since its Scottish Gaelic dimension undermines Ireland's position as a uniquely spiritual 'Other' capable of contrasting with modern industrialized England, or it is spurned in favour of more 'authentic' versions such as Brian O'Looney's translation of Mícheál Coimín's *Laoi Oisín i dTír na nÓg*. The challenge of Macpherson is contested directly by Sydney Owenson in her 1806 text *The Wild Irish Girl*. Later in the nineteenth century, Yeats takes an interest in the story of Oisín (or 'Oisin') but hardly engages with Macpherson's *Ossian*. In Irish Modernism, with the fading of early Celticism and a diminishing interest in cultural 'authenticity' and 'purity' (replaced by an emphasis on textual collage, psychoanalysis, and inauthenticity), allusions to *Ossian* appear in works by James Joyce and Samuel Beckett.

Although Celticism's first phase flourishes in the early nineteenth century, the origins of the phenomenon—and, arguably, the tone of Romanticism itself—lie in the publication of Macpherson's *Ossian* prose poems, starting in 1760.[6] The influence of *Ossian* occurred despite Macpherson's controversial claims regarding Irish history and his antagonistic stance towards Irish scholars.[7] Emerging from post-Culloden Scotland, Macpherson's English-language 'pseudotranslation'[8] of a supposedly newly discovered Gaelic epic

---

[5] However, Macpherson was a major influence on Scottish Revivalists such as William Sharp/Fiona Macleod.

[6] Macpherson created 'the tone at the root of Romanticism' (Crawford, 'Post-Cullodenism', 18). Furthermore, the 'construction of Celticism and the discourses associated with it effectively begin with [Macpherson's *Ossian*]' (Watson, George, 'Aspects', 130). See also: 'Macpherson virtually invented Romanticism' (Mercier, 230). As Fiona Stafford has suggested, Macpherson's text encapsulates the 'defining qualities' of Romanticism. She adds that 'if we were looking for a text to demonstrate the defining qualities of Romanticism, James Macpherson's *Ossian* would be hard to beat' (Stafford, 'Romantic', 27). Macpherson's work was published well before the generally accepted birth of English Romanticism, the publication of Coleridge and Wordsworth's *Lyrical Ballads* in 1798.

[7] In the 'Dissertation' attached to *Temora*, Macpherson rewrites Irish and Scottish history, claiming that 'Ireland was first peopled from Britain' (Macpherson, 208–9). In the same piece, Macpherson describes the work of the 'idle fabulists' Geoffrey Keating and Roderic O'Flaherty as 'Credulous and puerile' (Macpherson, 211). Incidentally, the 'Dissertation' also claims that 'Caledonians' means '*the Celts of the hill country*' (Macpherson, 207).

[8] Kristmannsson, 39.

appeared in an era searching for authenticity in place of artificiality, as James Pethica has discussed:

> The notion that folk stories are repositories of experience and emotion more powerful and authentic than the artificial culture and art of the educated had become popular in the late eighteenth century... [this] contributed to the sensational popularity of the poetry published by James Macpherson in the 1760s, which purported to be the work of Ossian, a Gaelic warrior-poet from an unspecified remote period of pre-history. Macpherson's 'Ossianic' poems – in fact merely adaptations and imitations of Gaelic material he had gathered in Scotland – were in vogue for more than a decade, and influenced many foundational Romantic texts, even after their recent origin had been exposed.[9]

It is important to note that not all of Macpherson's work had recent origins.[10] In terms of the repositories of emotion Pethica mentions, Macpherson's work expresses a sense of regret at the disappearance of an old, heroic culture.[11]

Macpherson's works, *Fragments of Ancient Poetry, Collected in the Highlands of Scotland, and Translated from the Galic or Erse Language* (1760), *Fingal, an Ancient Epic Poem in Six Books, together with Several Other Poems composed by Ossian, the Son of Fingal, translated from the Galic Language* (1761), and *Temora* (1763), faced immediate acclaim but also scepticism and investigation. As Stafford has discussed, initial hostility towards Macpherson's output involved protestations from Irish researchers and antiquarians:

> *Fingal* and *Temora* were greeted by a barrage of objections from Dublin, as scholars such as Charles O'Conor... criticised Macpherson's free-handling of Gaelic poetry, and particularly the way in which stories from the Fionn and Ulster cycles had been confused. Even more aggravating was his appropriation of Irish heroes, and the refusal to accept that the Scots were originally inhabitants of Ireland.[12]

---

[9] Pethica, 131.

[10] Macpherson's work was partly based on texts such as *Leabhar Deathan Lios Mòir* (*The Book of the Dean of Lismore*), *An Leabhar Dearg* (*The Red Book*), and *An Duanaire Ruadh* (*The Red Rhymer*). See Chapman, 39.

[11] According to Lesa Ní Mhunghaile, '*Ossian* represents a heightening and emphasising of the features of the Gaelic work in and through the language of eighteenth-century Sentimental writing in English' (Ní Mhunghaile, 37).

[12] Stafford, 'Introduction', vii.

Not only had Macpherson claimed national primacy for Scotland, in *Fingal* and *Temora* he had also presented Scotland as 'the cradle of civilization from which all the inhabitants of Britain emerged'.[13] O'Conor's criticism includes an imagined dialogue between the bard figure Ossian and his 'translator' Macpherson in *Dissertations on the History of Ireland* (1766). In this exchange, the two figures discuss how best to perpetrate an elaborate literary scam: 'Do, *Ossian*; make you a Collection of our old vulgar Tales about the *Tain-Bo-Cuailgne*, and *Fiana Ereann*...I will be your *Translator* and *Dissertator*...I alone will ensure your Wares, and make a good Market, before we are detected!'[14] As Seamus Deane has noted, 'All through the late eighteenth and well into the nineteenth century, Irish commentators...fought the *Ossian* battle over and over, denying the Scots the primacy they claimed in the Celtic hierarchy'.[15] A significant skirmish in the *Ossian* battle was launched within Irish fiction.

Sydney Owenson's *The Wild Irish Girl*, an epistolary 'national tale' influenced by the literature of sensibility,[16] tells the story of Horatio, 'a young landlord, long resident in England [who] finds his authentic identity in Ireland'.[17] This identity is found in the 'classic ground' of the west of the island:

> I leave Dublin to-morrow for M—— house. It is situated in the county of ——, on the northwest coast of Connaught, which I am told is the classic ground of Ireland. The native Irish, pursued by religious and political bigotry, made it the asylum of their sufferings, and were separated by a provincial barrier from an intercourse with the rest of Ireland, until after the Restoration; so I shall have a fair opportunity of beholding the Irish character in all its *primeval* ferocity.[18]

Owenson's novel has its defects, but its portrayal of Ireland—one heavily influenced by Macpherson's Celticism—is fascinating and revealing.[19] *The*

---

[13] Davis, 84.   [14] O'Conor, 47–8.   [15] Deane, *Strange Country*, 42–3.

[16] 'Owenson's contemporary readers would recognize the hallmarks of the earlier literature of Sensibility: apostrophe, ejaculation, heightened rhetoric, the trope of pleasing pain, and the literal multiplication of excess' (Nagle, 201). As Katie Trumpener has noted, 'The national tale, and out of it, the historical novel, develop...as essentially transnational genres, their generic breakthroughs transpiring alternately in works by Irish and Scottish writers' (Trumpener, 'Ireland, Scotland, and the politics of form', 177). See also Trumpener, 'National Character, Nationalist Plots'.

[17] Krielkamp, 63.   [18] Owenson, *The Wild Irish Girl*, 17.

[19] According to some recent critics, *The Wild Irish Girl* is 'a nebulous pastel over which some Ossianic coloring has been daubed' (Flanagan, 125), 'a work deficient in almost everything a novel should have, except success' (Deane, *Short History*, 97–8) and 'a poor novel' suffering from 'fulsome extravagance', 'pompous pedantry', and a 'welter of facts and pseudo-facts' (Andrews, 7, 7, 15, 15).

Wild Irish Girl contains a lengthy discussion between characters on the subject of Macpherson's texts. As Clíona Ó Gallchoir observes, 'a combination of manifest Ossianic influence and a rhetoric of denial and rejection is central to the novel's enormously influential construction of Ireland.'[20]

There are strong scholarly and intertextual aspects to *The Wild Irish Girl* and the book contains extensive footnotes citing non-fictional sources. Indeed, it has been suggested that the subject of *The Wild Irish Girl* is not Ireland itself but rather books about Ireland.[21] Part of this heteroglossic infotainment is an extended assertion of *Ossian's* Irish provenance. This is important for Owenson, because if Ireland cannot be understood as being the original and purest Celtic nation, then it is not uniquely placed to perfectly complement the Anglo-Saxon world. So, the Celtic primacy claimed for Scotland by Macpherson must be overturned.[22] In Owenson's text, Horatio deploys 'arguments used by Macpherson, Blair, etc. etc. etc. to prove that Ossian was a Highland bard.'[23] A priest informs Horatio that although 'Ossian is supposed to be a Scottish bard of ancient days... We are certain of his Irish origin, from the testimony of tradition, from proofs of historic fact, and above all, from the internal evidences of the poems themselves, even as they are given us by Mr Macpherson.'[24] The priest then embarks on a lengthy disquisition, pointing out Macpherson's errors, producing various proofs of *Ossian's* ultimately Irish origin, and submitting forms of textual evidence such as 'a bundle of old manuscripts' which turns out to contain a version of the *Agallamh Oisín agus Phádraig* ('The dialogue between Oisín and Patrick').[25]

Nevertheless, *The Wild Irish Girl* became a 'media event' (Connolly, Claire, 99), partly through Owenson's own 'simulation' of her character Glorvina at social events (see Donovan, 52).

[20] Ó Gallchoir, 117. The influence of Macpherson on Owenson's work can also be seen in the latter's *Twelve Original Hibernian Melodies with English Words, Imitated and Translated from the Works of Ancient Irish Bards*: 'Many of the poems which compose this little selection, were orally collected in what may be deemed the classic wilds of Ireland – where Ossian sung, where Fingal fought, and Oscar fell' (Owenson, *Original Hibernian Melodies*, 1). As Ina Ferris has noted, *Original Hibernian Melodies* was a model for Thomas Moore's *Irish Melodies*. See Ferris, *Achievement*, 123. The work of Robert Burns was also an important example for Moore.

[21] See Leerssen, *Remembrance and Imagination*, 60.

[22] As O'Halloran has noted, 'that the forgery question tended initially to obscure all other considerations is understandable, since Ireland was the only country which seemed, at the time, to lose from the popular acceptance of Macpherson's creation' (O'Halloran, Clare, 'Irish Re-Creations', 74).

[23] Owenson, *The Wild Irish Girl*, 107. The 'Blair' Horatio refers to is Hugh Blair, supporter of Macpherson's *Ossian*, and first Regius Professor of Rhetoric and Belles-Lettres at the University of Edinburgh.

[24] Ibid., 106.

[25] Ibid., 113. *Agallamh Oisín agus Phádraig* is a set of Fenian poems all based on, as the title suggests, a conversation between Oisín and Patrick. See Ó Fiannachta. Patrick is 'airbrushed out' of Macpherson's work (Leask, 'Fingalian Topographies', 186).

Faced with such a learned and convincing defence, Horatio admits he is 'fairly routed'.[26]

In *The Wild Irish Girl*, the priest's victory in proving *Ossian*'s Irish origins aligns with an attempt to secure Ireland's status as the original and most 'authentic' Celtic culture. Previously, Macpherson had claimed that

> That dialect of the Celtic tongue, spoken in the north of Scotland, is much more pure, more agreeable to its mother language, and more abounding with primitives, than that now spoken, or even that which has been writ for some centuries back, amongst the most unmixed part of the Irish nation...*Scotch Galic* is the most original, and, consequently, the language of a more antient and unmixed people.[27]

To combat such assertions, Owenson's strategy praises the racial constitution of the west of Ireland: 'they were true Milesians bred and born...not a drop of *Strongbonean* flowed in their Irish veins'[28] as well as Irish linguistic purity: 'the Celtic dialect used by the native Irish is the purest and most original language that yet remains'.[29] This exposure to an 'unadulterated' culture—as well as a love affair with a feminine personification of Ireland in the shape of the red-haired '*natural* and *national*' princess Glorvina (from *glór bhinn*—sweet voice)—acts as a gendered stimulant for the drained Englishman:

> Wearied, exhausted...at a moment when I was sinking beneath the lethargic influence of apathy, or hovering on the brink of despair, a new light broke upon my clouded mind, and discovered to my inquiring heart, something

---

[26] Owenson, *The Wild Irish Girl*, 113–4. For a similar dispute regarding Macpherson's *Ossian*, see Walter Scott's *The Antiquary*: 'I used often of an evening to get old Rory M'Alpin to sing us songs out of Ossian about the battles of Fingal and Lamon Mor, and Magnus and the spirit of Muirartach.' 'And did you believe', asked the aroused Antiquary, 'did you absolutely believe that stuff of Macpherson's to be really ancient, you simple boy?' 'Believe it, sir?–how could I but believe it, when I have heard the songs sung from my infancy?' 'But not the same as Macpherson's English Ossian–you're not absurd enough to say that, I hope?' said the Antiquary, his brow darkening with wrath. But Hector stoutly abode the storm; like many a sturdy Celt, he imagined the honour of his country and native language connected with the authenticity of these popular poems, and would have fought knee-deep, or forfeited life and land, rather than have given up a line of them' (Scott, *The Antiquary*, 292–3).

[27] Macpherson, 216–17.

[28] Owenson, *The Wild Irish Girl*, 38. 'Strongbow or Richard Fitz Gilbert, an Englishman, invaded in 1170 on behalf of Mac Murchada, an exiled Irish king, and after that king died, succeeded him and settled Leinster in Ireland with tenants from his English and Welsh estates' (Kirkpatrick in Owenson, *The Wild Irish Girl*, 257).

[29] Owenson, *The Wild Irish Girl*, 88.

yet worth living for. What that mystic something is, I can scarcely yet define myself, but a magic spell now irresistibly binds me to that life....[30]

Weariness and exhaustion belong to England in Owenson's text, while Ireland offers a revivifying and magical experience: 'What a dream was the last three weeks of my life!...It seemed to me as if I had lived in an age of primeval simplicity and primeval virtue'.[31] Part of this is the charm of the 'original and primitive' locals who possess 'colloquial wit', and who display 'cordiality and kindness'.[32] In addition to the primeval simplicity of the people, the landscape and architecture in the west of Ireland offer a sublime and wild grandeur to the tourist: 'Grand even in desolation, and magnificent in decay—it was the Castle of Inismore. The setting sun shone brightly on its mouldering turrets, and the waves which bathed its rocky basis, reflected on their swelling bosoms the dark outlines of its awful ruins'.[33] The construction of Ireland in *The Wild Irish Girl* is that of the romantic, spiritual, dream-land that will complement the supposedly more prosaic traits of England as an act of 'reconciliation' (religious differences are also overcome in this optimistic vision).[34] Owenson's novel closes with marriage and the following hope: 'In this the dearest, most sacred, and most lasting of all human ties, let the names of Inismore and M—— be inseparably blended, and the distinctions of English and Irish, of protestant and catholic, for ever buried'.[35]

Malcolm Chapman has argued that the Celtic/Saxon system of opposition (and complementarity) demonstrated in the work of writers such as Owenson and Walter Scott originates to a large extent in Macpherson's work.[36] This

---

[30] Ibid., 124. As Julia Anne Miller has noted, 'Horatio is unable to openly woo Lady Glorvina because he is descended from one of Cromwell's generals (General M--) who murdered Glorvina's great-great-great-grandfather and stole the family lands...In the narrative of Horatio and Glorvina's union, protestations of mutual affection blur the embarrassing circumstances of the coercion that founds the union' (Miller, Julie Anne, 24–8).

[31] Owenson, *The Wild Irish Girl*, 123. As Ina Ferris has mentioned, there are strong similarities between *The Wild Irish Girl* and Scott's *Waverley*: 'Both narratives are built around the journey of an English hero to a Gaelic culture, an experience that serves as an initiation into adulthood and involves the crossing of various cultural and psychological borders' (Ferris, *Achievement*, 123).

[32] Owenson, *The Wild Irish Girl*, 45, 14, 16.   [33] Ibid., 45.

[34] For Seamus Deane, '[The Irish national novel] seeking to find some reconciliation between versions of the English and Irish national communities that would stifle the impact of the French Revolution...the provision of the ballast of the English national character for the volatility of the Irish' (Deane, *Strange Country*, 30). For Deane, this is a 'Whig dream of reconciliation' and an 'unreality' (Deane, *Short History*, 99).

[35] Owenson, *The Wild Irish Girl*, 250. The sense of reconciliation at the end of *The Wild Irish Girl* may be an illusion, masking both the suppression of Ireland and of the novel's central character. See Miller, Julie Anne, 13. The reconciliation also has a worrying hint of incest to it. See Kroeg, 225–6.

[36] 'The Ossianic controversy promoted a picture of the Celt as natural, emotional, naïve, and a failure in the rough and tumble of the modern world' (Chapman, 82).

Celtic/Saxon binary was revived in the mid nineteenth century by Matthew Arnold. Drawing on Macpherson's texts, Arnold conceptualized the Celtic and Saxon races as being fundamentally and essentially contrasting, but also perfectly matched. Arnold, in his lectures *On the Study of Celtic Literature* (1866) wished to find a perfect synthesis of 'the idealist Celt and the materialist Anglo-Saxon'.[37] This is undertaken for ideological and political reasons, as George Watson has discussed: 'In *On the Study of Celtic Literature*, Celticism is very much deployed for assimilative purposes: its subtext is how to bring Ireland more firmly into the Union'.[38] Being feminine and childlike dreamers, the Celts, in Arnold's view, always need the Saxons around to take care of all of the practical work. This text was also an important foundation for the Irish and Scottish Celtic Revivals of the late nineteenth and early twentieth centuries.[39]

An example of Macpherson's influence on the Irish Celtic Revival, via Arnold, can be found in W.B. Yeats' early work.[40] However, the 'marriage' of Celtic and Saxon cultures is no longer sought here. Although the text's Celticism was designed to appeal to an audience beyond Ireland,[41] 'The Wanderings of Oisin' (1889) is a nationalist work which makes pointed reference to 'Fenians' rather than the 'Fianna' or the 'Fena'.[42] In 'Oisin', Yeats rejects or ignores Macpherson's *Ossian*, opting for an origin-controlled Ossianic source text for 'Oisin' in the form of Brian O'Looney's translations of the work of Mícheál Coimín.[43] Macpherson's Scottish *Ossian* would not have suited Yeats' Irish nationalist purposes. Nevertheless, Yeats is working within, or against, a dualistic discourse founded upon Macpherson's *Ossian*.

[37]   Ibid., 94.
[38]   Watson, George, 'Aspects', 136. According to Howes, 'The publication of *On the Study of Celtic Literature* coincided with an increase in "Fenian fever" in Ireland and the United States' and 'an outbreak of Fenian violence in Ireland and England' (Howes, *Yeats' Nations*, 20).
[39]   'It was *Ossian* by way of Matthew Arnold who structured the Celtic Twilight in Ireland and Scotland' (Crawford, 'Post-Cullodenism', 18).
[40]   As Gregory Castle has pointed out, 'Yeats's mystical view of the Irish folk tradition, developed partly in response to Matthew Arnold's imperialist Celticism' (Castle, 174). See also: 'Arnold's interest in the Celt, and his belief in the power of art and criticism to raise the cultural level of a nation, and to stem the tide of vulgarity and of Philistinism, were … important to Yeats' (Watson, George, 'Yeats', 41).
[41]   See Foster, *Yeats I*, 86.
[42]   See 'Put the staff in my hands, for I go to the Fenians, O cleric, to chaunt', ('The Wanderings of Oisin' Book III, l. 201, Yeats, *The Poems*, 31 and 'On the flaming stones, without refuge, the limbs of the Fenians are tost' ('The Wanderings of Oisin' Book III, l. 213, Yeats, *The Poems*, 31). For a discussion of Yeats' use of the term 'Fenians', see Foster, *Yeats I*, 80–2.
[43]   'The principal source that Yeats drew on for "The Wanderings of Oisin" was Brian O'Looney's translation of Michael Comyn's "The Lay of Oisin in the Land of Youth" (1750), which Yeats accessed in the fourth volume of the *Transactions of the Ossianic Society*' (Gomes, 378).

Yeats' early work is also informed by the activities and literature of the Ossianic Society of Dublin, which was itself established as another Irish reaction against Macpherson's work:

> Ireland's attempts to wrest Ossian back from Scotland was ambitiously embodied in the Ossianic Society of Dublin, founded in 1853, whose learned *Transactions* Yeats studied... Yeats learned from a scholarly tradition instigated by Macpherson's celebrated work: and he also chose to base his first ambitious long poem on the matter which was most clearly related in the public mind to the essential qualities of the Celt.[44]

Earlier Irish publications attempting to discredit or correct Macpherson include Theophilus O'Flanagan's *Deirdri* (1808), published in the first (and only) volume of the *Transactions of the Gaelic Society of Dublin*. Here O'Flanagan attempts to redress the 'monstrous fabrication' of Macpherson's 'Darthula'.[45] Despite the activities of the society, Yeats did adapt Macpherson's work on one occasion, as Ed Larrissy notes:

> In his influential lectures, *On Celtic Literature* (well known to Yeats), Matthew Arnold had quoted (or slightly misquoted) a line from Macpherson's *Ossian*: 'They went forth to the battle but they always fell'... Yeats gave as a title to one of his poems the same misquotation from Macpherson... though he later changed it to 'The Rose of Battle'.[46]

Yeats' interest in Macpherson was fleeting; it did not last into the twentieth century.[47]

Despite Yeats' overall rejection of Macpherson's texts, the binary relationship set up by Arnold, based on Macpherson's work, survives into the purple glow and pavements grey of Yeats' era. In the 1880s, '[t]hough jeering at Matthew Arnold', Yeats still 'apparently subscribed to the Arnoldean view of

---

[44] Larrissy, xiv.

[45] O'Flanagan, 143. See Mathis, 'Mourning the Maic Uislenn' for a discussion of O'Flanagan's work on Macpherson.

[46] Larrissy, xiv. Elizabeth Sharp—wife of William Sharp—included 'They went forth to the Battle, but they always fell', under that title, in the 1896 collection *Lyra Celtica*. Also, a Dublin journalist quotes this line during a discussion on pyrrhic victories and lost causes amid the rhetoric of the 'Aeolus' episode of *Ulysses*: 'They went forth to battle, Mr O'Madden Burke said greyly, but they always fell' (*U*, 7.572–3).

[47] See Larrissy, xiv. In terms of early Irish literature, Daniel Gomes argues that 'Yeats's emphasis was predominately on recalling a prior mythological unity' rather than on the kind of fragmentation found in Macpherson's work. See Gomes, 378.

the Celt as dreamy, sensitive, and doom-laden.'[48] Conversely, English culture
was, for Yeats, characterized by rationalism and materialism. However, this
materialism could be countered by the 'Celtic Element'. As Yeats writes in
'The Celtic Element in Literature', 'The reaction against rationalism of the
eighteenth century has mingled with a reaction against the materialism of the
nineteenth century'.[49] Commenting on Yeats' article, Pethica observes that:

> In 'The Celtic Element in Literature' [Yeats] memorably claims that 'litera-
> ture dwindles to a mere chronicle of circumstance, or passionless fantasies,
> and passionless meditation, unless it is constantly flooded with the passions
> and beliefs of ancient times', thereby tarring the realism predominant in
> contemporary British fiction and drama as imaginatively bankrupt. Of all
> the European races... 'the Celtic alone' had sustained 'the main river' of lit-
> erary inspiration....[50]

It was partly this Horatio-like reaction against rationality and materialism
which had initially led Yeats into his occult adventures and paranormal
investigations.[51] As Foster has noted, Yeats was working in 'the tradition of
Matthew Arnold [and] the philosophical and anti-materialist side of
'Celticism'' in 1893.[52] Even after the decline of early Celticism, James Joyce
speaks of England having 'almost entirely a materialist civilization' and creates anti-materialist texts in an imagined lineage of 'Celtic' philosophy.[53] The
idea that English materialism must be countered by 'Celtic' culture survives
from the Revival into Modernism. However, as is discussed in Chapter 4,
there is also an anomalous merging of Celticism with materialism in the work
of the Scottish Modernist poet Hugh MacDiarmid.

Irish and Scottish Modernisms developed out of greatly changed political
situations from that of Irish and Scottish Romanticisms.[54] In the period from
the early nineteenth century to the early twentieth century, the 'Celtic world'[55]
went through rapid and drastic change, including the continued decline of the
Irish and Scottish Gaelic languages. During the Romantic period 'Celticism was
used as a tool in the construction and expansion of the post-1745 British

---

[48] Foster, Yeats I, 53.   [49] Yeats, Essays and Introductions, 187.   [50] Pethica, 134.
[51] 'The youthful Yeats "tried many pathways"... in the 1880s in search of anti-materialist forms of
truth' (Ibid., 130).
[52] Foster, Yeats I, 131.   [53] OCPW, 125.
[54] Irish and Scottish Romanticisms grew out of the different aftermaths of the 1745/46 Jacobite
Rebellion, the 1798 United Irish Rebellion, and the 1800 Act of Union.
[55] OCPW, 124.

state'.[56] At this point, before the rise of O'Connell and before the tragedy of the Famine, Owenson's 'Whig dream of reconciliation' between Ireland and England was still possible, if implausible.[57] But after O'Connell—and the Famine—no such reconciliation was forthcoming. Since the marriage of Celtic and Saxon cultures had failed to produce a harmonious 'end of history' in Ireland, Celticism could no longer be used to promote a discourse of convergence and balance. In Ireland, 'the Celtic Revival became the Gaelic Revival, and was rapidly politicized'.[58] As a result of these developments, Celticism in its early form recedes rapidly at the beginning of the twentieth century, coinciding roughly with Yeats' loss of interest in Macpherson and the sidelining of Fiona Macleod from the Irish Revival (to be discussed in the following chapter). However, English modernity, emanating from the centre of imperial power, was still seen as posing a grave threat to the essence and identities of the Celtic 'periphery'. As a consequence, we see in Modernism a marked interest in the isolated limits of the Celtic world—the Aran Islands, the Hebrides—especially to islands of imagined primitive vitality considered less contaminated by the 'filthy modern tide'.[59]

In contrast to the historical contexts of Irish and Scottish Romanticisms, the Modernist period saw the British Empire beginning to fall apart and cracks starting to show in the British state itself.[60] Importantly for the study of Irish Modernism, this period also follows the dawn of psychoanalysis. If notions of national or imperial wholeness were being undermined during this period, so were concepts of personal or psychic unity, especially in texts by Joyce and Samuel Beckett.[61] Similarly, following the Romantic period, Macpherson's *Ossian* ceases to be involved in debates concerning authenticity, racial purity, or place of textual origin. Instead, within Modernist texts *Ossian* gains a capacity to signify some of the concerns and methods of the new era: mental fragmentation, indeterminacy, textual recycling, and literary collage.

Publications of Macpherson's works stalled during the Modernist period, a fallow period following the texts published in 1896 to mark the centenary of

---

[56] Carruthers and Rawes, 1.   [57] Deane, *Short History*, 99.   [58] Foster, *Irish Story*, 99.
[59] Yeats, 'The Statues', l. 29, *The Poems*, 385. For a discussion of archipelagic issues in Irish and Scottish Modernisms, see Brannigan.
[60] As John Brannigan states: 'in the 1920s and 1930s...the very notion of the "wholeness" of "Britain", "England", or the "United Kingdom" was undermined politically and culturally by the emergent sovereignty of the Irish Free State (1922) and its constitutional claim to the 'whole island of Ireland' (1937), by the Scottish Renaissance of the 1920s, by the formation of Plaid Cymru (1925) and the Scottish National Party (1934), and by the palpable decline of British imperial power across the globe' (Brannigan, 147).
[61] However, the national and the mental are often conjoined in Joyce's works. See, for example, the phrase 'little brittle magic nation, dim of mind' in *Finnegans Wake* (FW, 565.29–30).

Macpherson's death.[62] However, aspects of 'Celtic' culture re-emerge within Irish and Scottish Modernisms in order to resist English culture rather than to marry it (examples of this trend include the various 'Celtic' features of Joyce's *Finnegans Wake*, and Hugh MacDiarmid's *In Memoriam James Joyce*). This is partly due to an anxiety in Irish and Scottish literature concerning the perceived threat of an English modernity of soulless materialism (a continuation of anxieties dating back to the nineteenth century), or as a response to the historical domination of Ireland or Scotland by England. As Deane has noted: 'History…must be countered by fiction'.[63] Indeed, the Modernisms of Ireland and Scotland were often designed to vandalize or subvert English culture.[64] Some of the texts of Irish or Scottish Modernism can be placed in a context of 'Celtic' culture, broadly understood (*Finnegans Wake*, for example). However, Ossianic elements also appear in texts that are difficult or impossible to place in any kind of 'Celtic' context, such as Beckett's *Murphy*. The remainder of this chapter considers the different ways Joyce and Beckett react to Macpherson's *Ossian*.

Joyce was very much aware of the *Ossian* controversy[65] and held three copies of Macpherson's work, including Italian and German translations, as part of his Trieste library,[66] a collection that predates the composition of *Finnegans Wake* (published in full in 1939). In a letter to Paul Léon dated 11 September 1937, written during the final stages of the composition of *Finnegans Wake*, Joyce requests a copy of *Ossian*.[67] *Finnegans Wake* notebook VI.B.45, comprising notes written in January and February 1938 in Paris and Zurich, contains a number of Ossianic entries. Unlike Yeats, Joyce never placed much faith in supposedly 'authentic' or 'pure' Celtic mythology; during the 'Cyclops' episode of *Ulysses* the 'twelve tribes of Iar' include 'the tribe of Ossian'.[68] Like Mangan and Wilde, Joyce understood 'the value of the false, the insincere and the artificial, over whatever purported to be "real," genuine or authentic art'.[69] However, *Finnegans Wake* can be read as a 'Celtic' text (if we accept Joyce's use

[62] The 1896 edition was published by Patrick Geddes with an introduction by William Sharp. Sebastian Mitchell notes that 'At the time of the publication of *The Poems of Ossian* [Howard Gaskill's edition, published in 1996] there had been no new edition of the poems produced by a British or American publisher since 1926' (Mitchell, 'Ossian', 160).
[63] Deane, *Celtic*, 93.   [64] See Gibson, Andrew.
[65] As were his detractors. In an *Observer* review Oliver St. John Gogarty declared *Finnegans Wake* 'the most colossal leg pull in literature since Macpherson's *Ossian*' (*JJ*, 722).
[66] See Ellmann, *Consciousness*, 122.   [67] Fahy, 27.   [68] *U*, 12.1125 and *U*, 12.1129.
[69] Sturgeon, 115. On the subject of Oscar Fingal O'Flahertie Wills Wilde, it is worth mentioning that 'Oscar' and 'Fingal' are both Ossianic names and that Jane Francesca Agnes, Wilde's mother, was an admirer of Macpherson's work.

of the term),[70] with its prominent use of the figures Fionn mac Cumhaill (from what Joyce called 'the amorphous Celtic *Odyssey*')[71] its allusions to Tristan and Isolde, and its opening setting within a Celtic coastal and island network.[72] The phrase 'Kilt by kelt shell kithagain with kinagain'[73] links Ireland (since 'kinagain' rhymes with Finnegan) and Scotland ('kilt') and suggests the sea-links of the Celtic nations of the Atlantic archipelago through 'shell' and the play on the word Celt (a kelt is a post-spawn Atlantic salmon).

Perhaps due to his long 'exile' from Ireland, it was, for some time, fairly standard to consider Joyce as a rootless, European cosmopolitan rather than as an Irishman (never mind as a 'Celt'). Joyce parodies the melancholic excesses of Celtic Revival poetry in 'A Little Cloud' and the ethnographic English tourist Haines is seen clutching 'a portfolio full of Celtic literature in one hand, in the other a phial marked *Poison*' in the 'Oxen of the Sun' episode of *Ulysses*.[74] Nevertheless, Joyce shared with Irish revolutionaries the conception of England as a prosaic, debased, and materialist nation and of Ireland as an oppressed and spiritual Celtic nation. As Seamus Deane notes, 'Joyce is as willing as Pearse to speak of Ireland's soul, to speak of the nation as a spiritual entity, and to conceive of her plight as one in which something ethereal has been overwhelmed by something base'.[75]

In 'Ireland: Island of Saints and Sages', Joyce compares the 'Celtic spirit' to English materialism (while arguing that Ireland is controlled by what Stephen Dedalus calls 'two masters' in *Ulysses*):[76]

> I confess that I do not see what good it does to fulminate against English tyranny while the tyranny of Rome still holds the dwelling place of the soul. Neither do I see the use in bitter invectives against England, the despoiler, or in contempt for the vast Anglo-Saxon civilization, even if it is almost entirely a materialist civilization.[77]

---

[70] 'Joyce uses the word Celtic in a very loose and atypical fashion...simply to denote the non-English nations and inhabitants of the Atlantic archipelago, regardless of period, place, or language. For example, the modern, lowland, non-Gaelic speaking Scot David Hume is described as Celtic [in] Joyce's notes for *Exiles*' (Barlow, *The Celtic Unconscious*, 18).

[71] *OCPW*, 148.   [72] See Brannigan, 98.   [73] *FW* 594.3–4.   [74] *U*, 14.1013–1014.

[75] Deane, *Celtic*, 96. Furthermore, critics have begun to explore the connections between Joyce's work and the Irish Revival as part of a wider movement away from the idea that the Revival and Irish Modernism were mutually exclusive phenomena. According to Declan Kiberd, 'there is good reason to see Joyce as someone who felt himself a part (however angular a part)' of the Irish Literary Revival (Kiberd, 'Joyce's Homer, Homer's Joyce', 245). See also: 'Joyce is not unsympathetic to the larger goal of the Revival—establishing a genuinely Irish culture—but...he is hostile to the specific means it employed' (Begam, 194).

[76] *U*, 1.638.   [77] *OCPW*, 125.

While Joyce considers English culture 'materialist' he associates 'Celtic spirit' with 'consciousness', therefore continuing the Arnoldian materialist Saxon/ spiritual Celt binary:

> Is this country destined some day to resume its ancient position as the Hellas of the north? Is the Celtic spirit, like the Slavic one (which it resembles in many respects), destined in the future to enrich the consciousness of civilization with new discoveries and institutions? Or is the Celtic world, the five Celtic nations, pressed by a stronger race to the edge of the continent—to the very last islands of Europe—doomed, after centuries of struggle, finally to fall head-long into the ocean?[78]

Joyce writes of Ireland as a Celtic nation despite it being an 'immense woven fabric' in terms of race.[79] For Joyce, the Celtic nature of Ireland is a cultural rather than an ethnic issue. With regards to Celtic languages, it should be pointed out that, unlike figures of the Irish Revival such as Yeats and Gregory, Joyce actually had a good knowledge of Irish.[80] In addition to his interest in Celtic language, Joyce's 1913 notes for his play *Exiles* show his interest in what he deemed Celtic philosophy: 'All Celtic philosophers seem to have inclined towards incertitude or scepticism—Hume, Berkeley, Balfour, Bergson.'[81] As Jean-Michel Rabaté has suggested, Joyce's comments on Celtic philosophy point to 'a tradition or a line of descent in which Joyce clearly wants to be inscribed'.[82] Joyce's interest in Hume helps to create the atmosphere of incertitude or scepticism generated by *Finnegans Wake* and the unconscious night-world of that work is Joyce's Celtic, interior, mental (rather than spiritual) response to English materialism (or, to use Andrew Gibson's phrase, his

---

[78] Ibid., 124–5.   [79] Ibid., 118.

[80] Joyce was taught some Irish by the future revolutionary Patrick Pearse in his student days (see *JJ*, 61). Later in life, Joyce briefly studied another Celtic language, Breton, and declared Irish to be 'FAR SUPERIOR' (*JJ*, 567). There is a large quantity of Irish in *Finnegans Wake*. See O Hehir.

[81] *Poems and Exiles*, 353. C.f. ' "Gulliver's Travels" and "Tristram Shandy" will be substitutes for the books I have named only when the books of Hume are considered Scotch literature in the same sense as the books of Burns and Barrie' (Yeats, *Uncollected Prose I*, 352). Joyce's categorization of Hume as a Celtic philosopher is ironic given Hume's views on the Celts: 'Hume's Scots, and still more his Irish, are often portrayed as "disorderly", "slothful", "barbaric", "barbarous", and "least civilized". The Irish are "from the beginning of time…buried in the most profound barbarism and ignorance", "savage and untractable"; the Scots were full of "native ferocity", a "barbarous enemy" who carry out "insidious and unjust" attacks on England. Independent Scotland was "the rudest, perhaps, of all European nations", while among Scots, Highlanders, "continually concerned to keep themselves from starving or being hanged", were the rudest of all, locked in a Hobbesian state of Nature, immune to the refinements of civility. Both Scots and Irish are seen by Hume as prone to fanaticism' (Pittock, *Scottish and Irish Romanticism*, 64–5).

[82] Rabaté, 24.

'Celtic Revenge').[83] As with Hume's idealist philosophy, the sleeping 'dreamer' of *Finnegans Wake* is buried or inhumed inside his own mind, dead to the world: 'Joyce's use of sleep as a "setting" for the *Wake* functions as an illustration of his general conception that we as individuals are limited to the internal functions of the mind, caught in a Humean—and therefore, for Joyce, a Celtic—void of interiority and doubt.'[84]

In *Finnegans Wake*, Shem, the Joyce-like writer figure, is compared to 'jameymock farceson'.[85] Here, by comparing himself through Shem to Macpherson, Joyce jokes about his own method of composition and its inauthentic or 'mock' status. Joyce himself wrote that he was 'quite content to go down to posterity as a scissors and paste man' as it seemed to him 'a harsh but not unjust description.'[86] Like Macpherson, Joyce is a gatherer and recycler of textual material. Elsewhere in *Finnegans Wake*, the phrase '*MacPerson's Oshean*'[87] suggests that dreams (a central theme of *Finnegans Wake*) and personal identities are mixed, fluid, and recycled (water often signifies repetition and return in *Finnegans Wake*). There is a considerable amount of Ossianic material in *Finnegans Wake*.[88] Joyce mainly works with *Temora* and *Fingal*—thus connecting *Finnegans Wake* intertextually with the most and least 'authentic' Macpherson texts.[89] There are 61 examples of textual transmission from *Fingal* and 52 from *Temora* in *Finnegans Wake*.[90] Partly, these fragments help to create a vaguely Ossianic tone at certain points in the text.[91] As Stafford has noted, '[t]he repetitious nature of the language, imagery, metre and even the plots [of *Ossian*], has an almost mesmeric quality' with 'imprecise' characters and sense of landscape.[92] The repetitive use of Macpherson in *Finnegans Wake* helps to create the obscured, uncertain experience of *Finnegans Wake* and its representation of

[83] Gibson, Andrew, 1.   [84] Barlow, *The Celtic Unconscious*, 21.   [85] *FW*, 423.1.
[86] *LI*, 297.   [87] *FW*, 123.25.
[88] A search for 'James Macpherson' in the online 'Finnegans Wake Extensible Elucidation Treasury' (fweet.org). returns 152 glosses. Details of the specific Macphersonian textual matter incorporated into *Finnegans Wake* are also to be found in Swinson, 'Macpherson in *Finnegans Wake*' and Senn, 'Ossianic Echoes'.
[89] According to Moore, '*Fingal* most closely corresponds to extant traditional ballads actually in Gaelic; *Temora* is furthest from the extant tradition' (Moore, 'Introduction', 3).
[90] However, Joyce also incorporates elements from Macpherson's poems 'Comala', 'The War of Caros', 'The War of Inis-thona', 'The Battle of Lora', 'Conlath and Cuthona', 'The Death of Cuthullin', 'Carric-Thura', 'The Songs of Selma', 'Lathmon', 'Croma', 'Cathlin of Clutha', 'Cath-loda', 'Oina-moral' and 'Colna-dona'.
[91] As Senn has commented, 'Sometimes Joyce seems to have been content merely to create an atmosphere reminiscent of the Ossianic poems' (Senn, 25).
[92] Stafford, 'Introduction' to Macpherson, James. *The Poems of Ossian and Related Works*, v-xix, xvi. Indeed, words such as 'cloud', 'storm', 'dark', 'ocean', 'wave', 'stream', 'roll', 'rolls', 'rolling', and 'rolled' begin to attain a mantra-like quality after prolonged reading.

night, dreams, and unconsciousness. Aside from this 'macro-level' usage, meanings at the 'micro-level' can also be deciphered.

An allusion to *Fingal* features at the onset of *Finnegans Wake* (in its fourth paragraph). The announcement of Conal in Book II of the poem, 'If fall I must, my tomb shall rise, amidst the fame of future times'[93] is repurposed by Joyce as 'Phall if you but will, rise you must: and none so soon either shall the pharce for the nonce come to a setdown secular phoenish'.[94] Macpherson's phrase already shares the Wakean themes of death and resurrection but Joyce adds another image of endings and rebirth with 'Phoenish', while making his phrase more suggestive—in both senses—of bodily, non-monumental erections ('Phall') and of sleeping and waking. The elegiac grandeur of *Fingal* is transformed into the comedy and farce of *Finnegans Wake* and Macpherson's prose poetry is subsumed into the word-music of Joyce's final text. An illustrative example of the use of *Temora* (Macpherson's name for Tara, seat of the high kings of Ireland) in *Finnegans Wake* comes slightly further into the first chapter: 'hoist high the stone that Liam failed'.[95] This line adapts 'When thou, O stone, shalt fail: and Lubar's stream roll quite away'[96] but adds an allusion to the Lia Fáil, the ceremonial stone at Tara. This construction-themed phrase is part of the building of the central figure HCE (his occupation is a hod-carrier and he is destined to fail/fall). This phrase retains the rising and falling dualism of the first example.

Both of these sections occur right at the beginning, or resumption, of *Finnegans Wake*, in Book I. A particularly striking example of direct derivation from an Ossianic text to *Finnegans Wake* occurs in Book IV, the final section and 'ricorso' of Joyce's work: 'Which the deers alones they sees and the darkies they is snuffing of the wind up'.[97] This phrase alludes to Macpherson's 'Carthon: A Poem' from *The Works of Ossian* (1765),[98] which was itself based on a version of the Scottish ballad 'Bàs Chonlaoich' ('The Death of Conlaoch').[99] The relevant section of Macpherson's text reads: 'Two stones, half sunk in the ground, shew their heads of moss. The deer of the mountain avoids the place, for he beholds the gray ghost that guards it: for the mighty lie, O Malvina, in the narrow plain of the rock'.[100] Macpherson's note to this section reads: 'It was the opinion of the times, that deer saw the ghosts of the dead. To this day, when beasts suddenly start without any apparent cause, the vulgar think that

---

[93] Macpherson, 66.   [94] *FW*, 4.15–17.   [95] Ibid., 25.31.   [96] Macpherson, 241.
[97] *FW*, 603.26–27.   [98] Swinson, 95.
[99] See Meek, 31. *Finnegans Wake* also contains Joyce's own work in the ballad genre: 'The Ballad of Persse O'Reilly'.
[100] Macpherson, 127.

they see the spirits of the deceased.'[101] The final section of *Finnegans Wake* is a chapter of resurrection and waking, so the apparition of this eerie Macpherson material is well suited to its surroundings. Joyce's 'book of the dark'[102] frequently blurs death and sleep, and is interested in anything interred, subterranean, or chthonic.

As Donald Meek has discussed, in working with the ballad 'Bàs Chonlaoich', 'Macpherson was…using at least one source-poem which originated in Scotland'.[103] This may be considered as an instance not only of textual transmission of Macpherson's prose poetry in Joyce's work but also of an accidental, miniature link—via Macpherson—between the Scottish Gaelic ballad tradition and *Finnegans Wake*. While Owenson and Yeats sought to sideline Macpherson and, in Owenson's case, to discredit Scottish claims to Ossianic material, Joyce's text actually contains a small amount of material with its roots in a genuine Scottish Gaelic ballad (although it is unlikely that Joyce knew of the Scottish Gaelic source of 'Carthon'). *Finnegans Wake* incorporates the kind of textual matter that critics such as Meek have used to indicate that 'it is quite incorrect to imply that the tradition tapped by Macpherson had no proper Scottish dimension' and that Macpherson was 'operating… within…a tradition which was well rooted in Scotland'.[104] Here Joyce makes use, for his own purposes, and probably unwittingly, of material that would later be summoned as a defence against two charges commonly directed at Macpherson: that Macpherson had appropriated Irish culture for Scotland and that he had not worked with actual source material.[105] However, it should be stressed that there is no evidence to suggest that Joyce knew he was doing this—the traces of genuine Scottish material are simply part of the large amount of Ossianic matter Joyce took from Macpherson's work. This Ossianic material is used by Joyce in his exploration of textual recirculation/transmission and of literary construction and fabrication. The material is also part of Joyce's representation of dreams as a kind of indeterminate, illusory 'hoax' (despite the presence of authentic ballad material in Macpherson's work), his preoccupation with different types of repetition, and his rendering of the linked histories of Ireland and Scotland.[106]

As was mentioned earlier, a Romantic focus on national or racial traits in Irish and Scottish literature, as seen in texts such as *The Wild Irish Girl*, is

---

[101] Ibid., 445, n. 3.   [102] *FW*, 251.24.
[103] Meek, 31. A version of 'Bàs Chonlaoich' is included in the *Book of the Dean of Lismore*. For further information on the 'Dean's Book', see Gillies.
[104] Meek, 19.   [105] For a range of criticisms levelled at Macpherson, see Mackenzie, Henry.
[106] See the chapter 'The Dream of Ossian' in Barlow, *The Celtic Unconscious*, 151–82.

largely replaced by Modernist conceptions of personal and national fragmentation. Furthermore, the fragmentary nature of *Ossian* is highlighted and engaged with in Irish texts following the decline of early Celticism. As we have seen, *Finnegans Wake* contains a large number of 'fragments' taken from the works of James Macpherson. According to Robert Crawford, the fragment

> is a form which speaks of cultural ruin, and of potential re-assembly...Just as the Ossianic fragments are part of the aftermath of Culloden, in [the twentieth century] the greatest uses of the fragment have come in the work of poets writing in the wake of a war which shattered the civilisation they knew. Pound used the form for much of his career and Eliot shored up fragments against his *Waste Land* ruins.[107]

We might add Joyce to this list. Furthermore, in addition to the sense of global collapse—or at least European fragmentation—in the early twentieth century, there was also the partial crumbling of the British state during this period. Personal and national divisions and splits frequently merge in *Finnegans Wake*. As opposed to the models of convergence offered in works like *The Wild Irish Girl*, *Finnegans Wake* is a text of deliberate instability. Significantly, the *Wake* was also composed in years following the partition of Ireland, a 'partitional of twenty six and six'.[108]

In *Finnegans Wake*, the phrase '*MacPerson's Oshean*' is associated with '*Schizophrenesis*',[109] partly because Joyce is linking *Ossian*'s status as something consisting of different elements to the fragmentation of the split or schizophrenic mind. Similarly, Beckett makes use of *Ossian*, and a character of unstable, scattered origin to signal the 'schizoid voice' in his early text *Murphy* (1938, French translation in 1947). *Murphy* is a fairly Joycean text as far as Beckett works go, written before the younger writer's turn to textual distillation and reduction. Much of the action, or inaction, in the later stages of *Murphy* takes place at the 'Magdalen Mental Mercyseat' hospital in London. As Shane Weller has noted, 'if *Murphy* contains a range of terms drawn from psychoanalytic and psychiatric discourse, it is undoubtedly the concept of schizophrenia that dominates that novel'.[110] Beckett uses a Scottish character with an evocative name and a remarkably archipelagic background—and, in the French version of Beckett's novel, a liking for *Ossian*—to explore the 'schizoid voice'.

Beckett's text tells us that 'Dr. Killiekrankie, the Outer Hebridean R.M.S., had some experience of the schizoid voice. It was not like a real voice, one

---

[107] Crawford, 'Post-Cullodenism', 18.   [108] *FW*, 264.22–23.
[109] Ibid., 123.25 and 123.18–19.   [110] Weller, 38.

minute it said one thing and the next minute something quite different.'[111] Killiecrankie's own speaking voice sometimes lapses into Groundskeeper Willie-style rolled Rs: 'severe burrrns', 'Mrs. Murrrphy', 'The essence of all cold storage...is a free turrnover.'[112] Chris Ackerley has discussed Killiecrankie's origins and interests:

> In the French text his background...is more complex: conceived in the Shetlands, born in the Orkneys and weaned in the Hebrides, he is a great admirer of Ossian, and 'croyait s'y connaître en voix schizoïdes. Elles ne res-semblaient guère aux voix hébridiennes, ni aux voix orcadiennes, ni aux voix shetlandiennes. Tantôt elles vous disaient ceci et tantôt cela.' Jung might on occasion use the phrase 'Ossianic emotions' for wild flights of fancy.[113]

As Ackerley has discussed, '*Murphy* marks an important stage in Beckett's quest for the voice. Its structure and argument were shaped by Beckett's visit (2 October 1935) with his therapist, Wilfred Bion, to the Tavistock Clinic [in London], to hear the third of Jung's five lectures (which Beckett later read).'[114] Jung uses the phrase 'Ossianic emotions' in 'On Spiritualistic Phenomena' (1905), when discussing Romanticism:

> The beginning of the nineteenth century had brought us the Romantic Movement in literature, a symptom of a widespread, deep-seated longing for anything extraordinary and abnormal. People adored wallowing in Ossianic emotions, they went crazy over novels set in old castles and ruined cloisters. Everywhere prominence was given to the mystical, the hysterical....[115]

Beckett uses the term 'Ossianic', in his attack on Celtic antiquarianism in a 1934 article titled 'Recent Irish Poetry', published under the pseudonym 'Andrew Belis'. However, he uses the term in a slightly different way compared to Jung. In the article, Beckett accuses Irish 'antiquarians' (i.e. Yeatsian Revivalists), of 'delivering with the altitudinous complacency of the Victorian Gael the Ossianic goods', succumbing to the 'Celtic drill of extraversion' and providing only 'cut-and-dried sanctity and loveliness'.[116] According to Anthony McGrath:

> Art's true point of origination is within the inner depths of the artist's con-sciousness, where, as 'pure subject of knowing' he apprehends the Idea that is destined to be expressed by his work...Beckett's notion of the 'Celtic drill

---

[111] Beckett, *Murphy*, 116.   [112] Ibid., 163, 167, 168.   [113] Ackerley, 41.
[114] Ibid., 41.   [115] Jung, 294.   [116] Beckett, *Disjecta*, 70, 73, 71.

of extraversion', whereby poets of the Celtic Twilight are engaged in a 'flight from self-awareness', amounts to a repudiation of those whose artistic focus resided within the mists of Celtic antiquity.[117]

In 'Recent Irish Poetry', as in 'Censorship in the Saorstat', Beckett argues 'against cultural isolationism, and for internationalism, for Ireland's literature to submit itself...to the influences of the French avant-garde and Pound'.[118] For Beckett, the 'Celtic drill of extraversion' is—somewhat paradoxically—a form of inwardness but not the right type. 'Recent Irish Poetry' suggest that Irish poets should be inward in the mental or personal sense, but not in a national or cultural sense, since that would lead to a parochial insularity. However, perhaps Beckett was not averse to thinking in terms of the English/Irish oppositional binary developed in Celticist discourse. As the possibly apocryphal story goes, when asked if he was English at the premiere of *En Attendant Godot* in 1953, Beckett replied 'Au contraire'.[119]

If Yeats used Ossianic material for nationalist reasons, Beckett uses the term 'Ossianic'—post-Irish independence in the 26 counties—to rail against areas of Irish culture that, in his estimation, had become too inward-looking (in a national sense). After the demise of the Celtic Revival, and the establishment of the Free State, figures from older Irish literature are treated with greater irony and humour, as in Joyce's *Finnegans Wake*, Flann O'Brien's *At Swim-Two-Birds*, and Beckett's *Murphy*, where Neary headbutts the statue of Cú Chulainn in the Dublin General Post Office. Beckett's 'Fingal', the second story in *More Pricks than Kicks* (1934) combines an Ossianic title ('Fingal' is Macpherson's name for Fionn mac Cumhaill, as well as an area in County Dublin) with comic and unheroic content. In 'Fingal', Belacqua and his companion Winnie climb the Hill of Feltrim and look down at the Portrane Lunatic Asylum below. The association between questionable legend and madness continues in the French language *Murphy*, with its reference to 'Ossianic emotions' (i.e. mental illness).

As Ackerley and Gontarski have commented, the name of Angus Killiecrankie in *Murphy* 'connotes, in English, killing the cranky, the mentally ill (G. *krank*, 'ill')'.[120] Perhaps Beckett was unaware of the charged nature of the word Killiecrankie, but it is the name of a village in Perth and Kinross that saw a victory by Irish and Scottish Jacobites over Hanoverian forces in 1689

---

[117] McGrath, 17–18.   [118] Mooney, 33.   [119] See Roche, 199.
[120] Ackerley and Gontarski, 298. 'The original of Dr. Killiecrankie...was the senior assistant at the Bethlem Royal, one Murdo MacKenzie, originally from Inverness, the pun on "murder" ("Killie") being further identification' (Ackerley and Gontarski, 298).

(there are no Ossianic connections). The battle became the subject of a song and was used as an anthem of Pan-Celtic solidarity by the United Irishmen in the late eighteenth century: 'the United Irishmen's use of [Killiecrankie] recalled an important rebel victory against the forces of the crown at which Scottish and Irish forces had successfully united in their common grievances, much as they were being urged to do in Ulster in 1795'.[121] So, a text that associates Celticism with mental illness features a doctor with the name of a song celebrating an Irish-Scottish military victory. Though he does not inflict any violence upon the living Murphy, Killiecrankie is tasked with incinerating Murphy's corpse towards the end of the text, since he has access to 'a small close furnace...in which the toughest body, mind and soul could be relied on to revert, in under an hour...to ash of an eminently portable quality'.[122] At the close of a novel interested in fragmentation and breakdowns, Murphy himself disintegrates and his remains are unceremoniously scattered: 'By closing time the body, mind and soul of Murphy were freely distributed over the floor of the saloon' and he is swept out into the street with 'the spits, the vomit'.[123] Fittingly, Killiecrankie is considered 'Unromantic to the last'.[124]

Killiecrankie's name is clearly associated with the killing of the mentally ill. However, that Killiecrankie, in the French *Murphy*, has his origins in the geographically separate Scottish island groups of the Hebrides, Orkney, and Shetland, is also noteworthy. These origins suggest not only the multiplications of isolated and discrete schizoid voices but also the gathering of elements from separate, disparate sources (similar to the *Ossian* texts themselves of which Dr. Killiecrankie is an admirer in the French *Murphy*).[125] Killiecrankie's origins are also fairly Ossianic, since episodes of *Fingal* and *Temora* take place in the Hebrides, Orkney, and Shetland.[126] So, Killiecrankie's archipelagic origins reflect the various cultures featured in the poems he so admires. The sea often

---

[121] Thuente, 255.   [122] Beckett, *Murphy*, 169.   [123] Ibid., 171.   [124] Ibid., 164.

[125] Joyce also had an interest in the Hebrides, Orkney, and Shetland. For example, *Finnegans Wake* notebook VI.B.32 contains material relating to the Hebrides and notebook VI.B.6 has notes on Orkney and Shetland. Allusions to Papa Westray on Orkney appear in *Finnegans Wake* at 26.07 and 104.22. On the subject of Orkney and Macpherson, the Orcadian Malcolm Laing disputed Macpherson's claims to authenticity in his *Poems of Ossian, containing the Poetical Works of James MacPherson in Prose and Verse, with Notes and Illustrations* (1805). This text was assessed by Walter Scott in the *Edinburgh Review* (6 July, 1805, 429–62). Scott's piece includes a famous conclusion: 'let us therefore hear no more of Macpherson', (Scott, 'Laing's Edition of Macpherson / Report of the Highland Society upon Ossian', 461).

[126] As Mitchell has pointed out, although the 'main events of both *Fingal* and *Temora* take place in Ulster', '[e]pisodes in these epics and in the shorter lyrical and dramatic pieces are also set...in the Hebrides, Orkney and the Shetland isles...The central plot of *Fingal* hinges on an invasion of Ulster by Swaran, a Scandinavian chieftain...The action culminates in the set-piece battle between the Gaels and the Scandinavians' (Mitchell, 'Landscape', 67).

functions as a site of cultural exchange and convergence in Joyce.[127] However, in this Beckett text, the sea (and island groups within it) are associated with disconnection and incoherence. In Beckett's text, these scattered and isolated locations are linked to what has been called 'a multivocal, indeterminate multiplicity'.[128] Unlike Yeats, Beckett had no intention to make something 'intended, complete' out of incoherence and fragmentation: 'I am not interested in a…"clarification" of the individual chaos'.[129] Sinéad Mooney has suggested that Beckett constructed a 'deconstructive brand of modernism' as opposed to 'the mythopoeic modernism of Yeats'.[130] As part of this, Beckett involves the work of Macpherson, a compiler and arranger of fragments.[131]

Macpherson's *Ossian* founded a regrettably long-lived understanding of two races or worlds—the spiritual Celtic realm and the practical Anglo-Saxon territory—and a discourse, Celticism, that began partly as a way of uniting or reconciling those worlds in literature, especially in texts such as *The Wild Irish Girl*. Yeats largely ignores Macpherson, but keeps the interest in older Celtic literature and the Celtic/Saxon binary that Arnold built upon Macpherson's work. In the twentieth century, *Ossian* shifts from a connection with national or racial concerns to personal matters, to become a signifier of mental fragmentation. Joyce's use of *Ossian* ties in with the essentially 'Celtic' nature of *Finnegans Wake* and with that text's model of consciousness as fragmented and recycled. *Finnegans Wake* also contains a unique, large-scale set of Ossianic textual transmission. Beckett, following the work of Jung, uses *Ossian* and disparate offshore Scottish locations to signify a multiplicity of schizoid voices. From the nineteenth to the twentieth century, *Ossian* moves from an involvement in the Romantic imagining of national identities to an echoing Modernist confusion of irreconcilable inner and textual voices.

---

[127] See Hegglund, 71.
[128] Gontarski, 20. See also: 'Voice as disembodied entity…in fragments…is the heuristic that drives Samuel Beckett's supreme fictions…Its sources are indeterminate, evasive, ghostly, receding, counterfeited, echoed, ventriloquized' (Ibid., 19).
[129] Beckett, qtd in McNaughton, 107.   [130] Mooney, 34.
[131] Stafford has discussed the attractions of *Ossian* for postmodernism: 'postmodern culture offers echoes, quotations, repetitions and correspondences…In such a climate, a work that insistently blurred the normal distinctions between text and annotation, author and translator, past and present, quoting freely from different traditions…was likely to attract new interest' (Stafford, 'Romantic', 35–6).

2

Gender, nationality, and Celticism
in Gregory and Macleod

In the famous 1897 statement published by Augusta Gregory,[1] Edward Martyn, and W.B. Yeats prior to the founding of their new theatre in 1899, the supposedly Celtic nature of the enterprise is initially played up, before a specifically Irish focus develops:

> We propose to have performed in Dublin, in the spring of every year certain Celtic and Irish plays, which whatever be their degree of excellence will be written with a high ambition, and so to build up a Celtic and Irish school of dramatic literature. We hope to find in Ireland an uncorrupted and imaginative audience trained to listen by its passion for oratory, and believe that our desire to bring upon the stage the deeper thoughts and emotions of Ireland will ensure for us a tolerant welcome, and that freedom to experiment which is not found in theatres of England, and without which no new movement in art or literature can succeed. We will show that Ireland is not the home of buffoonery and of easy sentiment, as it has been represented, but the home of an ancient idealism. We are confident of the support of all Irish people, who are weary of misrepresentation, in carrying out a work that is outside all the political questions that divide us.[2]

In a similar fashion to the way an initially 'Celtic and Irish' themed statement moves on to expressly Irish concerns, the planned Celtic Theatre eventually became the Irish Literary Theatre.[3] The 1897 manifesto sets up the new Irish

---

[1] This chapter refers to 'Augusta Gregory' and 'Gregory', rather than 'Lady Gregory'. As Anne Fogarty has noted, 'the very anachronism of the title that is still seen as an irremovable part of her name acts as a barrier to a critical appreciation of the significant contribution she made to the literary revival in her capacity as folklorist, translator, theatre producer, and playwright' (Fogarty, 101).

[2] Gregory, *Irish Theatre*, 8–9.

[3] 'The "Celtic" theatre would be renamed the 'Irish Literary Theatre' in October [1897], as [Yeats], Russell and Martyn thought this 'less dangerous'; partly a political decision, partly because [Yeats] had recently discovered that 'Celticism' was a highly problematic concept in historical or cultural terms...Yeats...realized that the concept of 'Celticism' was bogus through reading an article by Andrew Lang' (Foster, *Yeats I*, 185 and 571, n. 84).

Modern Irish and Scottish Literature: Connections, Contrasts, Celticisms. Richard Alan Barlow, Oxford University Press.
© Richard Alan Barlow 2023. DOI: 10.1093/oso/9780192859181.003.0003

Literary Theatre as a high-minded alternative to the supposedly commercial and sentimental melodrama of playwrights such as Dion Boucicault. In a letter to the Scottish author 'Fiona Macleod' (William Sharp), from January 1897, Yeats wrote that 'Our Irish literary & politico-literary organizations are pretty complete now…celtic plays…would be far more effective than lectures & might do more than anything else, we can do, to make the Irish, Scotch, & Other, celts recognize their solidarity'.[4]

In her 1913 text *Our Irish Theatre*, Gregory comments that the Irish Literary Theatre announcement was a 'little pompous' (despite the uncertainty regarding dramatic quality betrayed by the phrase 'whatever be their degree of excellence').[5] She then goes on to discuss the inclusion of the word 'Celtic' in the statement:

> I think the word 'Celtic' was put in for the sake of Fiona Macleod, whose plays however we never acted, though we used to amuse ourselves by thinking of the call for 'author' that might follow one, and the possible appearance of William Sharp in place of the beautiful woman he had given her out to be, for even then we had little doubt they were one and the same person. I myself never quite understood the meaning of the 'Celtic Movement', which we were said to belong to. When I was asked about it, I used to say it was a movement meant to persuade the Scotch to begin buying our books, while we continued not to buy theirs.[6]

There are strong Celticist elements to the Irish Literary Theatre statement; it aims to set up a theatre that will be partly defined in opposition to English drama which supposedly has no room for 'experiment', it imagines an 'uncorrupted' Irish audience—implying a 'corrupted' English audience—and it will reveal the 'real' Ireland of 'ancient idealism' which has been obscured or misrepresented by the vulgar modernity of commercial drama with its

---

[4] *CL II*, 73.   [5] Gregory, *Irish Theatre*, 8.
[6] Ibid., 9–10. The comment regarding the movement's supposed aversion to buying 'Scotch' books is interesting, given the influence of work by figures such as James Macpherson, Walter Scott, Robert Burns, Thomas Carlyle, Alexander Carmichael, and James Frazer on the Irish Revival, as well as the contributions of Fiona Macleod to the 'Celtic Movement'. George Watson has noted that 'Carlyle's ideas…permeated much that Yeats read and heard because they were mediated in the work of Carlyle's enthusiastic Irish disciple, Standish James O'Grady, whom Yeats and others saw as "the father of the Revival"' (Watson, George, 'Aspects', 140). J.B. Yeats read Scott's *Lay of the Last Minstrel* and *Ivanhoe* to Yeats when he was a boy (See Ellmann, *Yeats*, 28). According to Yeats, 'but for the legends and history of the Highlanders, who are in all things of one stock with ourselves…Walter Scott could hardly have begun that great modern mediaeval movement, which has influenced all the literature and art and much of the religion of the nineteenth century. Until our day the Celt has dreamed half the dreams of Europe' (Yeats, *Uncollected Prose II*, 70–1).

'buffoonery' and 'easy sentiment'. However, Gregory is surely right to consider the inclusion of the word 'Celtic' at least partly an act of straightforward practicality to cover the case of the self-styled Scotswoman Fiona Macleod, one of the proposed contributors of the new theatre.[7] In the end, as Gregory noted, the Irish Literary Theatre never produced a play by Macleod.

Fiona Macleod was supposedly a 'self-sequestered Hebridean visionary'[8] with William Sharp, a 'red-faced six-footer in plus-fours'[9]—the man Gregory mentions in *Our Irish Theatre*—being her second cousin from Paisley as well as her friend and literary agent.[10] A great deal of work was produced under the name Fiona Macleod in the 1890s and 1900s, with a number of Macleod texts appearing in *The Evergreen*, the influential Edinburgh Celticist journal edited by the polymath Patrick Geddes.[11] Geddes himself described Macleod as 'the High Priestess of the Celtic Renascence'[12] while Yeats suggested that she held the keys to 'those gates of the primeval world, which shut behind more successful races, when they plunged into material progress'.[13] Yeats regarded Scotland as being an important source for spiritual culture, despite describing the Scots as 'too gloomy'.[14] This interest in Scotland can be partly attributed to increased attention within Scotland during the late nineteenth century to its Gaelic heritage and to its links to Ireland:

> As the nineteenth century drew to a close, awareness grew among Scottish writers and artists of the mythological dimension to the Gaelic heritage their nation shared with Ireland. This was, in a sense, no surprise: Ireland and Gaelic Scotland had been part of a single cultural and linguistic zone in the Middle Ages, and thanks to James Macpherson's Ossianic poems, Scotland

---

[7] According to Foster, 'While Gregory was relieved that their enterprise was to abandon the "poor Sharp-ridden" identification of "Celtic", the Pan-Celtic idea was still to be encouraged for purposes of bringing in respectable supporters' (Foster, *Yeats I*, 197). In November 1898, Yeats wrote to Thomas Patrick Gill that 'People should be asked to support the Irish Literary Theatre on patriotic grounds, but they should first be made to feal [*sic*] that there is an actual school of Irish spiritual thought in literature & that their patriotism will support this. Ireland is leading the way in a war on materialism, decadence, triviality as well as affirming her own individuality. That is our case' (*CL II*, 302).

[8] Williams, Mark, 371.   [9] Ibid., 370.   [10] See Halloran, 'A Celtic Drama', 159.

[11] Yeats was asked to contribute to *The Evergreen*, but nothing by him appeared in the journal. However, pieces by the Irish figures Standish James O'Grady, Douglas Hyde, Katharine Tynan, Nora Hopper, and Rosa Mulholland did appear, so the publication had a pan-Celtic feel and strong Irish-Scottish connections.

[12] Geddes, 1. Geddes continues, '[Macleod] is by far the most poetical of the prose-writers that lead this curious movement; and her mind is more completely imbued with what has been called "the Celtic glamour" than that of any of her colleagues' (Geddes, 1).

[13] Yeats, *Uncollected Prose II*, 45.

[14] Yeats, *Celtic Twilight*, 178. Despite his interest in Pan-Celticism, 'Yeats [had] a broad anti-Scottish bias that extended to Presbyterian Ulster' and 'he always blamed Walter Scott, even Burns sometimes, for debasing the currency of poetry during the nineteenth century' (Longley, 2).

had been the fountainhead of romantic Celticism in English for more than a century. From the mid-1890s Scotland developed a parallel Celtic Revival of its own, an anti-industrial aesthetic movement centred in Edinburgh but that looked to Ireland for an example.[15]

Within this parallel Anglophone Celtic Revival, Macleod was the preeminent writer. In her letters, Macleod discussed the mystery surrounding her identity (while attempting to convince correspondents that she was not William Sharp):

> Heaven knows who and what I am according to some wiseacres...A friend of a friend told that friend that I was Miss Nora Hopper and Mr. Yeats in union—at which I felt flattered but amused. For some time, a year or so ago, there was a rumour that 'Fiona Macleod' was my good friend and relative, William Sharp. Then, when this was disproved, I was said to be Mrs. Sharp. Latterly I became the daughter of the late Dr. Norman Macleod. The latest is that I am Miss Maud Gonne—which the paragraphist 'knows as a fact'. Do you know her? She is Irish, and lives in Paris, and is, I hear, very beautiful—so I prefer to be Miss Gonne, rather than the Fleet Street journalist! Seriously I am often annoyed by these rumours. But what can I do? There are private reasons, as well as my own particular wishes, why I must preserve my privacy.[16]

Elsewhere, Macleod wrote that she came from 'an old Catholic family' and that she was born 'in the southern Hebrides'.[17]

In reality, as Gregory notes above, 'Fiona Macleod' was the 'contrasexual authorial persona'[18] of the Scotsman William Sharp.[19] This secret was not officially revealed until Sharp's death in 1905, although Yeats and Russell had their suspicions much earlier.[20] 'Fiona Macleod' seems to have functioned as a secondary personality for Sharp and his transgender self-fashioning can also

---

[15] Williams, Mark, 361. An important part of this revival was developed within in the visual and decorative arts: 'In 1890s Scotland the Celtic Revival manifested itself as the Glasgow Style, epitomized by the work of [Charles Rennie] Mackintosh, Herbert McNair and Margaret and Frances Macdonald, known as "The Four"' (Fowle, 248).

[16] Macleod letter to Katharine Tynan, March 24, 1897, reproduced in Tynan, *The Middle Years*, 131.

[17] Letter to Katharine Tynan, March 24, 1897, reprinted in Halloran, *Life and Letters of William Sharp and 'Fiona Macleod' II*, 324.

[18] Williams, Mark, 374.

[19] In this chapter, the name 'Macleod' is used when referring to the texts published under the name 'Fiona Macleod'. 'Sharp' is used when discussing the life of the man behind the feminine persona. Sometimes it will be necessary to refer to 'Macleod/Sharp'.

[20] See Williams, Mark, 371. Yeats puts inverted commas around the name Fiona Macleod in letter from May, 1897 (see *CL II*, 99, n. 5).

be considered in the context of developments in study of sexuality during this period.[21] In one letter to a friend, Sharp pleads 'Don't despise me when I say that in some things I am more a woman than a man.'[22] Indeed, Sharp sometimes signed off his letters with a portmanteau of his name and his alter-ego's, 'Wilfion', while Yeats and George Russell wrote about 'MacSharp' in 1900 once they had worked out what was going on.[23] While Sharp believed that 'woman would be the medium of a universal redemption' and frequently imagined living the life of a woman,[24] he did not participate in activism within feminist circles.[25] In using the name Macleod, Sharp was also tapping into 'the contemporary fashion for seeing the "Celt" as intuitive, visionary, and feminine'.[26]

Of course, it had been commonplace to think of the Celts as an essentially feminine race since the mid nineteenth-century texts of theorists such as Matthew Arnold and Ernest Renan (though the Irish and Scottish Celts are not the most feminine of the Celtic nations in Renan's estimation): 'the Celtic race, especially with regard to its Cymric or Breton branch, is an essentially feminine race'.[27] In addition to this, there is a longstanding tradition in Ireland of imagining the nation as abstract, feminine personifications—the Sean Bhean Bhocht and Kathleen Ni Houlihan being the most obvious examples.[28]

---

[21] See Alaya, 10–11 and 120. 'Sharp's kind of transvestism—a transvestism not of the flesh but of the imagination—was implicitly sanctioned by contemporary anthropological studies of prophetic and visionary types, and by the "new spirit" of humane, compassionate sexuality expressed in the writings of such men as Edward Carpenter and Havelock Ellis' (Alaya, 10–11). See also: 'Sharp's ... associates in the Edinburgh Celtic movement, Patrick Geddes and J. Arthur Thompson, in their *Evolution of Sex*, admitted the sociological consequences of their biological discoveries. "The social order", they proclaimed with splendid optimism, "will clear itself, as it comes more in touch with biology." For biology had, they certified, determined beyond a shadow of doubt that women were the guests through whom "altruism, patience, affection, intuition, subtlety, feeling, and memory" found their way into society' (Alaya, 120).

[22] Sharp, Elizabeth, 33.

[23] Sharp, Elizabeth, 423, and two letters postmarked 13 July, 1900 and 8 August, 1900 qtd in Foster, *Yeats I*, 197, 572 n. 137.

[24] See also: 'I remember he told me that rarely a day passed in which he did not try to imagine himself living the life of a woman, to see through her eyes, and feel and view life from her standpoint, and so vividly that 'sometimes I forget I am not the woman I am trying to imagine' (Sharp, Elizabeth, 53).

[25] Sharp held a belief that 'that woman would be the medium of a universal redemption, for in woman are summed up all the powers of continuum, all the beneficence of Nature, in fact all the love respondent to the pathos of mankind both individually and as a race ... Paradoxically, this messianic view of woman may explain Sharp's aloofness from the practical, activist branch of the feminist movement' (Alaya, 140–1).

[26] Williams, Mark, 374.   [27] Renan, 8.

[28] According to Seamus Heaney, 'There is an indigenous territorial numen, a tutelar of the whole island, call her Mother Ireland, Kathleen Ni Houlihan, the poor old woman, the Shan Van Vocht, whatever; and her sovereignty has been temporarily usurped or infringed by a new male cult whose founding fathers were Cromwell, William of Orange and Edward Carson and whose godhead is incarnate in a rex or Caesar resident in a palace in London' (Heaney, *Preoccupations*, 57). For a modern and feminist approach to the female personification of Ireland, see Eavan Boland's 'Mise Éire' (1987), written partly in response to Pearse's 1912 poem 'Mise Éire'. As Mark Williams has noted, the god Aengus

These figures took on a strongly nationalistic dimension in the Revival/ Revolutionary era in Ireland, and it became common to imagine the wronged, dispossessed female figure as in need of rescue or redemption through violence and redemptive bloodshed. The association of the nation with femininity is not as strong in Scotland. However, texts from the era of the Act of Union such as William Wright's *The Comical History of the Marriage-Union Betwixt Fergusia and Heptarchus* (1717) represent Scotland (or Fegusia) as a 'Lady of Venerable Antiquity' whose 'Chastity, tho' several Times attack'd, yet was never violated' and England (Heptarchus) as 'Young, and Lusty, very opulent and Rich'.[29]

In *The Trembling of the Veil*, Yeats records a bizarre story Sharp told him 'in 1895, or on some visit four or five years later'[30] in which Sharp encountered a mysterious woman in his hotel room and chased her through the streets of Paris. Eventually the woman vanished. At this point, Sharp went into some kind of trance and imagined he was in Scotland hearing the ringing of a sheep-bell. When Sharp regained consciousness he was soaking wet, lying on the street with a crowd gathered around him. He had, supposedly, thrown himself in the Seine in order to rescue the fleeing, mystery woman. Yeats did not believe this story. Still, Sharp seems to have ascribed symbolic importance to the aisling-like story/'event'. According to Halloran, 'When he jumped into the water, he was trying to save both the woman he loved (Edith Rinder) and the female self within him'.[31] In Sharp's life and work, fantasies of the death of women seem to be related to pity for a part of himself. Whatever happened in Paris, Sharp's time in the French capital was a turning point for him and his work:

> after his experience in Paris the nature of the writings changed...From writing stories about the simple people who lived out their lives amid tragedies and in close touch with spirits in the West of Scotland, Sharp turned to symbolic and ritualistic stories and essays. The plunge into the Seine in a failed

Óg became an effeminate or hermaphroditic personification of Ireland in the late nineteenth/early twentieth centuries (see Williams, Mark, 444–52). For a discussion of the emergence of Caitlín Ní Uallacháin and other female personifications of land in eighteenth-century Irish political poetry, see Nic Eoin.

[29] Wright, 3, 7. For analysis of Wright's text and metaphors of political union as sexual violence, see Davis, 27–8.

[30] Yeats, *Collected Works III*, 260.

[31] Halloran, 'A Celtic Drama', 168. Sharp also led a double life in his personal relationships, 'dividing his time between Elizabeth Sharp...and Edith Rinder, the beautiful young woman with whom he had fallen in love' (Halloran, 'A Celtic Drama', 160). Edith Wingate Rinder was an English Celticist and translator. According to his wife's *Memoir*, Rinder put him 'in touch with ancestral memories' (Sharp, Elizabeth, 222).

attempt to rescue a woman became itself a symbol of his immersion in a new occult quest.[32]

Further insights into William Sharp's life and work can be gleaned from *A Memoir*, a text put together by his wife Elizabeth and published in 1910, five years after William's death. In this book, Elizabeth provides a potted history of the Celtic Revivals of Wales, Ireland, and Scotland, linking them back to nineteenth-century continental Celtic scholarship, and mentioning a mixture of Anglophone Celticists and Gaels:

> Following on the incentive given by such scholars as Windische [*sic*], Whitly Stokes [*sic*], Kuno Meyer, and the various Folklore societies, a Gaelic League had been formed by enthusiasts in Ireland, and in Scotland, for the preservation and teaching of the old Celtic tongue; for the study of the old literatures of which priceless treasures lay untouched in both countries, and for the encouragement of natural racial talent. Wales had succeeded in recovering the use of her Cymric tongue; and the expression in music of racial sentiment had become widespread throughout that country. Ireland and the Highlands looked forward to attaining to a similar result; and efforts to that end were set agoing in schools, in classes, by means of such organisations as the Irish Feis Ceoil Committee, the Irish Literary Society and the Irish National Theatre. Their aim was to preserve some utterance of the national life, to mould some new kind of romance, some new element of thought, out of Irish life and traditions. Among the most eager workers were Dr. Douglas Hyde, Mr. W. B. Yeats, Mr. Standish O'Grady, Mr. George Russell (A.E.), Dr. George Sigerson, and Lady Gregory. In Scotland much valuable work had been done by such men as Campbell of Islay, Cameron of Brodick, Mr. Alexander Carmichael; by the Gaelic League and the Highland Mod and its yearly gatherings.[33]

It is noteworthy that all of the Scottish figures Elizabeth Sharp mentions are men (thereby omitting figures such as the poet Alice MacDonell) and that, on the Scottish side, all were Gaelic speakers whereas, on the Irish side, not all

---

[32] Halloran, 'A Celtic Drama', 169. 'A survey of Fiona Macleod's production from that point until Sharp's death shows two revealing things: that nothing like her first rush of stories and poems between 1894 and 1896 was ever conceived again; that by 1898 Fiona Macleod's capacity for imaginative production had been almost totally exhausted, and there was no work thereafter that adhered to the classic Macleod type—the bardic, visionary, or mystical treatment of life in the Celtic highlands or islands' (Alaya, 7).

[33] Sharp, Elizabeth, 256–7.

were Irish speakers. Beyond studying early literature, preserving Celtic languages, and 'national life', these movements aimed at countering modern materialism and rationalism through a 'new kind of romance'.[34] These trends and interests overlapped with attempts in Europe during this era to find spiritual alternatives to Christianity. This search led to a heightened interest in esoterica and the occult, the setting up of various new religions and orders, and an interest in paganism, seen by some adherents as a 'religion of joy, pleasure, and natural beauty'.[35] There was a particularly strong link between magic and Celtic revivalism during this period: 'Both occultism and cultural nationalism involve belief in hidden realities which must be made manifest'.[36]

Despite the fact that 'Mythological divinities had been of negligible importance in the culture of Gaeldom in Scotland',[37] William Sharp became a 'theorist' of the Tuatha Dé Danann (the god-people of Irish myth) and began to absorb Irish divinities into Scottish literature from 1894.[38] In Sharp's view (revealed via Macleod),

The Celtic paganism lies profound and potent still beneath the fugitive drift of Christianity and Civilisation, as the deep sea beneath the coming and going of the tides. No one can understand the islander and remote Alban Gael who ignores or is oblivious of the potent pagan and indeed elementally barbaric forces behind all exterior appearances.[39]

Here Celticism merges with paganism in resisting forms of modern civilization, including some aspects or forms of organized Christianity. Sharp had a particular loathing for Presbyterianism and an attraction towards Catholicism, especially the figure of the Virgin Mary.[40]

---

[34] Yeats, 'Literary Movement', 858.   [35] Williams, Mark, 307.
[36] Brown, Terence, 'Cultural Nationalism, Celticism and the Occult', 222.
[37] Williams, Mark, 405.
[38] Ibid., 370. Williams has commented on the sources of Sharp's work on the Gaelic gods: 'Sharp purported to be transcribing from Gaelic oral tradition, but a significant source of his imagery was the periodical literature of Dublin and the world of Celtic research, which he read shrewdly' (Ibid., 378).
[39] Letter to Grant Allen, 1894, reproduced in Sharp, Elizabeth, 231.
[40] See Williams, Mark, 374. For further anti-Protestant sentiment in modern Scottish literature, see Edwin Muir's poem 'Scotland 1941': 'But Knox and Melville clapped their preaching palms / And bundled all the harvesters away' (Muir, Edwin, 97). According to Watson, 'Muir is [one] who regrets that Scotland has been given history rather than imagination, courtesy of Calvinism. (This is notwithstanding the existence of places like the island of Lewis, at once quintessentially Gaelic/Celtic and Calvinist)' (Watson, George, 'Annulment', 215). For Willa Muir, Presbyterianism was a 'a kind of spiritual strychnine of which Scotland took an overdose' (Muir, Willa, 75–6). Indeed, this is a view shared by many Scottish authors: 'Characteristic...of the Scottish Renaissance writers was a sympathy towards Catholicism and opposition to Presbyterian Unionism' (Pittock, *Celtic Identity*, 85). In Hugh MacDiarmid's *To Circumjack Cencrastus*, the Reformation is described as a 'foul trap' (*CP*, 213).

In the late 1890s, Sharp moved frequently around Scotland, England, and other parts of Europe. In 1897, he spent time in Paris with Yeats, Maud Gonne, and Moina and Macgregor Mathers, carrying out occult experiments, doing drugs (hash and mescaline), and making plans for a Celtic Mystical Order.[41] Later that year, Sharp visited the west of Ireland. Before he left, he wrote a letter that could very easily be mistaken for the work of Horatio in Sydney Owenson's *The Wild Irish Girl*: 'I hope to be dreaming in that old castle in what the Gaels called Far Connaught. Think of me there at the extreme verge of the passing Celtic world. There I know that some spiritual tidings or summons await me.'[42] In a letter written at Tulira Castle in Galway[43] to his wife Elizabeth Sharp dated 4 October 1897, Sharp details the plans for his trip to the west of Ireland and describes his new surroundings:

The country is strange and fascinating — at once so austere, so remote, so unusual, and so characteristic...It is glorious autumnal weather, with unclouded sky, and I am looking forward to the trip immensely. We leave at 11, and drive to Ardrahan, and there get a train southward into County Clare, and at Ennis catch a little loopline to the coast. Then for two hours we drive to the famous Cliffs of Moher, gigantic precipices facing the Atlantic...and...in the afternoon, to the beautiful Clare 'spa' of Lisdoonvarna, where we dine late and sleep. Next day we return by some famous Round Tower of antiquity, whose name I have forgotten. Another day soon we are to go into Galway, and to the Arran Isles [*sic*].[44]

---

[41] See Halloran, 'A Celtic Drama'. As Halloran has discussed, 'W. B. Yeats and William Sharp became acquainted shortly after Yeats settled in London in 1887, but it was nine years later, in 1896, through the Celtic Revival, that they became friends...Yeats's friendship with Sharp reached its peak in early 1897. It was in 1897...that Sharp told Yeats he was the author of the writings of Fiona Macleod' (Halloran, 'A Celtic Drama', 159). However, Sharp once stole one of Yeats' visions and passed it off as a joint revelation (see Foster, *Yeats I*, 165) and in 1897 Yeats vetoed Sharp's chairing of an Irish Literary Society meeting (see *CL II*, 148–9).

[42] Letter to Catherine Ann Janvier, October 1897. In Halloran, *Life and Letters of William Sharp and 'Fiona Macleod' II*, 348. For an account of Scottish Celticist occultism, see Shaw.

[43] Also spelled 'Tillyra' and 'Tullira'.

[44] Sharp, Elizabeth, 287–8. Yeats had tested the veracity of Macleod's *The Washer of the Ford* on the Aran Islands: 'I have put them to a hard test, for I read the tales in "The Washer of the Ford," which are reprinted here, on the deck of an Arran [*sic*] fishing-boat and among the grey stones of Arran [*sic*] Island; among the very people of whom she writes, for the Irish and Highland Gael are one race; and when I laid down the book I talked with an Arran [*sic*] fisherman of the very beliefs and legends that were its warp and woof' (Yeats, *Collected Works IX*, 337). Sharp's 1897 trip to the Aran Islands is worth dwelling on. '[Yeats] had read Fiona Macleod's *The Washer of the Ford* during his trip to the Aran Islands the previous August. After reading a passage from one tale, "The Dan-nan-Ron," which featured a man who was descended from the seals, Yeats talked to a fisherman and found he knew the story and shared its beliefs' (Halloran, 'A Celtic Drama', 175). The previous year, Yeats had advised Synge to 'Go to the Aran Islands. Live there as if you were one of the people themselves; express a life that has never found expression' (Yeats, Preface to the First Edition of *The Well of the Saints*, 63). John

As will be discussed in the final chapter of this book, trips to the west of Ireland—often imagined as a space of pure, authentic Irishness or a place to escape from modernity—remain a staple of Irish literature, especially poetry, well into the twentieth century.

Further in the 1897 letter from Tulira Castle, Sharp writes of the imminent arrival of the leading lights of the Irish Celtic Revival:

> On Thursday Yeats arrives, also Dr. Douglas Hyde, and possibly Standish O'Grady—and Lady Gregory, one of the moving spirits in this projected new Celtic Drama. She is my host's nearest neighbour, and has a lovely place (Coole Park) about five miles southwest from here, near Gort. I drove there…yesterday, in a car, through a strange fascinating austere country.[45]

Sure enough, Gregory did arrive at the Castle Tulira Celtic gathering. Yeats also arrived, and this is the only time Sharp and Yeats spent time together in Ireland.[46] Unfortunately, Sharp got off on the wrong foot with Gregory, as the latter's diaries show:

> I spent a few days at Tillyra to meet a "Celtic" party—William Sharp, an absurd object, in velvet coat, curled hair, wonderful ties—a good natured creature—a sort of professional patron of poets—but making himself ridiculous by stories to the men of his love affairs & entanglements, & seeing visions (instigated by Yeats)—one apparition clasped him to an elm tree from which he had to be released….[47]

Wonderful ties aside, Sharp's appearance and tree-hugging antics seem to have bemused Gregory and there is a trace of pity to the phrase 'good natured creature'. Similarly, Sharp failed to make a good first impression on Yeats: 'I was introduced to Sharp…and hated his red British face of flaccid contentment.'[48] Unfortunately for Sharp, he became a *persona non grata* at Tulira after making a holy show of himself with his high jinks at the summer Celtic party in 1897. Yeats returned to Tulira in 1898 and seems to have used

---

Brannigan has suggested that it was Sharp's influence that had led Yeats to give this advice (see Brannigan, 35–6). So, if Sharp did make it to Aran, he was visiting islands that would find their most famous literary representation in Synge's *The Aran Islands* (1907), a text based on expeditions likely influenced by Sharp's work.

[45] Sharp, Elizabeth, 288.
[46] According to Foster, 'the summer of 1897 was [Yeats'] first real immersion in what would become the centre of his Irish life' (i.e. Coole Park) (Foster, *Yeats I*, 181).
[47] Pethica (ed.), *Lady Gregory's Diaries*, 153–4.   [48] *CL I*, 24.

the death of Edward Martyn's mother as a tactful excuse to keep Sharp at a distance (Tulira Castle was Martyn's home).[49]

Gregory and Sharp had very different national and class backgrounds as well as differing attitudes to Protestantism (Gregory never abandoned Protestantism whereas Sharp created a Catholic *alter ego* for himself and regarded Protestantism as having been a curse to Scotland). Nevertheless, Gregory and Sharp were part of connected literary scenes and they worked on the same source material. It also seems that, despite the rocky start, relations improved between Gregory and Sharp. Later in Sharp's trip, Gregory took him to visit Kilmacduagh, a nearby cromlech, and to hear some local 'Celtic tales', including 'legends of Finn & Ussian galore'.[50] Furthermore, in December 1897, Gregory intervened when a disagreement over the chairing of an Irish Literary Society meeting in London threatened to disrupt Yeats and Sharp's friendship. Discussing her intervention, Gregory signalled her position that there should be no 'merging' of Irish and Scottish Celticists: 'one morning I telegraphed [Yeats] for Sharp's address—then to Sharp himself—& when he came I told him that Yeats's friends were of the opinion the Celtic movement wd be injured by them merging into one camp—that they shd rather be allies like the Unionists & Tories'.[51] That Christmas, the Sharps sent the texts *Lyra Celtica* (an anthology of poetry edited by Elizabeth Sharp) and *Vistas* (by William Sharp) to Gregory as presents.[52] Still, Sharp was eventually ousted from the Yeats/Gregory social-artistic network. Discussing the adoption of the name 'Irish Literary Theatre' and the removal of the word 'Celtic' in 1898, Gregory wrote to Yeats that the new name was 'much better' than 'poor Sharp-ridden "Celtic"'.[53] Similarly, Yeats wrote—also in 1898—that 'The Irish Literary Theatre' was 'less dangerous than Celtic'.[54] Yeats disclosed the change in the name in a breezy, nonchalant letter to Sharp: 'I shall be away again to look after the Irish Literary Theatre (celtic theatre renamed) at the end or middle of January'.[55] As has been noted, 'this deft parenthesis glides over the fact that the theatre, which had originally been named so as to include Sharp

---

[49] According to Gould et al, 'WBY may be using [the death of Martyn's mother] as a diplomatic excuse for putting off a further visit from Sharp, who had made something of a spectacle of himself on his previous stay at Tillyra' (*CL II*, 249, n. 1). The letter in question is from Coole Park, 4 July 1898 (*CL II*, 249–51).

[50] Qtd in Halloran, 'A Celtic Drama', 184.

[51] According to Halloran, 'Thanks to Lady Gregory's intervention, the relationship between Yeats and Sharp, though rocked briefly over the chair, was preserved on an even keel' (Halloran, 'A Celtic Drama', 198).

[52] Gregory, *Diaries*, 164.   [53] Qtd in *CL II*, 277, n. 14.   [54] *CL II*, 277.

[55] Ibid., 284–5.

and Macleod...was now being renamed partly to exclude them'.[56] The eventual side-lining of Sharp/Macleod during the Celtic Revival echoes the rejection of Macpherson's *Ossian* in Ireland during Sydney Owenson's era.[57]

Tensions between William Sharp and Irish writers were increased by Sharp's unionist politics, which coloured Fiona Macleod's texts. George Russell came to regard Macleod's form of Celticism as pro-British.[58] This is understandable, given sections such as this from the Macleod text *Winged Destiny*:

> I am not English, and have not the English mind or the English temper, and in many things do not share the English ideals; and to possess these would mean to relinquish my own heritage. But why should I be irreconcilably hostile to that mind and that temper and those ideals? Why should I not do my utmost to understand, sympathise, fall into line with them so far as may be, since we all have a common bond and a common destiny? To that mind and that temper and those ideals do we not owe some of the noblest achievements of the human race, some of the lordliest conquests over the instincts and forces of barbarism, some of the loveliest and most deathless things of the spirit and the imagination?[59]

Daniel G. Williams has commented that 'Sharp's Celticism was deeply anti-nationalist'.[60] That is certainly true if the nation in question is Scotland.[61] However, Sharp displays a great admiration for English culture and is a nationalist of a sort (British unionism having the traits of nationalism but with a focus on a multi-nation state rather than a nation), in contrast to Gregory's gradual development from unionism to nationalism[62] and her slight anti-English streak.[63] This contrast reflects a larger division between the

---

[56] Ibid., 285, n. 2.

[57] Sharp, along with Patrick Geddes, was one of the few promoters of *Ossian* in nineteenth century Scotland.

[58] See Halloran, 'A Celtic Drama', 206, n. 58.   [59] Macleod, *Winged Destiny*, 177–8.

[60] Williams, Daniel G., 162.

[61] 'While Macleod's novels were regarded by Yeats as part of the Celtic movement, and "she" was invited to write plays for the Abbey Theatre, Sharp consistently used his *alter ego* to reject emphatically any association with a nationalist movement' (Williams, Daniel G., 163). See also: 'Sharp...argued that Celticism was not nationalistic: its strength was that it dispensed with nationality in favour of cosmopolitan openness' (Harvie, *Floating*, 125).

[62] 'I first feared and then became reconciled to, and now hope to see even a greater independence than Home Rule, my saying has been long, "I am not fighting for it, but preparing for it." And that has been my purpose in my work for establishing a National Theatre, and for the revival of the language, and in making better known the heroic tales of Ireland' (Gregory, *Seventy Years*, 54).

[63] She once remarked that it was impossible for anyone to read Irish history 'without getting a dislike and distrust of England' (Gregory, *Irish Theatre*, 55).

Irish and Scottish Celtic Revivals: 'In Scotland, the Celtic Renaissance was considerably less radical than its Irish counterpart, both linguistically and politically.'[64] However, Celticism combines with radical politics in Scotland in the twentieth century.

Indeed, Sharp's political unionism parallels his Christian approach to the gods of Irish myth. For Mark Williams, 'The political unionism of Scots such as William Sharp...was accompanied by the firm insistence on Christian themes in their work: both saw the gods of the Gael as complemented and indeed completed by Christian revelation.'[65] Celticism for Sharp is not an alternative to English culture, it balances and supports English culture—a stance with obvious political ramifications. In the introduction to *Lyra Celtica*, 'an anthology of representative Celtic poetry', Macleod writes that 'we may hope that the beautiful poetry of Ireland...the strange, elemental, sombre imagination of the West Highlander and of the Gael of the Isles...and...the vivid spell of the old Welsh bards, will, before long, become...a lasting force and influence in *our English literature*' (italics mine).[66] As such, Sharp's Celticism is fairly Arnoldian.[67] His thinking on these matters is reflected in pieces such as this, from the *Fortnightly Review*:

What is called 'the Celtic Renascence' is simply a fresh development of creative energy coloured by nationality...The Celtic writer is the writer the temper of whose mind is more ancient, more primitive, and in a sense more natural than that of his compatriot in whom the Teutonic strain prevails...the Celt comes of a people who grew in spiritual outlook as they began what has been revealed to us by history as a ceaseless losing battle, so the Teuton comes of a people who has lost in the spiritual life what they have

---

[64] Stroh, 216.   [65] Williams, Mark, 433.

[66] Sharp, 'Introduction', xxxvi. '*Lyra Celtica*...contains almost two hundred individual works, followed by forty or so pages of notes. Contributions include ancient and modern work by poets from Scotland, Ireland, Brittany, Cornwall, Wales, and the Isle of Man...ranging from Macpherson's *Ossian* to Yeats's *The Lake Isle of Innisfree* via Duncan Bàn MacIntyre, Douglas Hyde, Sir Samuel Ferguson, Kuno Meyer, John Stuart Blackie, Hall Caine, T. W. Rolleston and Fiona Macleod. It was, however, a determinedly English-language presentation of the Celt: that was the key to Sharp's agenda for he wanted to claim the future of Celtic culture for English speakers like himself' (Macdonald, 143). *Lyra Celtica* contains a Deirdre text, 'Deirdrê's Lament for the Sons of Usnach'. Commenting on this piece, Elizabeth Sharp writes, 'Of the many Irish-Gaelic and Scottish-Gaelic and English translations and paraphrases, I have selected the rendering of Sir Samuel Ferguson. The original Erse is of unknown antiquity' (Sharp and Matthay, 404). The use of Ferguson in *Lyra Celtica* is fitting, since Ferguson's antiquarianism—like William Sharp's activities—was bound up with his unionism. However, Sharp was writing at a moment of transition. From this point onwards, literary Celticism is often aligned with Irish and Scottish nationalisms. Deirdre is discussed later in this chapter.

[67] 'Sharp associated Celticity with sensitivity, mysticism, anti-Presbyterian sensuousness, antimaterialism, femininity, childhood, timelessness, an idealized golden age in the past, and a fated decline under the tragically irresistible onslaught of modernity' (Stroh, 218).

gained in the moral and the practical...All that the new generation of Celtic or Anglo-Celtic (for the most part Anglo-Celtic) writers hold in conscious aim, is to interpret anew 'the beauty at the heart of things', not along the line of English tradition but along that of racial instinct, coloured and informed by individual temperament.[68]

In the *Lyra Celtica* introduction, Sharp discusses racial types without limiting himself to Scotland and Ireland or to historically 'Celtic' areas:

The truth is, that just as in Scotland we may come upon a type which is unmistakeably national without being either Anglo-Saxon or Celtic or Anglo-Celtic, but which, rightly or wrongly, we take to be Pictish (and possibly a survival of an older race still), so, throughout our whole country, and in Sussex and Hampshire, as well as in Connemara or Argyll, we may at any moment encounter the Celtic brain in the Anglo-Saxon flesh.[69]

Sharp's racial theorizing meets his political unionism here: he claims that Celtic mentality can be found in Anglo-Saxon bodies in places as English and as far south as Sussex and Hampshire. Sharp's introduction points to a number of places on the map as a way of pulling the islands or 'our whole country' together.[70]

The idea of the Celtic (or Anglo-Celtic) brain recurs later in the introduction: 'The Celtic Renascence, of which so much has been written of late—that is, the re-birth of the Celtic genius in the brain of Anglo-Celtic poets and the brotherhood of dreamers—is, fundamentally, the outcome of "Ossian," and, immediately, of the rising of the sap in the Irish nation.'[71] The phrase 'the outcome of "Ossian"' is noteworthy, since Sharp's entire introduction—with its talk of 'tragic gloom', 'haunting charm', 'deep yearning emotion', 'strange melancholy' and (discussing Yeats) 'haunting sense of beauty', 'exquisite remoteness', and 'dream-like music'—is basically an outcome of the language of *Ossian.*[72] So, this focus on dreamy Celtic gloom is one of the ways the

---

[68] Fiona Macleod, 'A Group of Celtic Writers', 36–7.

[69] Sharp, 'Introduction', *Lyra Celtica*, xxiv–xxv.

[70] He temporarily forgets Wales, although he does later address that nation: 'In the preservation of her language is her safeguard. Without Welsh, Wales would be as English as Cumberland or Cornwall. In this way only, knit indissolubly to the flank of England as she is, and without any natural eastern frontier of mountain range or sea, can she isolate herself' (Sharp, 'Introduction', xxxiii–xxxiv).

[71] Sharp, 'Introduction', xxxv.

[72] Sharp, 'Introduction', xxix, xxvii, xxvii, xlix, xliv, xliv, xliv. See also: 'in the words of the most recent of those many eager young Celtic writers... "...The Celt falls, but his spirit rises in the heart and

Celticism of the late nineteenth century—roughly a midway point in the development of Celticism overall—connects with its earliest phase.

For Macleod, the Celts, though a 'passing race,'[73] had maintained their purity through their geographical isolation and through resistance to historical forces. However, modernity is a new and deadly enemy:

> Never has human family lived more isolated from the world, nor less affected by foreign admixture...The civilization of Rome hardly reached them, and left among them but few traces. The Germanic invasion flowed back on them, but it did not affect them at all. At the present hour they still resist an invasion, dangerous in quite another way, that of modern civilisation, so destructive of local varieties and national types.[74]

In this respect, Macleod shares with Scottish and Irish Modernisms an anxiety regarding the effects of modernity on indigenous culture. Often this anxiety is reflected in an interest in Scottish and Irish islands as possibly 'uncorrupted' and premodern spaces.[75]

The story of the contacts between Augusta Gregory and William Sharp reveals the connections between the Celtic Revivals of Ireland and Scotland but also the underlying political tensions. While both were Celticists, neither were pan-Celticists. Gregory's Celticism was focused specifically on Ireland, while Sharp's unionism prevented him from adopting a pan-Celtic or nationalist position. Gregory and Sharp also have contrasting approaches to gender. The remainder of this chapter compares the different positions regarding nationality and gender taken by Gregory and Fiona Macleod by looking at the divergent approaches they take to a common story, the Deirdre tale from the Ulster Cycle. This story will be discussed here as it takes place in both Ireland and Scotland and is recorded in both Irish and Scottish manuscripts. As such, an examination of the different interpretations of the story by Gregory and Macleod will shed light on their conceptions of nationality, nationalism, and the shared culture of Ireland and Scotland. It is unsurprising that Sharp would be attracted to the Deirdre story, with its 'passive', 'dependent', 'self-destructive', and 'hyper-feminine' central character (at least in its Irish Revival iterations).[76] As will be discussed later in this chapter, these characteristics can help explain why Gregory never wrote a Deirdre-themed play.

---

the brain of the Anglo-Celtic peoples, with whom are the destinies of the generations to come"' (Sharp, 'Introduction', li.).
[73] Macleod, *Pharais*, ix.   [74] Sharp, 'Introduction', xlviii.   [75] See Brannigan.
[76] Doyle, 34, 38, 38, 38.

In 1899, two years after meeting Gregory at Tulira Castle in Galway, Sharp visited Antrim in the north of Ireland. Sharp recognized that he was in Deirdre territory:

We are on the shore of a beautiful bay — with the great ram-shaped head-land of Fair Head on the right, the Atlantic in front, and also in front but leftward the remote Gaelic island of Rathlin. It is the neighbourhood whence Deirdrê and Naois fled from Concobar, and it is from a haven in this coast that they sailed for Scotland. It is an enchanted land for those who dream the old dreams: though perhaps without magic or even appeal for those who do not.[77]

Sharp is referring to the ninth century *Longes mac n-Uislenn* (the Exile of Uisliu's Sons) here, a tale from the so-called Ulster Cycle preserved first in a twelfth century manuscript. The earliest source for the Deirdre story is the ninth century *Longes mac n-Uislenn* recorded in the twelfth century *Lebor Laignech* (Book of Leinster) and in a slightly longer version in the fourteenth century *Leabhar Buide Leacain* (Yellow Book of Lecan).[78] 'Deirdriu' is the oldest form of the name, and the assumption that *Longes mac n-Uislenn* is 'her' story dates from the post-Ossian period. 'Deirdre' becomes the most common form of the name in the antiquarian era. Though the story existed in pre-Christian Ireland, it cannot be seen as offering totally reliable access into the realities or ideologies of that world, since it assumed textual form in the Christian era and was modified by the patriarchal 'ethos' of the monastic scriptorium.[79]

In the story, the cry of the baby Deirdre is heard from inside her mother's womb at a feast.[80] Before Deirdre's birth it is prophesied by the druid Cathbad that she will grow up to be very beautiful and that she will be the cause of war in Ulster. It is then ordered that she should be put to death. However, Conchobar, the king of Ulster, decides against this so that he can possess Deirdre himself when she grows up.[81] So, Conchobar has Deirdre brought up

---

[77] Letter to Catherine Ann Janvier, August 6 1899, in Sharp, Elizabeth, 311.
[78] See Mathis, 'An Irish Poster Girl?', 263–4.   [79] See Herbert, Máire, 14–17.
[80] 'Deirdre enters as disruption of the convivial male environment of the feast, as she cries out from the womb of the host's wife' (Herbert, Máire, 17).
[81] Social harmony is disrupted by this rash decision (see Herbert, Máire, 19). The decision also sets in motion the 'four main phases of public action in narratives of social drama: a breach of relations, a phase of resultant crisis, redressive action and, finally, either resolution or irreparable schism' (Herbert, Máire, 15).

in seclusion. When Deirdre is a young woman, she falls in love with the warrior Naoise. In order to escape from Conchobar, Deirdre and Naoise elope to Scotland, along with Naoise's two brothers (i.e. Uisliu's sons). The exiles live quite happily in Scotland until they are tricked into returning to Ulster. When back in Ireland, Naoise and his brothers are killed in a battle at Conchobar's fort at Emain Macha in County Armagh. Later, while in Conchobar's custody, Deirdre kills herself.[82]

In terms of English-language versions, James Macpherson's *Dar-thula* from *The Poems of Ossian* (1760-63) is, according to one scholar, a 'massacre of the Deirdre story'.[83] In Macpherson's text Deirdre (or Dar-thula) dies from an arrow-wound rather than by suicide:

> Her shield fell from Dar-thula's arm, her breast of snow appeared. It appeared, but it was stained with blood for an arrow was fixed in her side. She fell on the fallen Nathos, like a wreath of snow. Her dark hair spreads on his face, and their blood is mixing round…Dar-thula! awake, thou first of women! the wind of spring is abroad. The flowers shake their heads on the green hills, the woods wave their growing leaves. Retire, O sun, the daughter of Colla is asleep. She will not come forth in her beauty: she will not move, in the steps of her loveliness.[84]

In response to Macpherson's *Ossian*, Theophilus O'Flanagan published his translation—*Deirdri, Or the Lamentable Fate of the Sons of Usnach, an Ancient Dramatic Irish Tale, One of the Three Tragic Stories of Eirin*—in 1808.[85] However, as Kate Mathis has discussed,

> the most influential English-language text was published by Eugene O'Curry in 1862, entitled 'The 'Trí Thruaighe na Scéalaigheachta' of Erinn'…O'Curry's text was recommended by Yeats, who appears to have learned of its existence from William Sharp ('Fiona Macleod'), to Lady Gregory, then in the process of gathering material to assist her composition of the chapter dealing with Deirdre and the Sons of Uisliu in *Cuchulain of Muirthemne*.[86]

---

[82] Suicide in medieval Irish texts is often associated with sexual violence and subsequent trauma. See Ní Dhonnchadha, Máirín, 'Introduction', 169.

[83] Mercier, 230.   [84] Macpherson, 147.

[85] For a further discussion on Irish antiquarian responses to Macpherson's *Ossian*, see Clare O'Halloran's 'Irish Re-Creations of the Gaelic Past' and Mac Craith's 'The Irish Response to *Ossian*'.

[86] Mathis, 'An Irish Poster Girl?', 265.

Deirdre became a near constant presence on the stages of the Irish Revival.[87] The character and her story appear in works such as George Russell's 1902 play *Deirdre* ('the literary Celticist play *par excellence*'),[88] Yeats' *Deirdre* (1907),[89] Synge's *Deirdre of the Sorrows* (1910),[90] and Eva Gore-Booth's Theosophy-inspired *The Buried Life of Deirdre* (written in 1908, but not published until 1930).[91]

In April 1900, the year following his trip to Antrim, Sharp put on his own Deirdre play at the Globe Theatre in London.[92] A one act drama titled *The House of Usna*, the play was also published in *The Fortnightly Review* in 1900. *The House of Usna* was originally conceived as part of a series to be titled 'The Theatre of the Soul' or 'Psychic Drama'. In a note prefacing the play, Macleod explains that the action is set after Deirdre's death (and four years after her elopement with Naoise).[93] In other words, Deirdre's association with the Sons of Uisliu has already taken place. As such, the play is essentially devoid of action. Furthermore, in place of realism and the external world the play attempts to represent the psyche or the soul (hence the terms 'Theatre of the Soul' and 'Psychic Drama'). As Flavia Alaya has noted,

[Sharp] evidently believed that psychic figments possessed a reality so virtual that they could be dramatized into what he called the "psychic" or symbolic drama. Here his comments on Yeats are...appropriate, for one of the "later" works he was studying in this essay was "The Shadowy Waters." This was not, he said, a drama in the usual sense, but "lyrical thought become continuous, because it is the symbolic reflection of what is in the poet's mind, rather than the architectonic revelation of what his imagination has definitely shaped. It is not, strictly, a poetical drama, even structurally,

[87] According to Maria-Elena Doyle, 'Deirdre...was arguably the most popular female figure of the Revival' (Doyle, 38).

[88] Levitas, 68.

[89] Gregory had a hand in the composition of Yeats's *Deirdre*: 'I...wrote dialogue and I worked as well at the plot and the construction of some of the poetic plays, especially *The King's Threshold* and *Deirdre*; for I learnt by this time a good deal about play-writing, to which I had never given thought before' (Gregory, *Irish Theatre*, 82–3).

[90] Synge died before he could complete this play. As Noelle Bowles has noted, Gregory, 'along with Yeats, worked to piece *Deirdre* together when Synge's death in 1909 left it incomplete' (Bowles, 125).

[91] The story also features in novels such as *Deirdre* (1923) by James Stephens. Deirdre and Conchobar also show up in *Finnegans Wake* in the phrase 'deerdrive, conconey's run' (*FW*, 449.8). In addition, Deirdre was a major presence in the Scottish Celtic Revival, in the visual arts as well as in literature. For example, she is portrayed in John Duncan's sketch *Deirdre of the Sorrows* in 1905 as well as in numerous works by Macleod/Sharp.

[92] This was a venue on Newcastle Street in central London that usually specialized in commercial fare, mainly musicals and comedies. Not to be confused with the theatre associated with Shakespeare.

[93] Macleod, *The House of Usna*, 4–5.

for action and speech are subservient to the writer's entranced vision of the symbolism of the action and of the speeches."[94]

In the foreword to *The House of Usna*, Macleod writes that 'the emotional energy shall be along the nerves of the spirit, which sees beneath and above and beyond, rather than merely along the nerves of material life, which sees only that which is in the line of sight'.[95] In other words, *The House of Usna* is an attempt to apply the Celticist emphasis on spirit to drama. Written under the influence of the plays of D'Annunzio,[96] *The House of Usna* is an 'entranced vision' of death and grief, in the form of 'sonorous, oracular, almost somnambulistic speeches...uttered by abstracted figures'.[97] The figure of Deirdre is addressed as part of these speeches: 'Was it I who put death upon the sons of Usna? It was not I, by the Sun and the Moon! It was the beauty of Deirdrê. O beauty too great and sore! Deirdrê, love of my love, sorrow of my sorrow, grief of my grief!'[98] In *The House of Usna*, Deirdre herself is an entirely abstract and absent figure: 'I will see her eyes like stars, and her face pale and wonderful as dawn, and her lips like twilight water.'[99] Along with the influence of D'Annunzio, Macleod attempts to introduce a tragic atmosphere to the play through rather unsubtle Shakespearean allusions: '*So to sleep, and to dream perchance, and / know no other grace / Than to wake and look betimes on thy / proud queenly face*,'[100] 'Where stands Eiré [*sic*] that was to be one nation?'[101] Perhaps unsurprisingly, *The House of Usna* has not been performed since 1900.

A version of the Deirdre story also appears in Fiona Macleod's children's book *The Laughter of Peterkin* (1897). In this text, the character Peterkin is 'not merely a little child, a boy, a youth, who went through his years gladly laughing, mysteriously wondering, wrought to pain and joy, to suffering and delight, by all he saw and heard and inwardly learned; but a type of the Wonder-Child, and so a brother to all children, to poets, and dreamers'.[102] As Alaya has pointed out, 'Peterkin is without doubt Sharp himself, liberated from perspective and restraint by the camouflage of pseudonymous authorship'[103] and his identification with children is in line with 'a view of life which consistently favors innocence'.[104] Predictably, Peterkin has amassed his poetic powers while living among the rural folk of the 'Celtic wonder-world' that is the Highlands and Islands of Scotland. In the story, he knows

---

[94] Alaya, 186.   [95] Macleod, 'Foreword', *The House of Usna*, xxviii.   [96] See Alaya, 187.
[97] Ibid., 187.   [98] Macleod, *The House of Usna*, 25.   [99] Ibid., 26.   [100] Ibid., 56.
[101] Ibid., 70.   [102] Macleod, *The Laughter of Peterkin*, 26.   [103] Alaya, 23.
[104] Ibid., 41.

'every shepherd on the hillsides of Strachurmore, and every fisherman on the shores of Loch Fyne'.[105] These rural contacts put him in touch with the 'old ballads, the old romances, the strange fragments of the Ossianic tales, the lore of fairydom, fantastic folk-lore, craft of the woodlands'.[106] In Macleod's work as a whole, Celticism is strongly related to infancy and childhood. As Silke Stroh has noted, Macleod's novel *Green Fire: A Romance* (1896) associates childbirth with the survival of Gaelic culture in Scotland. When the character Ynys becomes pregnant she hopes that her baby will grow to become a 'Celtic messiah'.[107] However, as Stroh points out, this hope is forlorn as the child is stillborn, suggesting that, for Sharp, there is no future for the Gaelic community and culture.[108]

The *Foam of the Past* section of the collection *From the Hills of Dream: Threnodies, Songs and Later Poems* (1907) also mentions Deirdre and contains a poem titled 'Deirdrê is Dead'. This poem uses a line taken from *The House of Usna* as an epigraph and quotes lines from the play ('*The grey wind weeps, the grey wind weeps, / the grey wind weeps; / Dust on her breasts, dust in her eyes, the / grey wind weeps!*') as a refrain. In his introduction to *The Foam of the Past* (dedicated to Yeats), Sharp writes that 'Like Deirdrê, we, too, look often yearningly to a land from which we were exiled in time, but inhabit in dream and longing'.[109] 'Deirdrê is Dead' is a fairly short poem and, while it is hardly great poetry, it is worthy quoting in full and examining, since it is a good example of Macleod's listless, morbid Celticism:

> '*Deirdre the beautiful is dead... is dead!*'
> (*The House of Usna*)

---

[105] Macleod, *Peterkin*, 25–6.

[106] Ibid., 26. *The Laughter of Peterkin* also contains a reference to Deirdre (in the form of 'Darthool'): 'Is a child more likely to be hurt, or to be nobly attuned to the chant-royal of life, by acquaintance with stories of vivid and beautiful human love such as that of Nathos and Darthool, or Dermid and Grainne?' (Macleod, *Peterkin*, 29). Macleod's notes for that book include her sources: 'In my renderings of the three famous ancient Gaelic tales, collectively known as "The Three Sorrows of Story-Telling" (*Trí 'Ihruaighe na Scéalaigheachta*), I have followed Professor Eugene O'Curry (*In Atlantis, Manners and Customs*, and *MS. Materials*); Dr. Douglas Hyde (*The Three Sorrows of Story-Telling*, translated into English verse); Dr. Joyce (*Old Celtic Romances*); Dr. Cameron (*Reliquiæ Celticæ*); Alexander Carmichael (*Trs. Gael. Socy. of Inverness*); Dr. Angus Smith (*Loch Etive and the Sons of Uisnach*)' (Macleod, *Peterkin*, 281). The 'Darthool and the Sons of Usna' story is based on 'the literal prose rendering by Dr. Cameron and the metrical translation of Dr. Douglas Hyde' (Macleod, *Peterkin*, 281).

[107] Stroh, 229.   [108] Ibid., 230.

[109] Macleod, *Hills of Dream*, 35. *From the Hills of Dream* contains another section, titled 'The Hour of Beauty'. That section contains a poem called 'A Cry on the Wind', which also refers to Deirdre: 'O sorrowful face of Deirdrê seen on the hill! / Once I have seen you, once, beautiful, silent, still: / As a cloud that gathers her robe like drifted snow / You stood in the mountain-corrie, and dreamed on the world below' (Macleod, *Hills of Dream*, 168).

The grey wind weeps, the grey wind weeps, the grey wind weeps:
Dust on her breast, dust on her eyes, the grey wind weeps!

Cold, cold it is under the brown sod, and cold under the grey
    grass;
Here only the wet wind and the flittermice and the plovers pass:

I wonder if the wailing birds, and the soft hair-covered things
Of the air, and the grey wind hear what sighing song she sings

Down in the quiet hollow where the coiled twilights of hair
Are gathered into the darkness that broods on her bosom bare?

It is said that the dead sing, though we have no ears to hear,
And that whoso lists is lickt up of the Shadow, too, because of
    fear—

But this would give me no fear, that I heard a sighing song
    from her lips:
No, but as the green heart of an upthrust towering billow slips

Down into the green hollow of the ingathering wave,
So would I slip, and sink, and drown, in her grassy grave.

For is not my desire there, hidden away under the cloudy night
Of her long hair that was my valley of whispers and delight—

And in her two white hands, like still swans on a frozen lake,
Hath she not my heart that I have hidden there for dear
    love's sake?

Alas, there is no sighing song, no breath in the silence there:
Not even the white moth that loves death flits through her hair

As the bird of Brigid, made of foam and the pale
    moonwhite wine
Of dreams, flits under the sombre windless plumes of the pine.

I hear a voice crying, crying, crying: is it the wind
I hear, crying its old weary cry time out of mind?

The grey wind weeps, the grey wind weeps, the grey wind weeps:
Dust on her breast, dust on her eyes, the grey wind weeps![110]

---

[110] Macleod, *Hills of Dream*, 40–1.

This nihilistic, repetitive work—a series of long, rhyming couplets of irregular meter—has a drab, muted palette of brown, green, grey, and white (as well as the sense of darkness expressed by 'twilight', 'cloudy', 'night', and 'Shadow') and evokes a dismal atmosphere with wind that is both 'wet' and 'grey'. This crepuscular gloom and dullness stands in high contrast to the brightness and colour in O'Curry's translation of the lively original language of *Longes mac n-Uislenn* (Macleod's probable source text). See, for example, this beautifully detailed description, part of one of Deirdre's laments over Noisi:

'Two crimson cheeks of most beautiful tint,
Red lips, eye-lashes of chafer colour,
A mouth with shining pearly teeth,
Like the brightest colour of snow.

'Distinguished was his bright array
Among the warriors of the men of *Alba*,
A beautiful crimson cloak in graceful gird,
With its bindings of red gold.

'A satin tunic,—a wonderful jewel,—
Beset with a hundred gems of various hues,
And in its splendid embroiderment
Fifty ounces of *Findruiné*.[111]

'A gold-hilted sword in his hand,
Two green spears with victory-promising points,
A shield with a rim of yellow gold,
And a face of silver upon it.[112]

In Gregory's novelistic treatment, this section is rendered as follows:

when Naoise went to the court of the king, his clothes were splendid among the great men of the army of Scotland, a cloak of bright purple, rightly shaped, with a fringe of bright gold; a coat of satin with fifty hooks of silver; a brooch on which were a hundred polished gems; a gold-hilted sword in his hand, two blue-green spears of bright points, a dagger with the colour of yellow gold on it, and a hilt of silver.[113]

---

[111] O'Curry glosses *findruiné* as 'silver, or white bronze, or both, but more probably the latter'. O'Curry, 415, n. 47.
[112] O'Curry, 415. For the original text in Irish, see O'Curry, 414.
[113] Gregory, *Cuchulain*, 114–15.

Alongside an absence of bright colour in Macleod's text, there are only small, fleeting signs of life. The life in the poem belongs to small, flying creatures—bats ('flittermice'), plovers, and moths, linking to the emphasis on air in the text, so that even the living creatures are seen as insubstantial and ephemeral. Swans are also mentioned in the poem, in connection to Deirdre's hands. But they are life-less like Deirdre, fixed 'still…on a frozen lake'. The poem—with its 'brown sod' and 'grassy grave' has earthy associations but its geographical location is vague—there are no references to any Irish or Scottish places as there are in Gregory's text (nor is there any use of Irish or Gaelic). Still, the cold, damp weather of the poem suits the location of its source material while the references to waves and seabirds hint at the sea-journeys of the story. In the introduction to the poetry collection *Lyra Celtica*, Sharp writes that the 'lyric love of Nature…is so distinct-ively Celtic'.[114] However, in this poem there is no love of nature as such, only the use of nature to externalize a sense of gloom and desolation.

There is a turn in the poem from the thought 'that the dead sing' and a consideration of the possibility that 'the wailing birds, and the soft hair-covered things / Of the air, and the grey wind' hear the songs of the dead, to a bitter realization that 'there is no sighing song'. However, the speaker[115] seems ultimately unsure: 'I hear a voice crying, crying, crying: is it the wind / I hear, crying its old weary cry time out of mind?' Along with this confusion regard-ing the presence or absence of the dead (or our ability to hear their singing), there is a tension in the poem between sound ('sighing', 'wailing') and 'the silence there'. The speaker of the poem is confused but also seems to harbour a death-wish. Like 'the white moth that loves death', the speaker seems to want to join Deirdre in oblivion: 'I slip, and sink, and drown, in her grassy grave.'[116]

Reading pieces like 'Deirdrê is Dead', with its Ossianic Romantic Celticism and its clear associations between Gaelic culture and stylized, romantic death, it is easy to see why the work of Macleod/Sharp has had a strongly negative reception in Gaelic Scotland. As Mark Williams has noted,

Sharp and his alter-ego have long been held in contempt by Gaels…[Domhnall Uilleam] Stiùbhart labels Sharp a 'Symbolist poetaster' while Murdo Macleod

---

[114] Sharp, 'Introduction', xli.
[115] Who is the speaker of Macleod's poem? A figure of the story? Or a modern figure acting as though Deirdre were a real person? Of course, the figure cannot be Naoise, since he dies before Deirdre in the story.
[116] Sharp seems to have had a preoccupation with drownings and near-death experiences in water. In addition to the Paris story mentioned earlier, see also: 'For an hour or more thereafter, till the river-police discovered it, a woman's body was tossed to and fro in the Pool, idly drifting and bumping against the slimy piers, along the gaunt, deserted wharves' 'Madge o' the Pool: A Thames Etching' in Macleod, *The Gipsy Christ*, 125.

has excoriated him for 'cultural necrophilia' on the grounds that he evidently preferred Gaelic culture and its language fetchingly doomed. Both find the Macleod writings essentially distasteful and exploitative.[117]

Macdonald has suggested that Sharp had a 'fantasy yearning for the death of the Gael'.[118] It is difficult to argue with these accusations and assessments. However, it should also be considered that in Macleod's oeuvre, and in Sharp's thinking, death is not the end of people or of races. In Macleod's poem 'The New Hope', 'never-dying death' is 'Eternal change'.[119] As Alaya has noted, 'The source of all the thrust [Macleod] gave to the Celtic movement lay in her conviction that the very passing of the Celtic races would be evidence of a "spiritual rebirth" that could move the world'.[120]

As will be discussed in Chapter 4, Celticism in Scottish Modernism also focuses on dead Irish figures—but in the work of MacDiarmid and MacLean the figures in question are historical—James Joyce, James Connolly[121]—rather than characters from traditional culture. Furthermore, dead men such as Joyce and Connolly are sources of power, potential, and renewal in the work of MacDiarmid and MacLean respectively, not the focus of gloomy death fantasies. Seamus Heaney's *Sweeney Astray* also focuses on a cold, wintry Celtic world but there is no relationship in that text between coldness and death or oblivion, as here. Neither is there a sense in *Sweeney Astray* that the Celtic world is 'fetchingly doomed'.[122] On the contrary, *Sweeney Astray* is more concerned with exploring the similarities between Sweeney's world and our own. These issues will be examined in greater depth in Chapter 5.

For Macleod/Sharp, the Gaelic world is finished. In an introduction to a collection of Fiona Macleod stories, Sharp (as Macleod) discusses the fates of indigenous cultures in Wales, Ireland, and Scotland in language not dissimilar to his Deirdre poem: 'In Wales, a great tradition survives; in Ireland, a supreme tradition fades through sunset-hued horizons to the edge o' dark; in

---

[117] Williams, Mark, 379–80.   [118] Macdonald, 144.

[119] Sharp, *The Human Inheritance*, 107.

[120] Alaya, 39. See also: 'What fools are those vain men who talk of death: blinded, and full of the dust of corruption. As God lives, the soul dies not' (Qtd in Sharp, Elizabeth, 62). Sharp also wrote that 'human death is less painful than that of nature, for in the former I see but change, but in the latter—annihilation' (Qtd in Sharp, Elizabeth, 89) and that 'Without death…there could be no prolongation of what we call life…I deny death as an end of everything. Never say of me that I am dead!' (Qtd in Sharp, Elizabeth, 159). See also: 'Death is a variation, a note of lower or higher insistence in the rhythmical sequence of Life' (Qtd in Sharp, Elizabeth, 161), and Sharp's epitaph on his grave in Sicily: 'Love is more great than we conceive and Death is the keeper of unknown redemptions' (Qtd in Sharp, Elizabeth, 306).

[121] Connolly is a special case here, since he was born in Scotland to Irish parents.

[122] Williams, Mark, 380.

Celtic Scotland, a passionate regret, a despairing love and longing narrows yearly before a bastard utilitarianism which is almost as great a curse to our despoiled land as Calvinistic theology has been.'[123] As with Gregory (possibly), as well as later Scottish writers such as Hugh MacDiarmid, Sharp was an initially Protestant writer attracted to Catholicism, a faith he saw as a more spiritual, beautiful religion.[124]

Tellingly, Gregory never wrote a play about Deirdre. This is despite Gregory's art being 'gender-based'[125] with plays focused on female figures from Irish history and culture including Grania, Dervorgilla, and Kathleen ni Houlihan. Instead of writing a play about Deirdre, Gregory 'turned to Grania because so many have written about sad, lovely Deirdre, who when overtaken by sorrow made no good battle at the last. Grania had more power of will, and for good or evil twice took the shaping of her life into her own hands.'[126] It seems that Gregory considered working with the Deirdre story but rejected the idea as she disapproved of its sorrowful central character. Gregory sees the Deirdre character primarily as a victim and a woman lacking in will, preferring stronger women for her plays to 'passive heroines'[127] like Deirdre, even if they have committed some great act of national betrayal (as is the case with Dervorgilla).

However, in 1900 (the same year that Sharp put on *The House of Usna* in London), Gregory began work on what was to become her *Cuchulain of Muirthemne* (published in 1902).[128] *Cuchulain*, a synthesis of a number of translations, now reads as a slightly odd mixture of primitivism and late nineteenth-century ethics conveyed in 'Kiltartanese',[129] with Deirdre featuring

---

[123] Sharp, William, *The Sin-Eater*, 13.

[124] See Williams, Mark: 'For Sharp, the pagan-Christian blend of his imagined version of Gaelic culture was more precisely a pagan-Catholic one, with relics of the "beautiful old cults" surviving in the Catholic heartlands of South Uist and Barra, where they were protected from the sterilizing effects of Calvinism… His fictional biography for Fiona expressly made her a Roman Catholic, even though this was apt to alienate Protestant Scots his alter-ego might otherwise have been expected to flatter. For Sharp, the key attraction of Catholicism was the prominence it gave to Mary, which drew him because of the centrality of the feminine to his imagination' (Williams, Mark, 374).

[125] Murray, 55.

[126] Gregory, *Irish Folk-History Plays*, 195. As Elizabeth Coxhead has commented, for Gregory, 'Deirdre in the ancient legend is the good lover, who dies rather than give herself to the oppressor. Grania is the bad one' (Coxhead, 142).

[127] Doyle, 34. According to Bowles, 'Gregory's plays express an awareness of women's marginalized role within the cause of Irish nationalism and object to ways in which women serve as passive symbols of nation within patriotic discourse' (Bowles, 116).

[128] Yeats encouraged Gregory to put together *Cuchulain of Muirthemne*. He was then inspired by *Cuchulain of Muirthemne* to compose his play *On Baile's Strand*, first performed in 1904.

[129] 'Just as *Ossian* was a primitivist projection of eighteenth-century values, so *Cuchulain of Muirthemne* was of its age, and the nature of its primitivism depended upon that fact: the primitive was treated as an expression of the best contemporary values' (Garrigan Mattar, 224).

as a 'domestic angel' rather than a 'new woman' in the section titled 'Fate of the Sons of Usnach'. As Maria-Elena Doyle writes,

> No controversial new women disturb the pages of Gregory's *Cuchulain*, and characters who might fit the bill, like Deirdre herself—who not only chooses her own lover instead of marrying the old ing Conchubar who has raised her to be his bride, but also demonstrates a marked individuality early on by screaming from the womb—are refashioned to fit the Victorian ideal of the domestic angel...The Deirdre of Gregory's *Cuchulain*...cannot imagine herself as an independent being...Dependent and self-destructive, the hyper-feminine Deirdre of Gregory's translations and the Revival stage exudes a sorrowful nobility.[130]

Gregory worked with a number of manuscripts in preparing her Deirdre story. As Yeats put it in the preface to *Cuchulain*, 'Sometimes, as in Lady Gregory's version of *Deirdre*, a dozen manuscripts have to give their best before the beads are ready for the necklace.'[131] Gregory's sources included a Scottish Gaelic version of the Deirdre tale published in 1886–8 by the folklorist Alexander Carmichael:[132]

> Gregory's sources are revealed, by her diaries, as 'a bundle of "Irische Texte"' donated by Douglas Hyde, and Carmichael's *Deirdire*, from which she has borrowed both the year-long deferral of Deirdre's wedding to the king, and her insistence that she receive adequate training for the role of wife (his 'modest maidens', in particular, are imported verbatim to *Cuchulain of Muirthemne*).[133]

---

[130] Doyle, 37–8.

[131] Yeats, 'Preface' to Gregory, *Cuchulain of Muirthemne*, vii.

[132] Carmichael published two Deirdre texts in *Transactions of the Gaelic Society of Inverness*: 'Deirdre', *Transactions of the Gaelic Society of Inverness* (1886–7): 241–57 and 'Deirdire, English translation of Deirdire', *Transactions of the Gaelic Society of Inverness* (1887–8): 370–87. Carmichael published a full version, *Deirdire*, in 1905. Carmichael tells us that 'the story of Deirdire was written down on 16th March 1867, from the recital of John Macneill, known as "Iain Donn," brown John, cottar at Buaile-nam-bodach in the island of Barra...his brother Alexander...was a famous "seanchaidh"–reciter, and a practiced dictater' (Carmichael, *Deirdire*, 3–4). Carmichael adds that 'The people of the Highlands have retained more of the tales of the Fiann cycle, while the people of Ireland have retained more of the tales of the Cuchulain cycle. The present is, I believe, the only version of this tale that has been got from oral sources in Scotland' (Carmichael, *Deirdire*, 7–8). According to Hugh Cheape, 'Research has now shown how highly contrived this text is' (Cheape, 131).

[133] Innes and Mathis, 128. As Innes and Mathis have observed, 'Carmichael's English translation is littered with alterations to his informant John Macneil's original Gaelic, one of the most telling of which occurs when the brothers attempt to protect her from the effects of the surging waves. Macneill's statement that Naoise "set Deirdire on his shoulders with a leg on either side of his neck" becomes in

The 'bundle' Gregory mentions—a version of the Deirdre tale in Whitley Stokes and Ernst Windisch's *Irische Texte* (1887)—is based, in turn, on a translation of part of the fifteenth-century Glenmasan manuscript now held at the National Library of Scotland.[134] Furthermore, much of Gregory's Deirdre tale in *Cuchulain* takes place in Scotland (this is the setting of the Glenmasan text, which itself is probably based on a twelfth-century 'Scottish' version).[135] Indeed, Gregory's version, following previous iterations of the story, makes numerous references to Scotland (as 'Scotland', 'Alban', and 'Alba') and to Scottish places such as Loch Ness, Inverness, and 'Glen Eitche' (Glen Etive): 'Glen Eitche, it was there I built my first house; beautiful were the woods on our rising; the home of the sun is Glen Eitche.'[136] However, Deirdre has an ambivalent attitude towards Scotland in Gregory's text. Gregory has Deirdre say, 'Dear to me is that land, that land to the east, Alban, with its wonders; I would not have come from it hither but that I came with Naoise' and 'I would never have come out from it at all but that I came with my beloved!'[137] These might look like nationalistic or patriotic insertions by Gregory placed in order to lessen the sense that Deirdre has formed a significant attachment to Scotland. However, the phrases are not Gregory's. An earlier version of them appears, for example, in Alexander Cameron's 1894 text *Reliquiae Celticae*: 'I would not have come hither thence / If I had not come with Naesi!', translated from 'Nocha ttiocfainn aiste alé, / Muna ttagain*n* le Naoise.'[138]

---

the printed translation: "Naoise placed [her] on the summit of his shoulders" – with the English version implying...that she "sits side-saddle rather than astride" him, and removing the possibility of "offend[ing] Victorian sensibilities by mentioning a lady's legs' (Innes and Mathis, 128).

[134] MS 72.2.3. Previously held at the Advocate's Library, also in Edinburgh, and listed as MS 53. 'The bulk of the following saga is taken from the so-called Glenn Masáin manuscript, which belongs to the Highland society and is now deposited in the Advocate's Library, Edinburgh...The conclusion of the saga is taken from a small quarto paper ms., marked "LVI Highland Society, Peter Turner, No. 3" and also deposited in the Advocate's Library' (Stokes and Windisch, 109). Gregory's other sources are as follows: 'Text and Translations published by the Society for the Preservation of the Irish Language; Hyde, *Literary History of Ireland*; Hyde, *Zeitschrift Celt. Philologie*; O'Curry; Whitley Stokes, *Irische Texte*; Windische, *Irische Texte*; Cameron, *Reliquae Celticae*; O'Flanagan, *Transactions of Gaelic Society*; O'Flanagan, *Reliquae Celticae*; Carmichael, *Transactions of Gaelic Society*; *Ultonian Ballads*; De Jubainville, *Epopée Celtique*; Dottin, *Revue Celtique*' (Gregory, *Cuchulain*, 359–60).

[135] See Innes and Mathis, 126.

[136] Gregory, *Cuchulain*, 121. For further references to Scotland in *Cuchulain*, see 100, 113–114, 122, and 134.

[137] Ibid., 120, 120.

[138] Cameron, 432–3. Like Whitley Stokes and Ernst Windisch's *Irische Texte*, Cameron's *Reliquiae Celticae* is based on the Glenmasan manuscript. Cameron transcribed the Glenmasan text, but he did not translate it; the English translation in *Reliquiae Celticae* is of the nineteenth century Peter Turner version. Gregory may have read the latter, but it is not specified in her diaries.

Despite the Scottish setting of much of Gregory's Deirdre story and the use of Carmichael's *Deirdire* (which is itself based on a Scottish Gaelic source),[139] there is no pan-Celtic angle to Gregory's text. *Cuchulain* even has Deirdre making excuses for her love of Scotland (though that sentiment also exists in her sources). In other words, there is no sense that Gregory is creating a combined 'Celtic' textual space in her work—her book is designed as a specifically Irish text. In her notes Gregory admits that she has 'occasionally used Scottish Gaelic versions' of the stories in the text.[140] However, her dedication in the text mentions only 'Irish things' and pitches her book as a 'history of the heroes of Ireland told in the language of Ireland'.[141] As such, Gregory's Celticist texts tend to have a more insular, solely Irish focus as compared to earlier and later examples of Irish Celticism (and there is certainly none of the 'Union of Hearts' sentiment seen in texts such as *The Wild Irish Girl*). This focus is in keeping with the disavowal of the term 'Celtic' by Gregory in relation to theatrical matters mentioned above.

There are very important Irish-Scottish intertextual connections involved in Gregory and Macleod's texts (in a neat symmetrical exchange, Gregory used Scottish sources while Macleod/Sharp used an Irish source). Furthermore, Gregory and Macleod/Sharp are both working with a body of scholarly work created in the wake of Macpherson's *Ossian*. In addition to these links, both Ireland and Scotland appear as locations in the sources they are working with. Despite all of these connections, neither writer stresses Irish-Scottish connections in their text or appeals to any ideas of pan-Celtic solidarity or identity. The Celtic Revivals in Ireland and Scotland in the 1890s/early 1900s ran parallel to an actual pan-Celtic movement founded in 1888, the Celtic Association set up by Bernard FitzPatrick and Edmund Edward Fournier d'Albe, with its neo-druidic Pan-Celtic congresses held in Dublin (1901), Caernarfon (1904),

---

[139] Stiùbhart has discussed the production of Carmichael's *Deirdire*: 'When...we compare the printed text to the original recorded text, we find that Carmichael has not only polished up MacNeil's oral account, but effectively rewritten it, even to the extent of interpolating a major episode quite absent in the original...Carmichael had not in fact taken down a complete text. As a narrative, the original *Deirdire* is extremely problematic. Half of it was taken down from MacNeil by Carmichael himself on 16 March 1867. Then he broke off...The remainder of the story was written down later...transcribed, and then retranscribed by amanuensis in 1872. *Deirdire* was an awkward text from the start, and this perhaps is why Carmichael felt able to rewrite it substantially for his presentation to the Gaelic Society of Inverness' (Stiùbhart, 26). As Donald Black has commented, 'Carmichael made changes big and small in nearly every line. These are changes for the sake of improving the language, cleaning it up, heightening the style, developing the story, archaiseing, and for the sake of change itself' (Black, Donald, 64).

[140] Gregory, *Cuchulain*, 359.

[141] Ibid., vi.

and Edinburgh (1907).[142] Gregory and Sharp were involved with this movement, though not to major degrees, and the key Irish and Scottish Celtic
Revival texts display little pan-Celticism in terms of an ideological project
seeking to draw Ireland and Scotland together through literature. That type of
ideologically or politically inflected literary Celticism, together with a strong
sense that there is (or was) a 'Celtic world', can be found later in the century,
especially in works by Joyce, MacDiarmid, and Heaney.

Gregory's Celticism is largely about creating a new and dignified form of
Irishness based on ancient culture, not about imagining Ireland as a spiritual
partner for a supposedly materialist England or creating links with the other
Celtic nations. The writing of the Celtic Revival in Ireland is something of an
anomaly in the history of literary Celticism since, unlike the era of Owenson
in the early nineteenth century or texts by Joyce and Heaney in the twentieth
century, Celtic Revival texts are, in general, specifically interested in Ireland
alone, not in Union with England or in links with the broader 'Celtic world'.
While Yeats was involved with the Pan-Celtic Society, and he cultivated a relationship with Fiona Macleod/William Sharp and read 'their' works with great
interest, there is little evidence of significant Scottish influence on his work
(unlike Joyce or Heaney). Furthermore, Yeats rarely discusses Scottish matters (or the cultures of other Celtic nations), with the notable exception of his
analysis of Scottish folklore in 'A remonstrance with Scotsmen for having
soured the disposition of their ghosts and faeries'. J.M. Synge's work is clearly
influenced by the work of the Scottish anthropologist James Frazer but, again,
Synge's interest is in Ireland—particularly the west of Ireland—not in the
'Celtic world'.

The Ireland-focused Celticism of the Celtic Revival can partly be explained
by the politics of the era. Any attachment to pan-Celticism would have complicated the Irish nationalist politics of figures such as Gregory and Yeats. As
an Irish nationalist (albeit an ambivalent one who moved gradually from an
earlier Unionist, anti-Home Rule position), Gregory's Celticism focused on
Ireland specifically. She states clearly that she was bemused by the use of the

---

[142] The Celtic Association is discussed in Elizabeth Sharp's *Memoir*: '"The Celtic Association" was
formed, with Lord Castletown [Bernard FitzPatrick] at its head, with a view of keeping each of the six
branches of the movement in touch with each other: the Irish, Scots, Welsh, Manx, Breton, and
Cornish or British. This Society desired to make a Federation of these working sections an actuality,
and to that end decided to hold a Pan Celtic Congress every three years. The first of these was held in
Dublin, and to it my husband subscribed as W. S. and as F. M., though, as an obvious precaution
against detection, he did not attend it' (Sharp, Elizabeth, 321). Yeats eventually realized that 'that
nation was to be the primary vehicle for folk revival, not the vague racial union represented in the
strange costumes and sword-wielding Druids of the Pan-Celtic Congress' (Brannigan, 34).

term 'Celtic' and she attempts to downplay Irish-Scottish links in her texts. Sharp's unionist politics, on the other hand, prevented him (or Fiona Macleod) from attaching an interest in Gaelic or Irish culture to pan-Celticism, since that movement sought the revival of power in the Celtic nations. Furthermore, Macleod/Sharp presents the Celtic race as essentially weak and its culture as being in a state of terminal decline. This is in contrast to the Pan-Celticist idea of Celtic culture as a source of untapped political energies. As Kaori Nagai has discussed, 'Pan-Celticism... idealised the Celtic heritage as a vital source of power, and sought to use this to further its modern political agenda: the liberation and creation of the Celtic nations.'[143] In addition to this, Sharp/Macleod avoided bringing politics into cultural matters. Elizabeth Sharp wrote that 'F. M. deplored the uniting of the political element to the movement—and naturally had no inclination towards any such feeling.'[144] In summary, there is a division between Celticism and pan-Celticism in this period. It might be said that while Gregory and Macleod were both Celtic Revival writers, for Gregory the movement was not really Celtic (at least not in the international sense—it was specifically Irish) and for Macleod it was not really a revival (at least not politically).

The division between Gregory and Macleod can be seen as representative of a larger split in the movement (if we can use that term).[145] As Elizabeth Sharp writes in the *Memoir*:

the Highland Celt and the Irish Celts did not quite understand one another; an animated correspondence ensued in private and in the press. The Irish press was divided in its opinion on 'Celtic', because the writers were not of one mind among themselves in their methods of working towards the one end all Celts have at heart. There were those, who being ardent Nationalists regarded the Celtic literary movement as one with the political, or as greatly coloured by it. This factor gave a special element to the Irish phase of the movement which sharply differentiated it from the movement in Scotland, Wales or Brittany.[146]

The different approaches to nationalism in Gregory and Macleod have important connections to their thinking on gender. Women in Gregory's texts make decisions and take action, often making history in the process and

---

[143] Nagai, 64.   [144] Sharp, Elizabeth, 321.
[145] Alongside a wider split between Irish/Gaelic linguistic vs. Anglophone Romanticist forms of revivalism.
[146] Sharp, Elizabeth, 320–1.

sometimes with negative or tragic consequences. Conversely, women in Sharp's thought and texts are frequently sidelined or absent or are frozen, aesthetic figures although they can be also objects of veneration. These differing depictions of women have political contexts since they are linked to the authors' visions of Irishness and of the Celts respectively.

Macleod associates the Celts with femininity and therefore—in 'her' mind—weakness (another manifestation of Ossianic discourse). As such, Macleod's work mixes gender essentialism with national or racial essentialism. One of the strange contradictions or ironies in Sharp's life and his work (as well as Macleod's work) is that he seems to have strongly identified with femininity while simultaneously associating femininity with death and destruction. So, the sexism encoded within forms of early Celticism persists even when a male writer adopts a female persona and even when a male writer considers himself to *be* a woman to some extent or to contain a feminine self. While Gregory avoids Deirdre in her dramatic works because she considered the character too passive, noting that she made 'no good battle', Deirdre largely disappears in Macleod's versions of the story. Gregory's work involved revival, in bringing 'dead' culture back to life as part of a larger political and cultural movement,[147] Macleod's work, on the other hand, focuses on death and disappearance. In Scotland, Anglophone literary Celticism is mainly a masculine business.[148] Generally, women writers in Scotland have not been attracted to Celticism. The main 'woman' who is interested in Celtic discourses associates the Celts with femininity, weakness, hysteria, and annihilation.

As the works of Gregory and Macleod are categorized as texts of the Celtic Revival, along with sections of Yeats' work, i.e. part of a larger movement—albeit a fissiparous one—and since Celticism as a whole is sometimes thought to have finished in around 1900,[149] it is tempting to think of them as representing the climax of Celticism. However, since we can find significant examples of Celticism (or late Celticism) in Irish and Scottish writing later in the twentieth century (as will be discussed in Chapters 3, 4, and 5), 1890s/1900s texts such as *Cuchulain of Muirthemne* can be thought of as transitional texts—albeit core texts—in the development of Celticism, rather than

---

[147] See Welch.

[148] However, there were prominent women visual artists interested in Celticism, including the Irish-born, Scottish-based Phoebe Traquair. The absence of women from Anglophone Scottish literary Celticism is an example of the division between Anglo-Highland Anglophone revivalism and Gaelic linguistic nationalism, as there were many vocal women involved in the latter, with Ella Carmichael being the the most obvious example.

[149] See Watson, George, 'Aspects', 142.

the culmination and terminus of a discourse or tradition. In other words, the Irish and Scottish Celtic Revivals occur at a midway stage in the overall chronology of literary Celticism (including late Celticism), not at the end. As such, we can consider how these texts are influenced by earlier Celticism and Celtology as well as how they anticipate or contrast with examples of late Celticism. These later works—such as Joyce's *Finnegans Wake*, MacDiarmid's *In Memoriam James Joyce*, and Heaney's *Sweeney Astray*—do not belong to Celtic Revival movements in the same way as the works of Gregory et al. However, they do continue and develop the Celticist literary discourse in different ways and in different contexts. After the Celtic Revival, much of the energy in Irish literature transfers to Modernism. However, as will be discussed in the following chapter, Modernism and Celticism are not necessarily mutually exclusive categories. Following the Celtic Revivals of Ireland and Scotland, Irish-Scottish literary connections continue in the Irish Modernist texts of James Joyce.

3

Joyce and Scott

Sex, history, and Celticism

While Walter Scott was the leading novelist of nineteenth-century literature, especially in terms of sales,[1] James Joyce is perhaps the major novelist of the twentieth century in terms of stature and influence. The two writers emerge from contrasting political traditions and national contexts—Scott's Toryism and unionism are at odds with Joyce's family connections to Fenianism and Parnellism. Furthermore, Scott and Joyce take very different approaches to the novel form. However, there are some important similarities between Scott and Joyce as authors—both were fascinated by the histories of their respective nations, in the relationship between their home country and English power, and in the historical development of societies. Furthermore, Joyce owned some of Scott's poetry and prose, and there is a network of intertextual links between Scott's work and Joyce's texts *Dubliners* (1914), *A Portrait of the Artist as a Young Man* (1916), *Ulysses* (1922), and *Finnegans Wake* (1939). This chapter studies Joyce's reading of Scott and examines allusions and references to Scott and his work in Joyce's texts. Special attention is paid here to the links between Scott, incest, and masturbation in Joyce's work, as well as to the different conceptions of history offered by these two writers—Scott's quasi-Smithian view of history is contrasted to Joyce's interest in the theories of Giambattista Vico. These areas—forms of sterile, onanistic sexuality linked to Scott in Joyce's texts, and the Smithian model of history terminating with capitalism adopted by Scott—both, for Joyce, negate the possibility of future development or change.

In the summer of 1825, Walter Scott visited Ireland with his daughter Anne and his son-in-law and biographer John Gibson Lockhart. The party sailed to Belfast before visiting Drogheda, Dublin, Longford (where they visited the

---

[1] According to William St Clair, 'During the Romantic period, the "Author of Waverley" sold more novels than all the other novelists of the time put together' (St Clair, 221).

Modern Irish and Scottish Literature: Connections, Contrasts, Celticisms. Richard Alan Barlow, Oxford University Press.
© Richard Alan Barlow 2023. DOI: 10.1093/oso/9780192859181.003.0004

Edgeworths), Cork, Blarney Castle (where Scott kissed the famous stone), and Glendalough (where Scott climbed up to St. Kevin's Bed, a cave associated with the famous saint). Also at Glendalough, the party's tour guide was subtly informed by William Plunket that Scott was a 'great man and a poet'. 'Poet!' the guide replied incredulously. 'Not a bit of him; but an honourable gentleman—he gave me half-a-crown.'[2] Scott's reception as a writer was better established in the rest of the island in 1825, and he was still massively popular and influential in late nineteenth/early twentieth-century Ireland, the scene of James Joyce's youth:

> Scott's novels had [an] effect not only upon the European novel in general— Manzoni and Tolstoy, for instance, are inconceivable without Scott—but upon the Irish novel in particular. In his study of the Irish historical novel, James Cahalan cites a 1919 study by Steven J. Brown that described more than twelve percent of the 1,713 novels published in Ireland before 1920 as historical novels after the pattern of Scott. Between 1880 and 1919...there was a great burst of historical fiction, 83 historical novels appearing from the hands of many different authors.[3]

However, as Scott Klein has noted, Irish interest in Scott declined rapidly after 1916, perhaps because there was no need for historical fiction and nostalgia when Irish political life had become so dramatic.[4] The widespread availability of Scott's work in Ireland during this period seems to have driven down the monetary value of his texts, as Joyce found out to his disappointment. Richard Ellmann has described one of Joyce's early, ill-fated money-making schemes:

> A medical student had given Joyce a pawn ticket for some books, supposedly expensive technical volumes like Gray's *Anatomy*. Joyce proposed to [Padraic] Colum that they pay seven shillings to the pawnbroker, Terence Kelly, in Fleet Street, and sell the books at a big profit to George Webb, the bookseller on Crampton quay. Colum put up the seven shillings. But after removing the books from pawn they found them to be only Scott's *Waverley Novels*, with one volume missing.[5]

---

[2] Qtd in Cuming, 53.   [3] Klein, 1021–2. See also Brown, Stephen J., *Ireland in Fiction*.
[4] See Klein, 1022.
[5] *JJ*, 141. Joyce and Colum's entrepreneurial activities seem to have occurred in 1903, although it is unclear in Ellmann's biography.

Perhaps this commercial misadventure embittered Joyce towards the 'Wizard of the North'. When Joyce's brother Stanislaus discusses his own juvenile and 'questionable' literary tastes in *My Brother's Keeper*, he mentions his interest in Scott, a writer his brother James supposedly 'could not stand'.[6] Be that as it may, Joyce kept a key Scott text in his Trieste library: *The Bride of Lammermoor*.

The Bride of Lammermoor (1819) is referred to twice in Joyce's works—late in Chapter 5 of *A Portrait of the Artist as a Young Man* and in the 'Cyclops' episode of *Ulysses*. Klein has pointed to the similar political contexts of *The Bride* and *A Portrait*:

> Post-Parnellite Ireland, like late seventeenth-century Scotland, presented an empty political space of possibility not yet resolved, in Joyce's case not by imminent Union but by the looming possibility of the Irish Free State...Thus, *The Bride* serves as a generic predecessor for Joyce as ironic historiography.[7]

On the subject of predecessors, Fiona Robertson and others have pointed out the numerous similarities between *The Bride of Lammermoor* and Charles Maturin's *The Milesian Chief* (1812). Furthermore, Robertson notes that *The Bride of Lammermoor* and *The Milesian Chief* share a common source in Sydney Owenson's *The Wild Irish Girl*.[8] So, a continuum in modern Irish and Scottish texts can be plotted from Owenson and Maturin, through Scott, to Joyce. Of course, the novels of Edgeworth and Owenson were the models for Scott's national tales.

In Joyce's *Portrait*, the 'thin', 'dwarfish', and 'monkeyish' 'captain' (a minor character in the text who is an acquaintance of Stephen Dedalus and his friends Cranly and Dixon) with his 'shrunken brown hand', says he is reading *The Bride of Lammermoor* and announces that Scott 'writes something lovely'.[9] Here Scott is associated with dwarfishness (elsewhere in Joyce's work Scott is associated with vastness). The captain adds that 'There is no writer can touch sir Walter Scott'.[10] Obviously the primary or surface meaning of this phrase is something like 'There is no writer who can rival Scott's literary prowess'. However, the word 'touch' lends the phrase a vague erotic undertone, given the context: 'The captain has only one love: sir Walter Scott'.[11] Here Scott's text is associated with shrinking, with a character who seems not fully human, perhaps due to a family history of inbreeding: 'was the story true and was the

---

[6] Joyce, Stanislaus, 79.   [7] Klein, 1028.   [8] See Robertson, 218–19.   [9] *P*, 228.
[10] Ibid., 228.   [11] Ibid., 228.

thin blood that flowed in his shrunken frame noble and come of an incestuous love?'[12]

The captain's preferred reading material, the works of Scott, also have strong associations with incest. As Patrick Parrinder has discussed, Scott popularized a style of plot wherein the hero and heroine are virtually brother and sister.[13] In Scott's texts, Parrinder argues,

> there is the 'light heroine' whom the official hero, the blond hero, must marry; she is usually a kind of sister to him, an adopted member of his own family. This is true of Rowena [in Ivanhoe], of Alice Lee in Woodstock, of Alice Bridgenorth [in Peveril of the Peak], and several others. Amy and Tressilian have a similar relationship in Kenilworth—Tressilian obtains her father's power of attorney in order to plead Amy's case before Queen Elizabeth—but they are not able to marry. Scott's novels therefore run counter to traditional romance and aristocratic values in that they seem to favour inbreeding and endogamy.[14]

The subject of incest also features in Scott's non-fiction. In a section on Spain in his Life of Napoleon Buonaparte, Scott discusses incest, and its attendant after-effects, in language similar to Joyce's: 'The incestuous practice of marrying within the near degrees of propinquity, had long existed, with its usual consequences, the dwarfing of the body, and degeneracy of the understanding.'[15] In Joyce's work, the issue of incest is treated to a sustained engagement in the 'Scylla and Charybdis' episode of Ulysses, as part of Stephen's discussion of Shakespeare's life and works. In that episode, as Katherine Mullin has observed, Stephen

> asserts that incest is 'an avarice of the emotions,' since 'the love so given to one near in blood is covetously withheld from some stranger who, it may be, hungers for it'...Incest is here presented as a perversely obsessional form of self-absorption, where sex, like gold, is hoarded from the outside world. The onanistic ramifications of this suggestion are elaborated: 'we walk through ourselves, meeting robbers, ghosts, giants, old men, young men, wives, widows, brothers-in-love, but always meeting ourselves.'[16]

---

[12] Ibid., 228.
[13] 'Scott did not invent the kind of plot that skirts the notion of incest by introducing a hero and heroine who are virtually brother and sister, but he did a great deal to popularize it' (Parrinder, 161).
[14] Ibid., 160–1.   [15] Scott, Walter. Napoleon Buonaparte, 58.   [16] Mullin, 83.

In other words, incest and inbreeding are, for Joyce, warped forms of self-absorption and have onanistic dimensions. In Joyce's works, the desire for family members is, ultimately, a desire for the self. The attention paid to the hands of the captain in *A Portrait* and the suggestive use of the word 'touch' add to the masturbatory connotations of the earlier passage. That the captain reveres Scott to the exclusion of other writers—'There is no writer can touch sir Walter Scott',[17] 'The captain has only one love: sir Walter Scott'[18]—reveals a preference for literature that 'favour[s] inbreeding and endogamy'. Furthermore, the captain's exclusion of all writers other than Scott reflects a fitting onanistic impulse to reject other possibilities in favour of one particular male.

In *A Portrait*, Scott is associated with racial and familial decline (as opposed to the development of society through fixed phases—a subject this chapter will return to in due course): 'The Captain acts thus as a figure for Stephen's national and sexual fears, a potentially apocalyptic image of the end of Ireland through inbreeding and Romantic absorption in its own past.'[19] It is noteworthy that the captain is obsessed with the work of Scott, who worked primarily on Scottish history, rather than an Irish novelist with an Irish focus (although Scott's national tales were heavily influenced by the regional novels of Maria Edgeworth and Sydney Owenson so, in reading Scott, the captain is engaging with texts with strong Irish connections). In other words, the captain is not *directly* absorbed in Ireland's past. However, since Joyce viewed Scotland as Ireland's 'Poor sister' and part of the 'Celtic family',[20] the captain is captivated by the past of a 'close relation' of Ireland's. Furthermore, since Joyce sees attraction to family members as a form of self-obsession, the captain's reading of Scott and Scottish historical fiction can be read as a warped, indirect form of Romantic obsession with Ireland and Ireland's past. This fascination is in keeping with the rumoured incestuous nature of the captain's family. Essentially, incest is a form of paralysis in Joyce's work since it leads to stasis or decline, as indicated in the figure of the captain. Similarly, as this chapter will discuss, for Joyce, Scott's conception of history ends with a form of stasis (or resolution). Joyce's work avoids this sense of stasis by adopting a Viconian vision of history as cyclical.

---

[17] *P*, 247.   [18] Ibid., 247.

[19] Klein, 1033. According to Klein, these 'dwarfish' and 'monkeyish' images are 'both Gothic and post-Darwinian' and draw on 'pervasive late-Victorian anti-Irish stereotypes that Joyce decries elsewhere, and associates [the captain] distastefully with racial decline...Like the subjects about which he reads in Scott, he is the end of a familial and national line' (Klein, 1033).

[20] Joyce, James, 'Gas from a Burner' in *Poems and Exiles*, 109, and 'Ireland: Island of Saints and Sages' in *OCPW*, 119.

In contrast to the 'dwarfish' and 'shrunken frame' of the diminutive captain of *A Portrait*, the *Bride of Lammermoor* also appears amid the gigantism of the 'Cyclops' episode of *Ulysses*.[21] The inclusion of Scott's *Bride* amongst 'giant' figures such as 'Napoleon Bonaparte' and 'Julius Caesar'[22] and within a comically bloated episode seems, initially, to suggest the gigantic bulk of Scott's work, the huge, prodigious nature of Scott's output in general, and the massive presence of the writer in 1904.[23] However, given that Joyce associates *The Bride* with dwarfishness in *A Portrait*, the reference to Scott's text acts, in a small way, to puncture the overinflated form of the episode. Furthermore, the appearance of a Scottish text such as *The Bride of Lammermoor* also contaminates the national 'purity' of the list of 'Irish heroes and heroines of antiquity'[24] (as do the ludicrous inclusions of figures such as 'Ludwig Beethoven' and the 'Queen of Sheba'),[25] thus undermining and satirizing the extreme nationalist rhetoric of the xenophobic Citizen who dominates the episode. The appearance of 'the tribe of Ossian' as part of a list of the 'twelve tribes of Iar' serves the same function.

On 24 June 1924, Joyce wrote to Harriet Shaw Weaver from the Victoria Hotel in Paris, where he was recovering after one of his many eye operations:

> I found that my memory was getting lame so in the clinic I started to learn by heart the Lady of the Lake by sir Walter Scott, Bart. In three days I learnt 500 lines and can repeat them without a mistake. Neither of my children can do this. It is not a sign of intelligence... but it is very useful.[26]

Lines from *The Lady of the Lake* appear in *Finnegans Wake* notebook VI.B.5 but not in *Finnegans Wake* itself.[27] Perhaps Joyce was only reading Scott's text because the poem, with its rhymed tetrameter couplets, was useful material for a mnemonic exercise. However, it seems unlikely that Joyce 'couldn't

---

[21] *U*, 12.189–190. *The Bride* also figures obliquely in the 'Hades' episode, since Bloom thinks of Gaetano Donizetti's opera *Lucia di Lammermoor* (1835) during Patrick Dignam's funeral: 'Last act of Lucia. Shall I nevermore behold thee? Bam! He expires. Gone at last' (*U*, 6.852–53). According to James Porter, *Lucia di Lammermoor* is part of a genre in opera with its roots in Macpherson's *Ossian*, via Scott. See Porter, James, *Beyond Fingal's Cave*, 298–9.
[22] *U*, 12.187, 12.188.
[23] Indeed, it is possible that Joyce saw the massive Scott monument on Princes Street in Edinburgh. Joyce visited Glasgow with his father in 1894 and, as Jackson and Costello have noted, 'Joyce's notes for *Stephen Hero*...strongly suggest that their final destination was beyond Glasgow and that a visit to Edinburgh featured in the lost chapters of that book—the existing parts of which are firmly rooted in fact' (Jackson and Costello, 186).
[24] *U*, 12.176.   [25] Ibid., 12.194, 12.198.   [26] *L I*, 216.
[27] As Scarlett Baron has pointed out, these jottings are part of a preoccupation of Joyce's during that time with stags and deer (Joyce's interest in matters cervine features as early as the image of flashing antlers at the close of the 1904 poem 'The Holy Office'). See Baron, n. p.

stand' Scott's work, as Stanislaus Joyce had previously suggested, since Joyce was administering himself a heavy dose of it at this point. Other than the appearance of *The Bride of Lammermoor* amongst the giants of 'Cyclops' and alongside the dwarfish captain in *A Portrait*, Scott's texts are also referred to in *Finnegans Wake* and *Dubliners*.

In the unsettling *Dubliners* story 'An Encounter', a lecherous old man asks a group of boys if they have read any of Scott's works. It has been suggested that the man's liking for Scott is in keeping with the 'corrupted' nature of his character.[28] However, as we have seen, Joyce associates Scott with incest and inbreeding, which for Joyce are closely linked to self-obsession and masturbation. Indeed, it is heavily implied that the old man goes off to masturbate during the story:

> After a long while his monologue paused. He stood up slowly, saying that he had to leave us for a minute or so, a few minutes, and, without changing the direction of my gaze, I saw him walking slowly away from us towards the near end of the field. We remained silent when he had gone. After a silence of a few minutes I heard Mahony exclaim:
> – I say! Look what he's doing!
> As I neither answered nor raised my eyes Mahony exclaimed again:
> – I say… He's a queer old josser![29]

Clearly, the 'queer old josser' has been sexually aroused by his meeting with the young boys. However, he uses that arousal to pleasure himself on his own and in isolation, another image of self-absorption or self-obsession. As with the figure of the captain in *A Portrait*, 'An Encounter' links Scott with solitary self-indulgence and with a sterile form of sexuality. It is noteworthy that Joyce makes connections between Scott and sterility in two separate texts, *Dubliners* and *A Portrait*.

In 'Araby', a copy of Scott's novel *The Abbot* (1820), is left behind—by a priest—in a pile of 'old useless papers'.[30] In Joyce's story it is a worrying sign that a priest would leave behind a Scott novel, since Joyce associates Scott with corruption and perversion. Furthermore, the narrative arc of Roland

---

[28] 'From the narrator's point of view, the pervert is 'well spoken' and 'well read,' though the pervert's taste in literature, in keeping with his character, is apparently for a kind of decadent romanticism' (Degnan, 92).

[29] *D*, 26.

[30] Ibid., 29. Perhaps, through some strange collision of real and fictional worlds, this discarded Scott text is the volume missing from Joyce's incomplete set of the *Waverley* novels.

Graeme in *The Abbot* forms an ironic counterpoint to that of the boy in 'Araby'. Joyce's nameless boy is never plucked from obscurity, never placed in the society of powerful individuals, and never finds himself in the midst of important events. Dublin is the centre of stasis and paralysis for Joyce (at least in *Dubliners*), not of political turbulence and adventure. Joyce once wrote to his friend Arthur Power that 'in realism you get down to facts on which the world is based; that sudden reality which smashes romanticism into a pulp. What makes most people's lives unhappy is some disappointed romanticism, some unrealisable misconceived ideal.'[31] There are many instances of 'disappointed romanticism' in Scott's texts. For example, *Waverley* (1814) ends with the defeat of the Jacobite rebellion and the destruction of the clan system in the Scottish Highlands. Scott's texts are often concerned with the demise of certain families or societies (though also with the survival of other families or traditional social structures), points of historical transition, or the recollection of youthful adventures from the standpoint of maturity or old age.

In some ways 'Araby' and 'An Encounter' have similar structures to that of a Scott novel, in that many of Scott's works end with a powerful sense of regret or disappointment after an initial spell of enchantment. The papers of Scott's text might not have been 'useless' to the boy in 'Araby', since the novel could have helped the boy in warning him of his imminent disappointment at the bazaar, which turns out to be a place of dreary commerce rather than Eastern enchantment. Scott's *The Abbot* ends with the defeat of Mary, Queen of Scots following her escape from Loch Leven Castle. Mary's forced flight to England is the anticlimactic failure of an initially exciting and romantic situation for Roland Graeme. So, the boy's dismissal of Scott's works in 'Araby' can be read as a kind of Joycean negative-epiphany, a missed opportunity to anticipate his coming 'disappointed romanticism'. Critics have often seen references to Scott in Joyce as part of a discourse linking perversion with Romantic self-absorption.[32] However, this approach tends to overlook the 'disappointed' features of many of Scott's texts, the 'renunciation of Romanticism, [the] conquest of Romanticism, a higher development of the realist traditions of the Enlightenment in keeping with the new times'.[33] A key feature of Scott's Enlightenment thinking is his understanding of the way in which societies develop towards 'completion' over time. Indeed, Scott's texts suggest that 'history can only be rationally possessed, recognized, *as romance*—as a private aesthetic property, in the imagination, materially signified by the book we are

---

[31] Joyce quoted in Power, 98.   [32] See Davison, Degnan, and Stone.   [33] Lukács, 33.

holding'[34] and, literature, for Scott, can help the movement towards political resolution. Scott, in his 'General Preface' to *Waverley*, states that Maria Edgeworth's novels had done more 'towards completing the Union, than perhaps all the legislative enactments by which it has been followed up'.[35]

In Joyce's texts, Scott is associated with sterility, 'apocalyptic' Romantic self-absorption, and endings, rather than with possibilities for future development or change. These readings neglect Scott's emphasis on improvement and the successful establishment of domesticity and modernity in texts such as *Waverley*. In other words, Joyce associates Scott with sterility in spite of resolutions in Scott's novels that express the opposite (the future-oriented fertility suggested by the marriage plot and the improvement and endurance of the landed estate in *Waverley*, for example). Scott's optimistic view of history as moving towards a fixed goal is rejected in Joyce's work in favour of a cyclical vision of the chaos of human civilization. Furthermore, in rejecting Scott's historical novels Joyce is also rejecting an important legacy of Irish literature, since texts such as *Waverley* drew inspiration from Edgeworth and Owenson's regional tales.[36] The remainder of this chapter will study Scott and Joyce in relation to Enlightenment and Modernist conceptions of historical progress.

Joyce's work was influenced by one particular branch of the Scottish Enlightenment—David Hume's scepticism and idealism.[37] Hume's work forms part of what Joyce regarded as 'Celtic philosophy',[38] an idea that informs the incertitude and indeterminacy of *Finnegans Wake*. However, Joyce rejects another vitally important part of the Scottish Enlightenment—Adam Smith's model of historical development as reflected in the teleological structure of Scott's novels.[39] As Kathryn Sutherland has discussed, Scott's thought regarding economics and societal progress were consistent with contemporary Scottish philosophy:

> Scott, in line with the Scottish speculative or philosophical historians of the later eighteenth century—Adam Smith, Adam Ferguson and the younger Dugald Stewart, for example—regarded commercial man, for good or ill, as

---

[34] Duncan, *Modern Romance*, 61.   [35] Scott, 'General Preface', 352.

[36] See Trumpener, 'National Character, Nationalist Plots'.

[37] See Barlow, ' "Hume Sweet Hume": Skepticism, Idealism, and Burial in *Finnegans Wake*'.

[38] 'All Celtic philosophers seem to have inclined towards incertitude or scepticism—Hume, Berkeley, Balfour, Bergson' (Joyce, James, *Poems and Exiles*, 353). Joyce was also influenced by Scottish literature, such as James Hogg's masterpiece of indeterminacy, *The Private Memoirs and Confessions of a Justified Sinner* (1824) and Robert Louis Stevenson's famous study of human duality, *Strange Case of Dr Jekyll and Mr Hyde* (1886). See Barlow, *The Celtic Unconscious*.

[39] For a discussion on Smith, Celticism, and sympathy, see Gibbons, 'This Sympathetic Bond: Ossian, Celticism, and Colonialism'.

the type to which all societies, however rude, inevitably tend... That Smith's economic theory as expounded in *An Inquiry into the Nature and Causes of the Wealth of Nations* (1776) influenced Scott needs no general proof: at Edinburgh University in 1789–90 Scott attended the classes held by Dugald Stewart, Professor of Moral Philosophy and Smith's chief contemporary commentator and popularizer.[40]

In his *Lectures on Jurisprudence*, Smith states that societies move through four distinct phases or states: '1st, the Age of Hunters; 2dly, the Age of Shepherds; 3dly, the Age of Agriculture; and 4thly, the Age of Commerce'.[41] Scott shared the idea that the commercial, capitalist world was the end state for human societies. However, Scott disagreed with Smith's feeling that the landowning classes should be replaced by businessmen. Furthermore, Scott's texts balance the power of commerce with the preservation of traditional social structures and some Scott novels question the Enlightenment model of historical progression.[42] Still, we can see a kind of Smithian barbarism to refinement thinking reflected in the conclusion of *Waverley*, when Scott discusses post-Culloden Scotland:

There is no European nation which, within the course of half a century, or little more, has undergone so complete a change as this kingdom of Scotland. The effects of the insurrection of 1745,—the destruction of the patriarchal power of the Highland chiefs,—the abolition of the heritable jurisdictions of the Lowland nobility and barons,—the total eradication of the Jacobite party, which, averse to intermingle with the English, or adopt their customs, long continued to pride themselves upon maintaining ancient Scottish manners and customs, commenced this innovation. The gradual influx of wealth, and extension of commerce, have since united to render the present people of Scotland a class of beings as different from their grandfathers, as the existing English are from those of Queen Elizabeth's time...But the change, though steadily and rapidly progressive, has, nevertheless, been gradual; and, like those who drift down the stream of a deep and smooth river, we are

[40] Sutherland, 97–100. As Raleigh has noted, 'Scott was a second-generation member of the Scottish Enlightenment, whose original proponents, Hume, Smith, Ferguson, Stewart, Miller...[were] the first sociologists' (Raleigh, 582).
[41] Smith, Adam, 14.
[42] In *Rob Roy* (1818), 'the Enlightenment model of linear progression comes into question. It is not that the novel rejects the notion of progress but that it complicates the stadial scheme by overlapping and intertwining its stages' (Ferris, 'Authorizing', 562).

not aware of the progress we have made until we fix our eye on the now-distant point from which we set out.[43]

Scott's river image, suggestive of both gradual changes and a sudden breach,[44] is based on the distance travelled from one point to another: 'Ah that Distance!... what a magician for conjuring up scenes of joy or sorrow, smoothing all asperities, reconciling all incongruities, veiling all absurdness, softening every coar[se]ness, doubling every effect by the influence of the imagination'.[45] As Ian Duncan has noted, Scott's fiction 'stakes its modernity on the claim of having superceded primitive modes of ideological identification (superstition and fanaticism) through a capacity to stand back and reflect on its own historical conditions'.[46] Civil war was, for Scott, the 'paradigm of historical progress'.[47] In terms of the relationship between history and the present, Scott's texts are based on differences, distances, and progress whereas Joyce's works stress similarities, repetitions, and parallels.

The obvious comparison to Scott's river image in a Joycean context is, of course, Joyce's use of flowing rivers as a symbol of history and the passage of time in *Finnegans Wake*: '[Joyce] conceived of his book as the dream of old Finn, lying in death beside the River Liffey and watching the history of Ireland and the world—past and future—flow through his mind like flotsam on the river of life'.[48] On the face of it, Scott and Joyce have similar ways of conceiving of, and presenting history. However, Scott's river brings society to a new position or location. Joyce's river of history is integrated into a greater, repetitive water-cycle. The river of history flows to the sea, but then returns through evaporation and rain to where it began. This process is mimicked by the cyclical structure of *Finnegans Wake*, a circular text that resists its own closure. Joyce uses water imagery to suggest the fluidity and flux of history, while Scott's river image suggests that history has a fixed direction and goal. Furthermore, following the thinking of Adam Smith, historical development is seen as inevitable and to some extent predetermined in Scott's work.[49]

---

[43] Scott, *Waverley*, 340.   [44] See Ferris, *Achievement*, 119.   [45] Scott, *Journal*, 127–8.

[46] Duncan, 'Scott and the Historical Novel', 110. Elsewhere, Duncan has discussed 'the condition of romance as modernity's vision of worlds it has superseded, charged with a magic of estrangement, peril and loss: a cultural uncanny' (Duncan, *Modern Romance*, 9).

[47] Ibid., 52.   [48] *JJ*, 544.

[49] In Joyce's work, the possibility of alternative realities is at least entertained by Stephen in the 'Nestor' episode of *Ulysses*: 'Had Pyrrhus not fallen by a beldam's hand in Argos or Julius Caesar not been knifed to death. They are not to be thought away. Time has branded them and fettered they are lodged in the room of the infinite possibilities they have ousted. But can those have been possible seeing that they never were? Or was that only possible which came to pass?' (*U*, 2.48–52).

However, Joyce associates Scott with decline and paralysis, not progress or improvement.

While Scott's thinking was informed by Adam Smith, Joyce famously used the cyclical model of history devised by the 'roundheaded Neapolitan' Giambattista Vico in his *La Scienza Nuova* (1725) as a 'trellis' for *Finnegans Wake*.[50] In Vico's system, a theocratic or divine age is followed by an aristocratic or heroic age, and then a democratic, human age. A 'ricorso' begins a new cycle, returning the world to the divine age. In *Finnegans Wake*, Joyce links this cyclical system to water imagery and Vico's plan guides the structure of his text. *Finnegans Wake* begins (or begins again) at a river and with a subtle allusion to Vico: 'riverrun, past Eve and Adam's, from swerve of shore to bend of bay, brings us by a commodious vicus of recirculation back to Howth Castle and Environs'.[51] There are some similarities in the thought of Vico and Smith, aside from their stadial conceptualizing. For example, both were interested in the relationship between the individual and society.[52] However, Smith's vision of history is linear whereas Vico's is cyclical. Furthermore, Smith's stages are based on materialism whereas Vico's interest is in morality and culture.[53] Joyce had little time for strictly materialist conceptions of the world, speaking of 'the science undergraduate's fatuous belief in headlong materialism' in 'Realism and Idealism in English Literature'.[54]

For Scott, progress is largely about the 'gradual influx of wealth' and the 'extension of commerce', as mentioned at the conclusion of *Waverley*. To paraphrase Garrett Deasy, Stephen Dedalus' boss in *Ulysses*, all human history in Scott moves towards one great goal: the manifestation of commercial man.[55] However, Scott is also interested in the persistence of tradition, especially traditional social structures, in the face of the rising power of capital. The emergence of this power is often presented as a natural, organic process. Indeed, Scott's work is informed by a 'poetics of distance',[56] the exploration of how present society came into being, and an emphasis on the differences between 'then' and 'now'. In contrast, Joyce's work is structured by what might be termed a poetics of parallel. His use of the *Odyssey* as a scaffolding for

---

[50] *JJ*, 554.   [51] *FW*, 3.1–3.   [52] See Miller, Cecilia.

[53] See Simon, 46. Furthermore, 'what Vico attributes to God's divine providence is precisely that which the Scots seek to explain in secular sociological terms' (Smith, Craig, 4).

[54] *OCPW*, 179.

[55] Bloom is a 'commercial man' in *Ulysses* (in two senses, since his job is an advertising canvasser) but capitalism is not a new phase of history for Joyce. Joyce's comments suggest that capital has always influenced the course of civilization, even in ancient times. For example, he thought that the Trojan war was fought because Greek merchants were looking for new markets. See *JJ*, 416.

[56] Jones, 59.

Ulysses is the best-known example of this feature of his work. Scott's characters are formed by their historical situations, whereas Joyce's—especially in *Ulysses* and *Finnegans Wake*—find themselves in warped or ironic recreations of historical or mythical situations.

As Ellmann has reported, 'if someone mentioned a new atrocity to Joyce, he at once pointed out some equally horrible old atrocity.'[57] If nothing is really new and the past is inescapable (or repetitions and variations of the past are inescapable), then, for Joyce, there is no need to set narratives in the distant past. *Ulysses*, published in full in 1922, is set in 1904. For Joyce, it is preferable to resurrect Odysseus in the modern world by way of metempsychosis—or to reincarnate Fionn mac Cumhaill as HCE—than to set a novel in a remote time (the subject of resurrections or rebirths in Irish literature will reappear in Chapter 5 of this volume). The presentation of parallels between past and present is common in *Dubliners*, *A Portrait of the Artist as a Young Man*, and *Ulysses*. In *Finnegans Wake*, the passage of time itself is negated: 'In all his books up to *Finnegans Wake* Joyce sought to reveal the coincidence of the present with the past. Only in *Finnegans Wake* was he to carry his convictions to its furthest reaches, by implying that there is no present and no past.'[58]

Novels such as *Waverley* present us with purposefully unremarkable main characters whose role is primarily to exist at a flashpoint of historical change as antagonistic sections of a society clash. In other words, Scott details the advance of a dialectical process which engulfs and shapes middling, average figures such as Edward Waverley or Roland Graeme.[59] Scott's novels, in which individuals are caught in the midst of vast and 'necessary' social change, display a belief in the advancement of societies through fixed stages towards harmonious resolutions. Often Scott's works attain this resolution through a quasi-incestuous relationship or marriage. However, this worldview and this type of fiction is, as we have seen, associated with self-absorption, paralysis, and sterility in Joyce's work. Scott's view of history contrasts with the presentation of history as cyclical and repetitive in *Finnegans Wake*. In *Finnegans Wake*, history occurs within the mind of the text's 'dreamer', and there is no

---

[57] *JJ*, 551.   [58] Ibid., 551.

[59] As Ina Ferris has observed, 'personal subjectivity is profoundly historical' in Scott's work (Ferris, 'Authorizing', 561). In addition to subjectivity, Scott is also interested in the 'manners' of his historical periods: 'the dress, customs, habits, and informal institutions that defined the way people inhabited particular times and places' (Ferris, 'Authorizing', 557) as well as in the 'local worlds' maintained through 'song, legend, joke, family tradition' and 'marginal kinds of writing and print like...letters, tracts, pamphlets, and private memoirs' (Ferris, 'The Historical Novel', 78).

real sense of a substantial change or progress, only a nightmarish or comical maze of repetition and resemblance.[60]

For Terry Eagleton, Joyce's Viconian cycles (as well as Yeats's gyres) 'compensate for different forms of powerlessness.'[61] Similarly, Alistair Cormack has argued that Joyce and Yeats 'attempt to approach history in a fashion that is not infected with an alienating positivism that both writers identify with colonialism and tyranny. They both try to appropriate history—to encompass it—rather than letting it encompass them.'[62] Scott can accept historical violence in Scotland as a price worth paying for what he sees as progress. Joyce's work contemplates the violence in Ireland but his work rejects the very idea of historical progress. As Lukács has written, commenting on Scott's *Waverley*, 'as a sober, conservative petty aristocrat, [Scott] naturally affirms the result of the 1745 rebellion, and the necessity of this result is the ground on which he stands.'[63] However, the Irish situation, is, as Cormack notes, 'a tale of invasion and colonialism—a tale that is ripped in two by the Famine' so it 'offers no stable means of constructing linear, organic narratives.'[64] Furthermore, 'the official discourse of materialism and linearity' was, for Joyce, 'generated by imperialism.'[65] In other words, the differing visions or models of world history offered by Scott and Joyce are determined to a great extent by their thinking on the recent past of their own nations, as well as by their respective readings of Smith and Vico.

The differing views of Scott and Joyce may also be discerned from their attitudes to Gaelic or Celtic matters and to the merging of different peoples or tribes in ancient times. The question of the ethnic origin of the Picts had been a charged debate in Scotland since 1787 and the publication of John Pinkerton's *Dissertation on the Origin and Progress of the Scythians or Goths*. Pinkerton claimed a Gothic and Germanic ethnicity for the Picts and branded the Celts a 'weak and brutish people' who, in ancient times had 'washed their bodies and cleaned their teeth with urine.'[66] Scott struggled with the question of the origin of the Picts but by 1830 had decided that both the Picts and the Scots were Celtic peoples.[67] Joyce was also interested in the history of the

---

[60] As Alistair Cormack has suggested, 'History [in Joyce's work] becomes not a journey towards a fixed point, but a field of shifting and competing states of mind' (Cormack, 59).

[61] Eagleton, 270.   [62] Cormack, 33.   [63] Lukács, 33.   [64] Cormack, 37.

[65] Ibid., 4.   [66] See Leask, '*The Antiquary* and the *Ossian* Controversy', 194.

[67] Ibid., 194. In 'Introductory Remarks on Popular Poetry' in the 1830 edition of *Minstrelsy of the Scottish Border*, Scott comments that 'It is now generally admitted that the Scots and Picts, however differing otherwise, were each by descent a Celtic race' (Scott, *Minstrelsy Vol. I*, 28). The Scottish origins debate also features in Scott's *The Antiquary* with Oldbuck arguing for the Gothic origin of the Picts, and Wardour in favour of a Celtic origin (see Leask, '*The Antiquary* and the *Ossian* Controversy', 193–4): 'Oldbuck dismisses the Celtic genealogy of the Pictish kings as "sprung from the tribe of

Picts and Scots and wove a thread of allusions and references to them through the text of *Finnegans Wake*, comparing their story to the Ulster Plantation and stressing the blended, diverse natures of the Irish and Scottish nations.[68] Unlike Yeats, Joyce had no time for ideas of racial 'purity'. Like Scotland, the Irish 'civilization' was, for Joyce, 'an immense woven fabric in which very different elements are mixed'.[69] In Scott's *The Antiquary* (1816), a text where the merging of Gothic and Celtic tribes in Scotland is discussed, 'Scott's eirenic vision of Britain resolves ethnic conflict between Goths and Celts in the interest of national unity'.[70] The difference between Scott and Joyce in terms of racial or tribal integration is that for Scott, these amalgamations stand for progress and lead eventually to peace and harmony while, for Joyce, they only signal repetition. In Joyce's work, new amalgamations will always happen, betrayals and divisions are constants, and national history can never be entirely 'resolved'. For Joyce, there is little prospect of an eternally 'paisibly eirenical' Ireland.[71]

The decline of Gaelic Scotland seems to be a *sine qua non* for Scotland's political and economic development in Scott's work. 'The Two Drovers' (1827) indicates that Highland forms of justice are admirable but outmoded and *Waverley* suggests that it was necessary for the indigenous Highland way of life to be wiped out in order for Scotland to develop (although its culture could be also appropriated in various ways). According to Ian Duncan,

> The rising's failure confirms the anachronistic character of the old regime and its organic base of support, the Highland clans, sacrificed in the irreversible drive of modernisation... *Waverley* renders clearly the imperial logic that rewrites Highland society as archaic, already superseded, doomed to pass, as the condition of its fascination for the modern reader.[72]

In terms of Scott's relationship with Celticism and historical development, a 'common theme uniting Macpherson's *Ossian* [and] Scott's *Waverley*... is the persistence of the "primitive" in spite of the relentless progress of modernity, and this is intimately linked to Scottish Enlightenment ideas concerning the development of societies "out of barbarism into refinement"'.[73] Of course,

---

Macfungus—mushroom monarchs every one of them; sprung up from the fumes of conceit, folly, and falsehood, fermenting in the brains of some mad Highland seannachie"' (Leask, '*The Antiquary* and the *Ossian* Controversy', 194).

[68] See Barlow, 'The "united states of Scotia Picta"'.   [69] *OCPW*, 118.
[70] Leask, '*The Antiquary* and the *Ossian* Controversy', 201.   [71] *FW*, 14.30.
[72] Duncan, 'Scott and the Historical Novel', 108.   [73] Robichaud, 136.

while the clan system may have been doomed to pass, its colourful symbols could be put into the service of the British Empire and British imperial ideologies. The public apogee of this process was Scott's elaborate stage-managing of the visit of George IV to Scotland in 1822—the first visit to Scotland by a reigning monarch for almost 200 years—where the king was persuaded to wear Highland dress amid grand scenes of clannish pageantry.

At the end of Volume I of *Waverley*, the young English captain is taken to a remote Highland location to hear Flora sing a 'lofty and uncommon Highland air, which had been a battle-song in former ages':

> ...Waverley found Flora gazing on the water-fall. Two paces farther back stood Cathleen, holding a small Scottish harp...'I have given you the trouble of walking to this spot, Captain Waverley, both because I thought the scenery would interest you, and because a Highland song would suffer still more from my imperfect translations, were I to produce it without its own wild and appropriate accompaniments. To speak in the poetical language of my country, the seat of the Celtic Muse is in the mist of the secret and solitary hill, and her voice in the murmur of the mountain stream....[74]

The lure of Celtic or Gaelic culture is, for Scott, a 'dangerous romantic folly',[75] whereas in Irish texts of the same period, such as Owenson's *The Wild Irish Girl*, the same imagery is deployed for nationalist purposes (albeit a form of cultural nationalism that aspires to match Irish wildness with English practicality). In *The Wild Irish Girl*, the Englishman Horatio is entranced by Glorvina, who stands for Celtic femininity, spirituality, and musicality:

> Slowly departing, I raised my eyes to the Castle of Inismore...At that moment a strain of music stole over me, as if the breeze of midnight stillness had expired in a manner on the Eolian lyre. Emotion, undefinable emotion, thrilled on every nerve. I listened. I trembled. A breathless silence gave me

---

[74] Scott, *Waverley*, 106–7. Scott is working with an image previously used in Macpherson's work. See Pittock's chapter 'Romance, the Aeolian Harp, and the Theft of History' in *Scottish and Irish Romanticism*, 59–91. See also: 'Irish and Scottish novels from Sydney Owenson's *Wild Irish Girl* (1806) to Charles Maturin's *Milesian Chief* (1812) and Walter Scott's *Waverley* (1814) have imbued the image of the harp-playing heroines with a great deal of picturesque and romantic charm, signifying a poetic soul and a reverence for national traditions. As a bardic instrument, the cherished vehicle of Irish, Welsh, and Scottish nationalism, and then as the emblem of a nationalist republicanism, the harp stands for an art that honors the organic relationship between a people, their land, and their culture' (Trumpener, *Bardic Nationalism*, 18–19). See also: Gibbons, 'From Ossian to O'Carolan: The Bard as Separatist Symbol'.
[75] Lincoln, 58.

every note. Was it the illusion of my now all awakened fancy, or the professional exertions of the bard of Inismore? Oh, no! for the voice it symphonized; the low wild tremulous voice, which sweetly sighed its soul of melody o'er the harp's responsive chords, was the voice of a *woman*![76]

Joyce also uses the image of a harpist in 'Two Gallants', a story in which a female domestic worker is (probably) swindled by a character named Corley while his acquaintance Lenehan waits nearby. In the story the harpist is a man, not a woman. However, the association of femininity with the harp continues:

> They walked along Nassau Street and then turned into Kildare Street. Not far from the porch of the club a harpist stood in the roadway, playing to a little ring of listeners. He plucked at the wires heedlessly, glancing quickly from time to time at the face of each new-comer and from time to time, wearily also, at the sky. His harp too, heedless that her coverings had fallen about her knees, seemed weary alike of the eyes of strangers and of her master's hands. One hand played in the bass the melody of *Silent, O Moyle*, while the other hand careered in the treble after each group of notes. The notes of the air sounded deep and full.[77]

Lenehan and Corley are in modern central Dublin, not in the romantic wilds of Connaught or the Scottish Highlands. However, the setting of the harp scene is still heavily symbolic, since the name Nassau Street recalls William of Orange.[78] Furthermore, the club mentioned in the story is the Kildare Street Club, a centre of Irish unionism and Protestant Ascendancy. Joyce wrote to his brother Stanislaus that '*Two Gallants*—with the Sunday crowds and the harp in Kildare Street and Lenehan—is an Irish landscape'.[79] According to Steven Doloff:

> The harp...a traditional symbol of Ireland, has been seen, in its forlorn description [in 'Two Gallants'], as a representation of Irish national decline.

---

[76] Owenson, *The Wild Irish Girl*, 52.

[77] *D*, 54. According to Klein, both *The Bride of Lammermoor* and *A Portrait of the Artist as a Young Man* 'present women coming to terms with sexuality as a pre-condition of a renewed national consciousness–and this has been implied earlier in Joyce's work by the symbolic presence of the song 'Silent, O Moyle' in 'Two Gallants'' (Klein, 1032).

[78] 'Nassau Street instantly recalls the Prince of Orange, who...presided over Ireland's defeat at the Battle of the Boyne and perpetuated the broken Treaty of Limerick' (Torchiana, 119).

[79] *JJ*, 231.

It has also been pointed out that the harper's 'heedless' and insensitive hand-ling of the instrument corresponds to, and combines with, Corley's misuse of the servant girl whom he meets to create a figurative motif of Irish self-betrayal. The harper's song, 'Silent, O Moyle,' in its mythological theme of mournful, long-suffering exile, has similarly been identified in the story with a sense of Irish cultural and spiritual despondency.[80]

In 'Two Gallants', an anthropomorphic and feminized harp is 'weary' of the hands of her masculine master, an image of the exploitation of women by men studied in the story as a whole. Regardless of the nationality of the harpist, the 'heedless' playing of the worn-out harp by its 'master' is also an image of a degrading colonial situation in which, for Joyce, the Irish were complicit. The symbol of the harp, a key Celticist image in literature and the visual arts from *Ossian* onwards, changes in these texts from a symbol of Irish beauty and spirituality—or Jacobite danger—in Romanticism to an image of Irish national misery in Modernism.

There are strong intertextual and thematic links between the works of Scott and Joyce. However, the two writers were working in two very different his-torical eras and national contexts. The violence and political instability in Ireland and Europe in the late nineteenth / early twentieth-century contrasts markedly with the 'end of history' feeling in the orderly, improved, and 'enlightened' sections of Scotland during the early nineteenth century. Scott's linear texts often find completion through quasi-incestuous relationships, situations that Joyce associates with sterility and self-obsession. Scott viewed Scotland's development as a story of progress towards commercial modernity, involving an inevitable abandonment and silencing of 'the Celtic muse'[81] (even though this muse will later be imaginatively captured and commodified by writers like Scott). In keeping with Joyce's reading of Scott, the characters in Joyce's texts who read Scott's works are perverted old men associated with familial and racial decline, who are associated with incest and, therefore, a paralyzing self-absorption.

---

[80] Doloff, 823.   [81] Scott, *Waverley*, 106.

4

Scottish Modernism and the Celtic world

MacDiarmid and MacLean

According to Augusta Gregory, Dublin was the 'Mecca' of the Celtic Revival.[1] While later Celticism is perhaps more of a Scottish phenomenon (with the exception of Seamus Heaney), there was a strong Irish influence on the Scottish Revival as whole, especially on the Scottish Modernist poet Hugh MacDiarmid (Christopher Murray Grieve). MacDiarmid once claimed that he had urinated in a Dublin alleyway together with Yeats after a heavy night on the lemonade at George Russell's house: 'I crossed swords wi' him – and I had the better flow!'[2] This poetic pissing contest—with its echoes of Leopold Bloom and Stephen Dedalus in the garden of 7 Eccles Street—may be one of MacDiarmid's tall tales. However, it does reveal MacDiarmid's desire to be aligned with figures from Irish culture and politics. Even the *nom de plume/nom de geurre* 'MacDiarmid' echoes the name of the 1916 Rising leader Seán Mac Diarmada.[3] It is also probable that 'MacDiarmid' was chosen as it has more of an obviously Celtic or Scottish ring and look to it than 'Grieve' (a use of nominative Celticism the poet has in common with Samuel Liddel MacGregor Mathers and Fiona Macleod). MacDiarmid saw Ireland's struggle for independence as a potential source of instruction and inspiration for Scotland:

> I believe that Ireland during its long struggle not only set a magnificent example of 'following the gleam', but that it had a prescience of the wider implications of the necessity of doing so...in short, that the true

---

[1] See Pethica, James (ed.). *Lady Gregory's Diaries*, 153. London was also an important centre of Celticist activities in the 1890s. See Foster, *Yeats I*.

[2] Qtd in Crotty, 'Swordsmen', 36. MacDiarmid claimed that this event took place in 1928.

[3] 'Grieve's poetic pseudonym was the gaelicized name adopted by [one] of the 1916 leaders executed by the British, Seán Mac Diarmada (originally John MacDermott)' (Lyall, *Hugh MacDiarmid*, 108). In the 1972 documentary *No Fellow Travellers*, MacDiarmid claims that he chose the name simply because it was more 'euphonious' than Grieve ["Hugh' and 'MacDiarmid' traditionally go together, you know, and it sounds well' (Marzaroli, 05:20-05:34)] but surely Lyall is correct to point to the figure of Mac Diarmada. Lyall has noted elsewhere that the name also evokes the figure of Diarmuid from the Fenian Cycle (see Lyall, 'Hugh MacDiarmid and the Scottish Renaissance', 178).

Modern Irish and Scottish Literature: Connections, Contrasts, Celticisms. Richard Alan Barlow, Oxford University Press.
© Richard Alan Barlow 2023. DOI: 10.1093/oso/9780192859181.003.0005

interpretation of its achievement was a deep intuition of the ruination a continued English ascendancy was enforcing on these islands...Ireland's breakaway – its power to sunder itself in the teeth of the entrenched English power – is one of the happy signs that all may not be lost. I welcome like tendencies in India, Egypt, South Africa and elsewhere, and think it is high time Scotland in particular was realizing what it is all about in terms not only of the crucial and immediate problems of our own country but in terms of world politics.[4]

MacDiarmid's admiration for modern Ireland covered both politicians and cultural figures. Writing in 1928, MacDiarmid praised Ireland as having

produced an astonishingly rich and varied crop of men and women during the past fifty to seventy years – a brilliant and restless generation...Think of these people – Yeats, 'A. E.' (George Russell), George Moore, J. M. Synge, Lady Gregory, Michael Collins, Arthur Griffiths [sic], James Connolly, Lord Dunsany, Maud Gonne, Eamonn de Valera [sic].[5]

Furthermore, MacDiarmid welcomed Irish immigration into Scotland at a time when anti-Irish sentiment was rife in sections of Scottish society.[6] Commenting on Irish migration to Scotland in the late nineteenth and early twentieth centuries, R.F. Foster writes that 'The Irish found prejudice to contend with [in Scotland]; anti-Irishness and anti-Catholicism took a special colouring where Presbyterian values saw the very existence of destitute Irish Catholics as an outrage...Catholics remained a disadvantaged minority there until the 1920s'.[7] Such prejudice is well illustrated by the Church of Scotland's 1923 report *The Menace of the Irish Race to Our Scottish Nationality*, anti-Irish texts such as George Malcolm Thomson's *Caledonia: Or the Future of the Scots*

---

[4] MacDiarmid, *Selected Essays*, 61–2.

[5] *RT II*, 219–20. Of course, it could be argued that Scotland help to 'produce' James Connolly. In a piece titled 'What Irishmen Think of Ireland: some prominent literary men', MacDiarmid suggests that this 'abnormal efflorescence of Irish genius could not be maintained' (*RT II*, 193). MacDiarmid had mixed feelings towards the Irish Revival: 'despite the excellent and durable work that some of the Irish writers did one of the reasons that Movement petered out was precisely that Kiltartan Irish and 'Celtic Twilight' stuff generally was too much relied upon...the earlier translations of Irish, Welsh, and Scottish Gaelic poetry were sadly befogged by Celtic Twilightism and yet they...paved the way for a great extension of genuine Celtic studies and for subsequent translations much truer to the origi-nals' (*RT III*, 310–11).

[6] Anti-Irish racism and anti-Catholic bigotry are still serious problems in Scottish society and are frequently evident at Orange marches and at Rangers Football Club matches.

[7] Foster, *Modern Ireland*, 368.

(1927) and Andrew Dewar Gibb's *Scotland in Eclipse* (1930),[8] and in the setting up of the anti-Catholic political parties the Scottish Protestant League (1920) and the Protestant Action Society (1933). For MacDiarmid, Scottish anti-Irishness was 'a profound mistake'.[9] Partly, this was because MacDiarmid saw Irish migration into Scotland as maintaining what he called 'the ancient Gaelic commonwealth'.[10]

As has been noted elsewhere, of all the modern writers of the Atlantic archipelago (with the possible exception of Yeats), MacDiarmid is the figure most interested and invested in the concept of the Celtic world and of a Celtic revival, one that will differ from the 'defeated Celticism' of the past.[11] In his political activities, MacDiarmid imagined establishing a 'Workers' Republic in Scotland, Ireland, Wales, and Cornwall, and indeed...a sort of Celtic Union in Socialist Soviet Republics'.[12] MacDiarmid's 'Gaelic commonwealth', or the idea of a modern united and resurgent Celtic front, is first expressed artistically in his long poem *To Circumjack Cencrastus or The Curly Snake*, published in 1930.[13] As Duncan Glen has observed, the 1930s 'saw MacDiarmid becoming increasingly concerned with Gaelic Scotland [and] with Celticism generally'.[14] During this period, MacDiarmid read texts such as William Ferris' *The Gaelic Commonwealth* (1923), Daniel Corkery's *Hidden Ireland* (1925), and Aodh de Blácan's *Gaelic Literature Surveyed* (1929). MacDiarmid's expressions of late Celticism can be understood as part of the political changes occurring in Scotland in the 1930s. As Murray Pittock has noted, 'The Depression of the 1930s, together with the incipient metropolitan bias of the electronic media and the first signs of decay in the British Empire, served to move Scotland and Wales, albeit very slowly, in the direction of a distinctive national politics.'[15]

---

[8] For Thomson, Irish migration was causing Scotland to suffer 'the gravest race problem confronting any nation in Europe today' (Thomson, 10). Gibb described 'the great Irish trek to Scotland' as 'a national problem and a national evil' (Gibb, 53).

[9] Qtd in Pittock, *Celtic Identity*, 85.   [10] Qtd in Pittock, *Celtic Identity*, 84.

[11] See Brannigan, 160 and Lyall, *Hugh MacDiarmid*, 13.

[12] MacDiarmid, *Lucky Poet*, 26. See also: 'In 1930, disaffected by the ca' canny Home Rule constitutionalism of the [National Party of Scotland], and the sectarianism of some of its leading members, MacDiarmid sought to develop Clann Albain, a nationalist organisation along the lines of Sinn Féin in Ireland' (Lyall, *Hugh MacDiarmid*, 39).

[13] As Lyall has discussed, MacDiarmid's interest in Scottish Gaelic is part of a broader interest in 'the Celtic genius' that is first expressed by the poet in *Cencrastus*. See Lyall, 'Hugh MacDiarmid and the Scottish Renaissance', 179–80. MacDiarmid explained under the name 'A. L.' in *The Scottish Educational Journal* in November 1930 that '"Cencrastus" is an ancient Gaelic snake symbolising the fundamental pattern of life, while "to circumjack" means "to encompass"' (*RT II*, 248).

[14] Glen, 150.

[15] Pittock, *Celtic Identity*, 110. MacDiarmid's Celtic turn came about in a post-WWI era of British imperial decline where 'Grieve hoped for a...renewal in what he saw as a now deracinated and bankrupt Scottish culture' (Watson, Roderick, 7). According to McCulloch, 'what made the Scottish Revival unique among Scottish cultural movements was the belief of those involved that any regeneration in

Much of *To Circumjack Cencrastus* is extremely pessimistic with regards to modern Scotland and its culture. In one section, MacDiarmid imagines haranguing a group of unlucky students who are seemingly unaware of locations mentioned in Macpherson's *Ossian*: '*I summoned the students /And spiered them to tell / Where Trenmore triumphed / Or Oscar fell /'Dammit,' I cried, /'But here is a mystery – / That nane o' ye ken / The first word in history!*'[16] Strangely, the places of *Ossian* are regarded as sites of authentic history rather than areas associated with a controversial and synthetic literary pseudotrans- lation, 'the very archetype of the inauthentic representation of national origins'.[17] Elsewhere in the poem, MacDiarmid laments 'It isna fair to my wife and weans, / It isna fair to mysel'. / The day's lang by when the Gaels gaed oot / To battle and aye fell'.[18] Here, MacDiarmid is alluding to the famous and fre- quently quoted (or misquoted) lines 'His race came forth, in their years; they came forth to war, but they always fell' from Macpherson's 'Cath-Loda'.[19]

MacDiarmid also conceives a conversation with a 'visitor from France', where a number of Scotland's literary greats are deemed unrepresentative. The visitor has never heard of them anyway:

I asked him if he'd heard
Of Burns or Sir Walter Scott,
Of Carlyle or R. L. S.
He said that he had not.
'Some people think that these
Are representative … I don't.
At least, you've little to forget,
And should assimilate with ease,
     From that false Scotland free,
And that's worth knowing yet.'[20]

---

the nation's aesthetic culture could not be separated from revival in the nation's wider social, eco- nomic, and political life' (McCulloch, 'Scottish Modernism', 766).

[16] *CP*, 203 (the italics, as with examples that follow, are in the original texts). For MacDiarmid, *Ossian* had some value despite its problematic nature: 'James Macpherson's Ossian, phoney as it was, was nevertheless perhaps the only way in which Gaelic qualities could be got over at that time to the non-Gaelic world… it rendered great service and led on in due course to the genuine article' (*RT III*, 310–11). See also the chapter '"Ossian" Macpherson and William Lauder' in MacDiarmid's *Scottish Eccentrics*, 212–60.

[17] Duncan, 'Hugh MacDiarmid's Modernist Nationalism', 256.   [18] *CP*, 253.

[19] For a brief discussion of uses of this line, see Chapter 1, footnote 46.   [20] *CP*, 208.

In this jaunty, irregular fragment the visitor is in the blessed situation—in MacDiarmid's estimation—of not knowing Scotland through the works of Burns, Scott, Carlyle, or Stevenson. As a consequence, the visitor will find it easier to access the 'reality' of Scotland since he is not suffering a form of cultural false consciousness and does not have to work to see through the illusions and mystifications conjured up by Scott et al. However, the general situation is, disappointingly for MacDiarmid, one in which the texts by these writers are considered 'representative'.[21]

In the face of a dire cultural state of affairs in which a 'false Scotland' is known (except to this somewhat unlettered French tourist) and the 'real' Scotland (of Macpherson's *Ossian*) is unknown, the poem envisages '*Gaeldom regained*',[22] a utopian space in which '*The Gaelic sun swings up again*'.[23] In a 1927 article, MacDiarmid proposed a renewal of Gaelic culture in order to 'repair the fatal breach in continuity which has cut us off from our own roots'.[24] For MacDiarmid, modernity had brought about a need to return to origins: 'civilisation...needs to renew itself at its original sources'.[25] In MacDiarmid's vision, this repair work will be achieved partly through Irish immigration into Scotland, something that will reverse the harm done to Gaelic Scotland over the centuries (and, through an influx of Catholicism, work to undo the damage done by the Reformation).[26] It should be kept in mind that although MacDiarmid had a fascination with Gaelic culture and had declared that 'The Scottish Renaissance Movement is even more concerned with the revival of Gaelic than of Scots',[27] he had minimal knowledge of the Gaelic language. According to Sorley MacLean, 'He had little Gàidhlig

---

[21] See also 'This Scotland is not Scotland' in 'Lament for the Great Music' (*CP*, 472).

[22] *CP*, 188. MacDiarmid claimed that *Cencrastus* embodies 'a very specialized view of Scottish nationalism depending upon an intimate knowledge of "our Gaelic background"' (*RT II*, 247).

[23] *CP*, 207. At one point in the poem MacDiarmid imagines a pan-Celtic friendship achieved through a kind of bardic time travel: 'I was a bard in Alba and Eire / Two hundred years ago. / Michael Comyn was one of my friends' (*CP*, 213). *Cencrastus* also gestures towards an imagined Gaelic resurgence through references to poetry such as 'A theachtaire tig ón Róimh', which MacDiarmid glosses as 'a noble poem in defence of the art of poetry...attributed by Miss Knott (vide *Irish Syllabic Poetry*) to the famous Gilbride Albanach MacNamee (Giolla-Bhrighde Albanach MacConmidhe)' (*CP*, 293).

[24] *RT II*, 40.   [25] *RT III*, 24.

[26] See Pittock, *Celtic Identity*, 84–5 and Lyall, *Hugh MacDiarmid*, 39–40. In an interview with Nancy Gish, MacDiarmid stated that 'if I had been attracted to any form of Christianity, it would certainly have been the Roman Catholic Church' (MacDiarmid qtd in Gish, 'Interview', 140). For MacDiarmid (writing under his orginal name), the Reformation had 'strangled Scottish arts and letters [and] subverted the whole national psychology' (Grieve, *Albyn*, 12).

[27] Grieve, *Albyn*, 4.

himself'.[28] As such, MacDiarmid left himself wide open to accusations of cultural appropriation.[29]

This injection of Catholic/Celtic spirit will, presumably, also reverse the anglicization of Scotland, since *'The great poets o' Gaelic Ireland'* were able to soar *'up frae the rags and tatters / O' the muckle grey mist o' Englishry'*.[30] In *Cencrastus*, the idea of Celtic regeneration is expressed in arboreal terms: *'the forests of Alba, / Cut down now, that may grow again / Thanks to the branch of Ireland / Growing among us'*.[31] Elsewhere in MacDiarmid's poetry, this pan-Celtic union is also imagined in heated and slightly alarming metallurgical language, *'Scots steel tempered wi' Irish fire/Is the weapon that I desire'*.[32] Scots steel—perhaps echoing the Scottish steel industry of the twentieth century—is tempered, in rather essentialist terms, by the intense 'fire' of the Irish. This Gaelic resurgence and Irish/Scottish amalgamation will, in MacDiarmid's grand plans for world reordering, form a new geopolitical or geocultural order in alignment with a resurgence in Russian power: *'the Russian Idea's / Broken the balance o' the North and Sooth / And needs a coonter that can only be / The Gaelic Idea / To mak' a parallelogram o' forces'*.[33] In 'Direadh III',

---

[28] According to Susan R. Wilson, 'MacDiarmid expressed a fascination with Scotland's Gaelic language and culture throughout his career, the result being a corpus of some fifty articles, essays, and poems related to the Gaelic tradition. Equally as well read in terms of critical studies of Irish language and literature, he recognized the regenerative creative impulse that the Gaelic traditions of Ireland and Scotland could stimulate in their respective countries. Although at times his advocacy exasperated even native Gaels like MacLean...MacDiarmid's literary legacy in this sphere may perhaps best be described as 'influence by association', largely comprising his mentorship of young Gaelic writers' (Wilson, 81).

[29] As Byrne has commented, 'MacDiarmid's ideas are impressive in their ambition but also in their sheer presumption. However glorious the world mission being bestowed on Gaelic, the "ur-Gaelic initiative" is clearly the latest in a long line of alien appropriations of the language and its culture' (Byrne, 2). For Peter Mackay, this is 'an appropriation which relies on an understanding of the world as structured by racial distinctions, and which finds MacDiarmid, in Scott Lyall's words "on indefensible fascist terrain", proposing a post-socialist nationalism similar to that found in Hitler's Germany, which is based on "race-consciousness" not "class consciousness"' (Mackay, 'Optik to Haptik', 280). See also the bizarre suggestion in *In Memoriam James Joyce* that 'the War was partly caused / By Hitler's innocent translators' (*IMJJ*, 44). On the subject of fascist terrain, MacDiarmid seems to link health with race (via language) in his text the *Islands of Scotland*: 'there is nothing surprising in the fact that the healthiest parts of Scottish Gaeldom – physically, psychologically, economically and otherwise – are precisely those in which Gaelic is still purest and most generally used, and English intrudes least' (MacDiarmid, *Islands of Scotland*, xii). See also: *'I took him to the islands / Where the wells are undefiled'* (*CP*, 208).

[30] *CP*, 210. MacDiarmid cites Antoine Ó Raifteirí, Aodhagán Ó Rathaille, Eoghan Rua Ó Súilleabháin, Piaras Feiritéar, Pádraigín Haicéad, and Seathrún Céitinn as examples here. See *CP*, 210. See also MacDiarmid's poem 'In Memoriam: Liam Mac'Ille Iosa' with its 'Lost world of Gaeldom' (*CP*, 415) where anglicization is a 'degrading and damnable load' (Ibid., 415).

[31] Ibid., 208–9.   [32] Ibid., 263.

[33] *CP*, 222. 'The opposing and complementary concepts of the "Russian Idea" and the "Gaelic Idea" were explained by MacDiarmid, shortly after the publication of *Cencrastus*, in an essay titled "The Caledonian Antisyzygy and the Gaelic Idea", published across two issues of *The Modern Scot*. Dostoevsky's "Russian Idea", "in which he pictured Russia as the sick man possessed of devils but who would yet 'sit at the feet of Jesus'", is extolled by MacDiarmid as "a great creative idea – a dynamic

MacDiarmid states that 'Georgia / Stalin's native country, was also the first home of the Scots'.[34] As Glen has noted, this rather bizarre Scottish/Georgian conjunction brings 'with some sign of strain ... [MacDiarmid's] pan-Celticism into contact with his communism'.[35] It might be said that MacDiarmid shares Joyce's 'amazing proclivity to make outlandish correspondences, connections, and associations between apparently unrelated things'.[36]

In *In Memoriam James Joyce: A Vision of World Language* (1955), the increased interest in the 'Gaelic' world first developed in *Cencrastus* converges with the development of MacDiarmid's 'poetry of fact'[37] from the second half of the 1930s onwards. In addition, Joyce's death in 1941 gave MacDiarmid the opportunity to add further 'Celtic' elements to the text through its dedication and through a number of moments in which he addresses the departed Irishman.[38] The work, complete with symbolic illustrations by John Duncan Fergusson based on ogham, the early Irish system of writing,[39] is a central text of MacDiarmid's Celticism, though it has been claimed that the use of 'world language' in the poem is an attempt to 'transcend nationality'.[40] The book is a 'rag-bag'[41] that throws short moments of intimate, conversational

myth – and in no way devalued by the difference of the actual happenings in Russia from any Dostoevsky dreamed or desired"' (McCulloch and Matthews, 64). See also: 'Only in Gaeldom can there be the necessary counter-idea to the Russian idea—one that does not run wholly counter to it, but supplements, corrects, challenges, and qualifies it ... This Gaelic idea has nothing in common with the activities of An Comunn Gaidhealach, no relationship whatever with the Celtic Twilight' (MacDiarmid, *Selected Essays*, 67–8). MacDiarmid's 'Gaelic Idea' develops through his articles 'Scottish Gaelic Policy' (1927), 'Gaelic Poetry' (1928), 'Towards a Scottish Renaissance: desirable lines of advance' (1929), as well as 'The Caledonian Antisyzygy and the Gaelic Idea'.

[34] MacDiarmid, *Selected Poetry*, 205.   [35] Glen, 151.   [36] Gibson, George Cinclair, 20.

[37] MacDiarmid, *Lucky Poet*, xxxii.

[38] As Peter Mackay has observed, MacDiarmid's 'evolving support for a "Gaelic Idea" had paralleled ... the development of his "poetry of wisdom", written in synthetic English, which attempted to find a "correct vocabulary, whether spiritual, technical, or purely associative" with which to describe the world' (Mackay, 'Optik to Haptik', 280–1). One of the sources for *In Memoriam* was Henri Hubert's *The Greatness and Decline of the Celts* (1934). See Benstead, 147.

[39] 'The ogam alphabet was an indigenous script of old Ireland named after Ogma the Celtic God of Literature and Eloquence [,] The Decorations are composed of Joyce's initials in Ogam and other characters together with other symbols that convey Joyce's concern with music, creation, feeling and his native Ireland' (Fergusson, John Duncan, 10). Fergusson's illustrations include shamrocks, treble clefs, nude figures, and Joyce's initials.

[40] See Freedman, 253.–4. If *Finnegans Wake*—with its Irish setting, use of Irish language, links to Irish literature, and borderline obsession with Irish history—is an attempt to transcend Irish nationality then it is a failed one. MacDiarmid commented on the Irish nature of *Work in Progress* (the project that became *Finnegans Wake*), and Joyce's recording of a section of it, in *At the Sign of the Thistle*: 'In *Work in Progress*, Joyce, using about a score of languages, becomes not less, but more, Irish. 'Anna Livia Plurabelle' may look incomprehensible on the printed page; but on the gramophone record, in Joyce's own voice, it gets right over to every hearer' (MacDiarmid, *Sign*, 118). MacDiarmid responds to this section of *Work in Progress/Finnegans Wake* in the 1932 poem 'Water Music': 'Wheesht, wheesht, Joyce, and let me hear / Nae Anna Livvy's lilt, / But Wauchope, Esk, and Ewes again, / Each wi' its ain rhythms till't' (*CP*, 333).

[41] *IMJJ*, 35.

address—'Welcome then, Joyce, to our *aonach* here... We who know'[42]—into a very long and monotonous information session on a wide range of subjects, with an emphasis on language and culture.

MacDiarmid began work on what was to become *In Memoriam James Joyce* in the 1930s—before Joyce's death—but it was not completed and published until the mid 1950s.[43] Similarly to the personal links between the Irish and Scottish Celtic Revivals, MacDiarmid had a number of contacts in Ireland and had visited the country in 1928 (he visited again in 1978). However, Joyce was long gone from Ireland by 1928 and the two never met (though MacDiarmid supposedly met *AE*, Yeats, Oliver St. John Gogarty, and Éamon de Valera).[44] Still, MacDiarmid felt a close affinity to Joyce and compared his own work to Joyce's in a number of articles published under a variety of pseudonyms.[45] Of course, it helped that Joyce was Irish. It is difficult to imagine MacDiarmid writing a late career *In Memoriam D. H. Lawrence* or *In Memoriam Virginia Woolf*. Such works would have been read as a form of identification with English culture, something MacDiarmid was usually at pains to avoid. Originally, the poetry that makes up *In Memoriam James Joyce*

[42] *IMJJ*, 27. MacDiarmid glosses *aonach* as 'Scottish Gaelic, meaning (1) a solitary place, (2) a place of union' (*IMJJ*, 27). One of the meanings of *aonach* in Irish is, appropriately enough perhaps, 'assembly' (see Ó Dónaill, 53). The term *óenach*, from which *aonach* is derived, originally meant 'a periodic assembly of the population of a *tuath*, or group of *tuatha*, for horse racing and athletic contests' in medieval Ireland (Connolly, S.J., 425). Fittingly, given the title of MacDiarmid's text, 'Óenaig apparently originated as funeral games, a number of the traditional sites being associated with mythical burials' (Connolly, S.J., 425).

[43] See Gish, *MacDiarmid*, 183. Roderick Watson states that *In Memoriam James Joyce* was begun by 1939 (Watson, Roderick, 20).

[44] See Bold, Alan, *Scots Steel*, 6. According to Bold, 'Yeats knew MacDiarmid's "O Wha's Been Here Afore Me Lass"... from *A Drunk Man* – by heart and included it, with three other MacDiarmid poems ("Parley of Beasts", "Cattle Show", "The Skeleton of the Future") in *The Oxford Book of Modern Verse* (1936)' (Bold, *Scots Steel*, 9–10). For a discussion on Yeats and MacDiarmid, see Crotty, 'Swordsmen'. Gogarty wrote a positive review of *A Drunk Man Looks at the Thistle* for the *Irish Statesman*, claiming that the book was 'significant, because in the wonderfully flexible and containing form [MacDiarmid] has chosen he has managed to become, as it were, a frenzied mouth letting the present-day soul of Scotland speak out with its metaphysic, its politic and its poetry' (Gogarty, 432). MacDiarmid, in turn, suggested that Gogarty's reputation would eventually eclipse Yeats' (see *RT II*, 221).

[45] Here is a selection: 'Grieve's first published work, apart from the monumental *Northern Numbers*, by far the best anthology of Scots poetry, was *Annals of the Five Senses*, consisting of marvelous experiments in the cerebral manner. Compared with Joyce at this period he was a more polished craftsman: his work had no blurred edges, but he had no spiritual upheaval similar to Joyce's to liberate a Scottish *Ulysses*' (*RT II*, 152). In another piece, published under the rather outlandish name J.G. Outterstone Buglass, the writer claims that 'Mr M'Diarmid... resembles Mr Joyce in his attitude to the religion of his countrymen, to sexual problems, to political and cultural nationalism, to humbug, hypocrisy, and sentimentalism, in his preoccupation with "interior revelation"... and in his European range in technique and ideas' (*RT I*, 237). However, in a 1932 piece published under the name C. M. Grieve and responding to a review of his work in *The Daily Record and Mail*, MacDiarmid attempts to distance himself from Joyce: '"E. de B." says I am increasingly under the influence of James Joyce. I know too much about Joyce not to know the full absurdity of this remark. A village idiot with half an eye could see that neither in technique nor subject-matter have Joyce and I one iota in common... why should the Editor of "Scotland's National Paper"... turn over my book to such a moron?' (*RT II*, 419).

was to be a part of a massive text usually known as *Mature Art*, but this project was never completed.[46] According to Roderick Watson, 'Having turned to scientific and Marxist materialism in the 1930s, MacDiarmid was determined to forge a poetry that could illuminate a world of material facts without recourse to...Romantic solipsism.'[47] One wonders what Joyce would have made of a work of materialist poetry being dedicated to him, given that he considered 'belief in headlong materialism' to be 'fatuous'.[48]

As Louisa Gairn has noted, part of MacDiarmid's Marxist materialism was an interest in the science of ecology and in the biodiversity of the Scottish landscape. This interest was influenced by the sociologist, biologist, town planner, and Celticist Patrick Geddes.[49] In poems such as 'Dìreadh I' from 1938, detailed descriptions of the natural world converge with MacDiarmid's interest in Gaelic poetry. Indeed, MacDiarmid saw a similarity between scientific field observation and Gaelic poetics.[50] In 1954, MacDiarmid wrote that he was 'concerned to dissociate myself from romantic idealisations of Gaelic "spirituality", etc., and a non-scientific attitude to Nature, in accordance with my own Marxist tenets.'[51] According to Gairn,

> While not always successful in his quest for a poetry of facts, MacDiarmid's attempt to bring together Gaelic poetics, Geddesian ecological practice and the philosophy of being can be read as an important Scottish contribution to the discourse of ecopoetics, and a vital link between the polymaths of the

---

[46] Benstead refers to this work as the *Mature Art/Cornish Heroic Song* urtext. See Benstead, 18. The prospectus for *Mature Art* promised an 'enormous poem of 20,000 lines, dealing with the inter-related themes of the evolution of world literature and world consciousness, the problem of linguistics, the place and potentialities of the Gaelic genius, from its origin in Georgia to its modern expressions in Scotland, Ireland, Wales, Cornwall, Galicia and the Pays Basque, the synthesis of East and West' (Qtd in Gish, *MacDiarmid*, 182–3). According to W.N. Herbert, there is also a 'Celtic branch' of this project, commenting that 'Obvious candidates for inclusion in this Celtic branch of the poem [alongside 'Cornish Heroic Song' and 'Once in a Cornish Garden'] are the 'Dìreadh' poems and miscellaneous pieces such as 'Island Funeral', 'A Golden Wine in the Gaidhealtachd', 'Happy on Heimeay', and 'The Glen of Silence'...A strong candidate for inclusion must also be 'Lament for the Great Music'...(Herbert, W.N., 165). For a summary of the Byzantine complications surrounding the composition and publication of *In Memoriam James Joyce* from 1932–1955, including its relationship to the MacDiarmid projects *In Memoriam Teofilo Folengo*, *A Cornish Heroic Song*, *Impavidi Progrediamur*, and *The Kind of Poetry I Want*, see Riach, 60–7.
[47] Watson, Roderick, 20.   [48] *OCPW*, 179.
[49] 'Geddes's own attempts towards a 'Scots Renascence' (focused on his 1895 periodical *The Evergreen*) may have been linked to the 'Celtic Twilight' and Kailyard MacDiarmid and his peers forcefully rejected, but MacDiarmid would later claim Geddes as one of his key influences in *The Company I've Kept* (1966)...*In Memoriam James Joyce* (1955), begun during MacDiarmid's Shetland years, names Geddes when calling for 'completeness of thought / A synthesis of all view points" (Gairn, 85).
[50] See Gairn, 94.
[51] Letter to Neil M. Gunn, 10 December 1954, in MacDiarmid, *Letters*, 271.

nineteenth century, the Scottish Renaissance movement and the radical eco- and geopoetics of our contemporary world.[52]

Since Macpherson's *Ossian*, nature has often been romanticized, idealized, or endowed with human emotion in Irish and Scottish literature, especially in work of the Celtic Revival era.[53] MacDiarmid's 1930s Gaelic-influenced nature poetry stands as a new development—a kind of Modernist eco-Celticism without any Macphersonian influence. In other words, this is poetry that attempts to approach and represent the natural world 'directly' or 'scientifically' without the elements of romance superimposed by Macpherson. Eventually the Celticist elements—and, arguably, any sense of human emotion—are also stripped away from this category of MacDiarmid's poetry, leading to the dry cairns of specialized vocabulary that make up works such as 'On a Raised Beach' (1934).

In the 1930s, MacDiarmid went through the break-up of his first marriage and suffered financial difficulties and a mental breakdown. During this time, MacDiarmid lived with his second wife and his son at Whalsay in Shetland, 'dependent on hand-outs from the islanders'.[54] The 1930s also saw a decisive change of direction in MacDiarmid's poetry:

> From [his nervous breakdown] the direction is clearly defined, and the later 1930s see a working out of the discursive poetry of fact and idea first developed in *Stony Limits and Other Poems*. From 1936 to his leaving Shetland in 1942, he wrote longer and longer poems based on a kind of journalistic collage of his reading and thinking on philosophy, language, culture, politics. Though much of this was not published until the 1950s or even 1960s, nearly everything, including *In Memoriam James Joyce* was written in the Shetlands.[55]

This change of direction also meant a movement away from Scots, the potential of which MacDiarmid had once compared to the liberatory power of Joyce's *Ulysses*:

> We have been enormously struck by the resemblance – the moral resemblance – between Jamieson's Etymological Dictionary of the Scottish language and James Joyce's *Ulysses*. A *vis comica* that has not yet been liberated lies bound by desuetude and misappreciation in the recesses of the

---

[52] Gairn, 96.   [53] See Frawley, especially 37–40.   [54] Gairn, 88.
[55] Gish, *MacDiarmid*, 122.

Doric: and its potential uprising would be no less prodigious, uncontrollable, and utterly at variance with conventional morality than was Joyce's tremendous outpouring....[56]

Numerous critics have pointed to the influence of *Ulysses* on MacDiarmid's book-length poem in Synthetic Scots, *A Drunk Man Looks at the Thistle* (1926), especially in terms of the focus on individual consciousnesses in both texts.[57] MacDiarmid's use of Scots was a reaction towards the English language that was, for him, 'suffering from a kind of Imperial elephantiasis' and that had 'vastly outgrown itself and [become] more and more useless for creative purposes.'[58]

The replacement of MacDiarmid's Scots with 'journalistic collage', transcription, and plagiarism[59]—or 'the habitual print out', as Seamus Heaney put it[60]—offered MacDiarmid the means to put together works that could rival the scale of Joyce texts like *Ulysses* and *Finnegans Wake* but with less strain on individual creativity (of course Joyce was no stranger to textual recycling or processing himself).[61] The composition of *In Memoriam James Joyce* involved a large amount of textual selection, accumulation, 'treatment' (i.e. the conversion of prose into poetry through the introduction of line breaks), and assembly, even if much of the material comes from a single source—the *Times Literary Supplement*.[62] However, MacDiarmid's efforts—the 'excessive cataloguing' in his own words[63]—still required a considerable degree of effort, regardless of the originality of the output. In the digital age, the copy and paste function means that moving text from a source into a new document—or creating textual 'collages'—has become a standard, everyday activity. A poem like *In Memoriam James Joyce* could be collated with much greater ease now, if anyone had the desire. Furthermore, the internet has allowed us to carry out deep and wide research at speeds impossible in MacDiarmid's time. As such, MacDiarmid's text has assumed a kind of quixotic grandeur since few would carry out such work manually now—surely it is one of the

---

[56] MacDiarmid, qtd. in McCulloch, *Modernism and Nationalism*, 27.

[57] See Bold, *Scots Steel*, Roderick Watson, 'MacDiarmid and International Modernism', and Sassi's 'Hugh MacDiarmid's (Un)making of the Modern Scottish Nation'.

[58] Qtd in Glen, 50–1.

[59] As Scott Lyall has noted, MacDiarmid had a 'blasé attitude to the laws of copyright' (Lyall, *Hugh MacDiarmid*, 63).

[60] *FK*, 295.

[61] For an extensive list of the sources of MacDiarmid's appropriations in *In Memoriam James Joyce*, see the appendix in Benstead's 'A Study of Hugh MacDiarmid's *In Memoriam James Joyce*'. The sources for the sections of *In Memoriam* quoted in this chapter have been given when known. However, not all of MacDiarmid's sources are known and some sections of the text are original.

[62] See Benstead, 16.   [63] MacDiarmid qtd in Gish, 'Interview', 143.

last of its kind, pieced together in the final decades of the pre-digital, pre-Internet world. However, *In Memoriam* is a precursor of modern citational and intertextual poetics, as well as the practice of 'uncreative writing'.[64] *In Memoriam* is also part of a category of modern poetics that challenges the notion that poetry ought to be the expression of emotion in a poet's own words.[65]

It has been suggested that *In Memoriam James Joyce* predicted hypertexts, databases, or the products and relations of the digital age and information technology.[66] The poem certainly does express the Modernist sense that the twentieth century saw a 'profound, rapid, irresistible, and total transform-ation of all / the conditions of human activity and of life itself'.[67] When asked for the controlling principle of *In Memoriam* by Nancy Gish, MacDiarmid suggested that the 'structure' of the text derives from the 'coherence' of the research efforts of the writer himself:

> There's the absolute coherence of the writer's intellectual quest into all the possibilities of the language, more particularly languages of small countries, their past times or dialects. I think personally it's a perfectly complete struc-ture, and I'm not disheartened because many people find the excessive cata-loguing of all things unpoetical.[68]

In the same interview, when asked what gives *In Memoriam* the 'clarity and intensity of poetry'[69] MacDiarmid spoke of 'the sheer tenacity of the develop-ment of intellectual ideas' suggesting that 'tenacity itself is infinitely valuable'.[70] Here, MacDiarmid conceives of poetry as an exhibition of scholarly exertion and determination. The central task of the poem is to 'heal the breach / Between genius and scholarship, literature and learning'.[71] *In Memoriam James Joyce* states MacDiarmid's desire for a 'perfect fusion' of 'Scientific data and aesthetic realization'[72] in his work and likens himself to 'a man who ... uses words from many dialects / To say what he has to say as exactly and directly as possible'.[73] However, *In Memoriam James Joyce* is more of a prescription for, or vision of, the future of poetry—similarly outlined in the text 'The Kind of

---

[64] For a discussion of these concepts, see Perloff.

[65] For a commentary on the expression of emotion and the use of original language in modern poetry, see Perloff, 2–3.

[66] See Crawford, *The Modern Poet*, 212. *Ulysses* and *Finnegans Wake* have also been discussed with reference to information technology. See Connor and Creasy, and also Derrida.

[67] *IMJJ*, 34.   [68] MacDiarmid, qtd in Gish, 'Interview', 143.   [69] Gish, 'Interview', 143.

[70] MacDiarmid, qtd in Gish, 'Interview', 143.   [71] *IMJJ*, 33.   [72] Ibid., 55.

[73] Ibid., 59.

Poetry I Want'—rather than the realization of that poetry. MacDiarmid's 1955 Modernist data poem is also an anomaly in the history of Celticism, since it is more interested in materialism and science—the science of linguistics in particular—than the 'spirit' of the Celtic world. The work is a convergence of the Celticist strain in MacDiarmid's work and the scientific/materialist strain.[74] This is a neat reversal of the Arnoldian Celticism of the nineteenth century in which it is the Anglo-Saxon world that is associated with rationality, the intellect, science, and materialism.[75]

Similarly to *To Circumjack Cencrastus*, *In Memoriam James Joyce* engages with what MacDiarmid calls elsewhere 'The Celtic genius.'[76] MacDiarmid's work shares a Celticist trope of thinking of the 'Celtic world' or the 'Gaelic countries' (including Wales, erroneously) in a binary, oppositional relationship with the 'Anglo-Saxon world' or simply, England itself:

> Our Gaelic forbears possessed their great literature
> As nothing is possessed by peoples to-day,
> And in Scotland and Ireland and Wales
> There was a popular understanding and delight
> In literary allusions, technical niceties, and dexterities of
>   expression
> Of which the English in Elizabethan times
> Had only the poorest counterpart,
> And have since had none whatever
> And have destroyed it in the Gaelic countries too.[77]

In this Celtic binary trope, the Gaelic or Celtic countries are generally seen as more civilized, spiritual, or artistic than England. For MacDiarmid, Celts are usually rich in spirit and in speech even if they are cash-strapped: 'Ah, in the Gaelic countries still—in Ireland / And Scotland and Wales—the poor man / Is seldom poor in spirit or address.'[78] On the other hand, the Anglo-Saxon is narrow-minded and inward-looking ('The magnificent insularity / Which is

---

[74] However, this combination of Marxism and Celticism has precursors in the thought of Ruaridh Erskine and John Maclean. See Pittock, *Celtic Identity*, 83 and 125.
[75] See the following list of perceived Anglo Saxon and Celtic oppositions: 'intellectual/emotional, rational/intuitive, science/religion, science/arts, externality/internality, instrumentality/creativity, practicality/sentimentality, culture/nature, materialism/idealism, objectivity/subjectivity, artificial/spontaneous, society/family, modern/ancient, male/female, Anglo-Saxon/Celt' (Chapman, 106).
[76] *CP*, 708.   [77] *CP*, 664.
[78] *IMJJ*, 87. MacDiarmid's source for this section was Orlo Williams' 'England Through Irish Eyes', an article in the December 25, 1937 issue of the *Times Literary Supplement*. See Benstead, 287.

the pride of the Anglo-Saxon mind').[79] Furthermore, literature in the English language would have become dull and dishonest had it not been for the Irishman Joyce (and other Modernists):

> I certainly agree with Mr. Emrys [sic] Humphreys that 'It is not too soon to say that Joyce saved us from being smothered in the spurious: without Joyce (without Eliot and Pound) the atmosphere of English literature today would be that of the bar of a suburban golf club. Honest, serious, sensitive communications would have become practically impossible.'[80]

Towards the end of the poem, MacDiarmid writes that 'Literature of the imagination in Anglo-Saxondom.../ Is not a very thriving national affair / Because it has lost touch completely / With racial life.'[81] These lines link the standard Arnoldian Celticist idea that England is lacking imagination with the problematic and worrying suggestion that this could somehow be countered with a return to 'racial life'.

It is difficult to defend MacDiarmid from charges of Anglophobia, though this has been attempted. According to MacDiarmid's biographer Alan Bold, 'the intelligent Englishman will understand that MacDiarmid's Anglophobic argument is not with individuals but with the impact of England's imperialism.'[82] Yes, part of MacDiarmid's problem with England certainly was the 'English Ascendancy, the hideous khaki Empire.'[83] However, in *In Memoriam James Joyce* alone we find a number of examples of quite extreme Anglophobia that have little or nothing to do with English imperialism: 'In England where the men, and women too, / Are almost as interesting as the sheep'[84]; 'I cherish the following passage quoted by F.O. Matthiessen in *The James Family...* "They (the English) are an intensely vulgar race, high and low .... They are not worth studying..."';[85] 'Only an Englishman yet much to my liking'[86]; and, addressing Yeats, 'I who am infinitely more un-English than you.'[87] These examples are in addition to a section titled, fairly unambiguously, 'ENGLAND IS OUR

---

[79] *IMJJ*, 61. MacDiarmid lifted this line, and the surrounding section of *In Memoriam*, from *Europe Free and United* (1945) by Albert Léon Guérard. See Benstead, 281.
[80] 'Author's Note' in *IMJJ*, 13.
[81] *IMJJ*, 123. MacDiarmid took this, and a large section of the 'England is our Enemy' part of *In Memoriam*, from Ford Madox Ford's 1924 text 'Stocktaking: Towards a Re-valuation of English Literature'. See Benstead, 292.
[82] Bold, *Scots Steel*, 20.   [83] *CP*, 708.
[84] *IMJJ*, 106. This section of *In Memoriam* comes from a 1945 *Observer* article by William Beach Thomas titled 'Open Air'. See Benstead, 290.
[85] 'Author's Note' in *IMJJ*, 18.   [86] *IMJJ*, 25.   [87] Ibid., 36.

ENEMY.'[88] Indeed, MacDiarmid states quite clearly that 'My love of the East, and my Anglophobia, are both evident in this poem.'[89] Had James Joyce been born an Englishman (something almost impossible to imagine, given the importance of Irish life, history, and culture to his work) Hugh MacDiarmid would never have attached such importance to him as a writer. Indeed, MacDiarmid's Anglophobia is very closely linked to his Hibernophilia.[90] In a 1916 letter to his former teacher George Ogilvie, MacDiarmid mentions his composition of some 'Anti-English verse, not dissimilar to certain products of [the] Irish revival.'[91] This anti-Englishness is another new development in Celticism and is a contrast to the then-recent Celticist Anglophilia of Fiona Macleod. Macleod's *Winged Destiny* described English culture as producing 'some of the noblest achievements of the human race, some of the lordliest conquests over the instincts and forces of barbarism, some of the loveliest and most deathless things of the spirit and the imagination.'[92] It is unlikely that MacDiarmid shared this assessment.

Despite its title, the relationship between MacDiarmid's *In Memoriam James Joyce* and Joyce's own work is fairly tenuous. Indeed, the book's title may have been a late addition when the project was virtually complete and designed partly to 'appeal to all Joyce enthusiasts'.[93] Furthermore, the text contrasts starkly to the late Celticism of the actual writer it is dedicated to. However, a comparison between MacDiarmid's text and Joyce's work, especially *Finnegans Wake*, can help us understand MacDiarmid's unique form of late Celticism, and the points of communality between the two writers, as well as some clear areas of divergence. It is also worth considering why MacDiarmid would choose to link Joyce's precedent to his work by naming it *In Memoriam James Joyce* if most of the text had been written without Joyce's work in mind. In *In Memoriam James Joyce*, MacDiarmid's admiration for Joyce is partly based on an appreciation of the Irishman's indifference to the way in which his work was received, as he selflessly worked to increase a cultural 'inheritance':

---

[88] Ibid., 119.   [89] 'Author's Note' in *IMJJ*, 17.

[90] As Lyall has noted, the Easter Rising was 'fundamental to Grieve's developing nationalism...In barracks in Sheffield when the Rising took place between 24 and 29 April, MacDiarmid recalled, "If it had been possible at all I would have deserted at that time from the British Army and joined the Irish." Claiming to have been a gunrunner for the Irish, he relates his notorious anglophobia to disgust at the killing of the 1916 leaders: "The picture of [Roger] Casement hanged, and [James] Connolly taken out on a stretcher and executed, are two of the great rallying points of my spirit in its eternal and immeasurable hatred of everything English"' (Lyall, *Hugh MacDiarmid*, 32–3).

[91] See Bold, *Scots Steel*, 3.   [92] Macleod, *Winged Destiny*, 178.

[93] MacDiarmid, *Letters*, 453.

> I praise you then, Joyce, because you too
> Were—like all Gongorists—one of those altruists
> (However their conscious motives may be mixed)
> Risking contemporary misunderstanding, personal
>   obloquy even,
> For the sake of enriching the inheritance
> Each administers in his generation.[94]

Clearly, MacDiarmid is inviting comparisons with himself here.

MacDiarmid's poem displays a confidence in the human capacity to understand and classify the world. This stems partly from MacDiarmid's own interpretation of *Finnegans Wake* and of Joyce's work in general—that Joyce's texts are displays of knowledge (despite Joyce's late Celticism—based partly on the work of David Hume—stressing our inability to fully access external reality). A brief examination of one section of Joyce's *Ulysses* might illustrate the difference between MacDiarmid and Joyce in terms of attitudes to knowledge. Here is a section from the opening page of the 'Aeolus' episode, set in the offices of the *Freeman's Journal* newspaper in Dublin: 'Grossbooted draymen rolled barrels dullthudding out of Prince's stores and bumped them up on the brewery float. On the brewery float bumped dullthudding barrels rolled by grossbooted draymen out of Prince's stores.'[95] Discussing this section, Karen Lawrence has noted that this chiasmus

> shifts our attention from the meaning of a sentence to its spatial arrangement on the page. The figure makes us aware of the difference between the words and the things they represent, for it flaunts the fact that language and print are reversible, whereas the movement of life and the movement of the plot that mirrors life are not. It reminds us that the rules of the text are distinct from the rules of life.[96]

So, Joyce suggests that texts operate in a radically different way to life (*Ulysses* also invites readers to move backwards and forwards in narrative 'time' in order to understand its puzzles and intricacies). Elsewhere in the text, the

---

[94] *IMJJ*, 91. As Nancy Gish has noted, the term 'Gongorist' here refers to the Spanish poet Luis de Góngora y Argote, whose work featured 'strange words, allusion, obscurity, and borrowings from other sources and languages' (see Gish, *MacDiarmid*, 191).

[95] *U*, 7.21–24.

[96] Lawrence, 69–70. Similarly, on the subject of the different styles in *Ulysses*, Lawrence writes 'what the seemingly limitless number of details and styles suggests is the awareness that no matter how comprehensive the text, it can never exhaust reality' (Lawrence, 78).

difficulties in aligning in text and reality are made evident when Bloom reads the attendees of Dignam's funeral in the 'Eumaeus' episode. According to the report, 'Stephen Dedalus, B. A.' was at a funeral earlier that day (which the reader knows is not 'true' in the world of the novel), as was someone called 'M'Intosh'[97] (this is based on an amusing misunderstanding between Bloom and the journalist Hynes about a man wearing a Macintosh jacket at the funeral of Paddy Dignam in the earlier 'Hades' episode), and Bloom's name is misprinted as 'L. Boom',[98] something that slightly irritates him. So, for Joyce, texts are often sources of error and inaccuracy. Newspapers—or Modernist novels—either mangle or fail to encapsulate life or reality or they 'behave' in ways that life does not. On the other hand, MacDiarmid's language in *In Memoriam James Joyce* is confident and direct, with no anxiety that language and text might not possess the capacity to faithfully represent or capture the world: 'the unity of thing and word, / Of feeling and its articulation...is the essence of poetry'.[99]

Some of *In Memoriam James Joyce* is less a display of MacDiarmid's undoubted poetic talent (as in his early work) and more of a slightly insecure attempt to convince his readers of his polymath genius and supposedly vast knowledge. *In Memoriam James Joyce* is the polar opposite of a Joycean lack of faith in knowledge and in the ability of texts to contain or express reality, since it is designed to showcase the 'impact / Of the whole range of *welt literatur* on one man's brain'.[100] Beyond the attempted demonstration of this supposed impact, the poem contains a number of declarations of knowledge, understanding, and mastery of academic or arcane subjects: 'We who know', 'Even as we delight in the letter of Aristeas', 'And even as we know', 'Even as we know', 'Or even as we know', 'So we have read', 'I have known', 'Even as I know'.[101]

Strangely, an early MacDiarmid lyric like 'The Watergaw' is much closer in spirit and technique to Joyce's work than *In Memoriam James Joyce* itself:

> Ae weet forenicht i' the yow-trummle
> I saw yon antrin thing,
> A watergaw wi' its chitterin' licht
> Ayont the on-ding;

---

[97] *U*, 16.1259 and 16.1261.   [98] Ibid., 16.1260.
[99] *IMJJ*, 49. These lines are taken from Sidney Barrington Gates and Erich Heller's 1953 *TLS* article 'Satirist in the Modern World'. See Benstead, 278.
[100] *IMJJ*, 35.   [101] Ibid., 27, 40, 40, 40, 41, 82, 86, 86.

An' I thocht o' the last wild look ye gied
Afore ye deed!

There was nae reek i' the laverock's hoose
That nicht – an' nane i' mine;
But I hae thocht o' that foolish licht
Ever sin' syne;
An' I think that mebbe at last I ken
What your look meant then.[102]

Like *Finnegans Wake*, 'The Watergaw' experiments with alternatives to the English language and, like the stories of *Dubliners*, it hints at what Seamus Heaney has called a 'sort of epiphany'[103] or 'something not quite clearly apprehended but very definitely experienced'.[104] MacDiarmid's early poem, like much of Joyce's output, focuses on moments that are a mixture of perception and doubt. The phrase 'mebbe at last I ken' expresses a cautious, hesitant, uncertain experience of knowledge.[105] Joyce's works—aside from the uncertainties generated by the use of languages in *Finnegans Wake* and the 'riddles and enigmas'[106] Joyce famously worked into his texts—express the impossibilities of knowing anything for sure and explore the gaps between reality and fiction, including the ways the written word can falsify life, and the difficulties expressing knowledge even if it has somehow been fully accessed. The stories of *Dubliners* are structured around the 'epiphany' but these moments are often complex and highly ambiguous with crucial information sometimes withheld from the reader.[107] Poems like 'The Watergaw' may be MacDiarmid's most Modernist work in terms of its poetics of indeterminacy (and it is difficult to square this work with the sense of ideological certainty he expresses elsewhere in his writing, or with the 'Poetry of Fact' of an encyclopedic text like *In Memoriam James Joyce*). Furthermore, poetry like 'The Watergaw' is also where MacDiarmid comes close to Scottish philosophy—Hume's idealism and scepticism rather than the 'Common Sense' school.

A further disparity between Joyce and MacDiarmid is in their differing approaches to languages. In the introduction to *In Memoriam James Joyce*,

---

[102] *CP*, 17.   [103] *FK*, 297.

[104] Ibid., 297. Perhaps Heaney could relate to this line in particular—his early pseudonym was 'Incertus'.

[105] Not dissimilar from Beckett's supposed favourite word perhaps: 'perhaps'.

[106] 'I've put in so many enigmas and puzzles that it will keep the professors busy for centuries arguing over what I meant, and that's the only way of insuring one's immortality' (*JJ*, 521).

[107] As I have written elsewhere, Hume's philosophy is an important 'Celtic' precursor to the atmosphere of incertitude, and obscurity in *Finnegans Wake*.

MacDiarmid notes approvingly that 'Finnegans Wake of James Joyce...uses twenty languages as a sort of keyboard'.[108] However, as W.N. Herbert has discussed, the 'basic difference between MacDiarmid's method and that of Joyce, his example in multi-linguistic work, seems to have eluded him. Instead of creating a medium in which several languages are intermingling, MacDiarmid drops a phrase or verse into a basically intact journalistic English'.[109] As Dorian Grieve has noted, these languages include Welsh, Breton, Greek, Hebrew, Sanskrit, Chinese and others (MacDiarmid's command of these languages is not necessarily perfect—one Hebrew word is printed upside down).[110] Indeed, In Memoriam James Joyce does admit to MacDiarmid's comparative lack of ability with languages in one of the few passages of the book that displays any real emotion:

> I might be found so speaking too
> fhios dom fhéin some fine day
> Tho' I appreciate Euripides' use
> Of archaic diction too,
> But alas I can speak no Greek
> And am now too old to learn
> And nil leiyas ogam air[111]

There is a sense of a weakness and ignorance here which is rare in the text. The admission of a struggle with language is matched, perhaps appropriately, by the use of some questionable Irish (for example, the Irish alphabet has no letter 'y'). The use of multiple languages, as well as wordplay, allusions, references, and motifs, in Joyce's writing creates difficulties, opacities, possibilities and a generally evasive attitude towards fixed meanings. MacDiarmid's text, on the other hand, is much more straightforward in its assertions. Discussing Joyce's use of the Encyclopædia Britannica in the composition of Finnegans Wake, Len Platt has suggested that 'Finnegans Wake is a text that has apparently swallowed or "digested" vast amounts of information only to return it in

---

[108] 'Author's Note' in IMJJ, 14.   [109] Herbert, W.N., 195–6.   [110] See Grieve, Dorian, 33.

[111] IMJJ, 67. According to Dorian Grieve, 'The last line...along with another Irish phrase a few lines before (and almost all of the rest of the stanza), is taken, with MacDiarmidian errors, from the Journals and Letters of Stephen MacKenna, where it is glossed "I have no cure for it"' (Grieve, Dorian, 34). In his piece 'The Case for Synthetic Scots', MacDiarmid admits the gap between himself and Joyce in terms of artistic-linguistic achievements: 'My synthetic Scots has not yet touched the fringe of Joycean experimentation...practically confined to the revival of Scots words with no equivalents, or precise equivalents, in English, on the one hand, and a use of Gaelic and foreign phrases and old allusions on the other' (MacDiarmid, Sign, 184).

ways that seem outside all reasoned discussion.[112] *In Memoriam James Joyce*, on the other hand, often reads just like an encyclopedia.

When MacDiarmid uses phrases such as 'Even as we know' in *In Memoriam James Joyce* the 'we' is unlikely to mean the poet and his readership and certainly not the human race at large. It refers to MacDiarmid's specially selected clique of poets and writers he regards as highly evolved and politically or racially aligned: 'So I think of you, Joyce, and of Yeats and others who are dead.'[113] MacDiarmid is, like Joyce, 'committed to a linguistically uncommon literature of complex generalist knowledge.'[114] This sense of artistic and intellectual exclusivity jars somewhat with MacDiarmid's socialism. However, MacDiarmid seems to have anticipated such criticism. In a piece from the *Daily Worker* titled 'Joyce is Hard, but so is Life', MacDiarmid claims that:

> The right to ignorance, the avoidance of the excruciatingly painful and unnatural business of thinking, cannot be conceded by anyone concerned with the interests of the masses of mankind. Defective education, limited sensibilities and a restriction to rudimentary interests can never be permitted to establish themselves as criteria of literary criticism. The cultural issue is the crucial and all-important one, and is the end, in the light of which everything else must be regarded simply as means.[115]

In other words, the 'masses' have no right to 'ignorance' no matter how hard their lives are, how limited their opportunities might be, or what obstacles stand in the way of their appreciation of texts like Joyce's. Challenging texts must be engaged with, since an improvement in intelligence and consciousness ('the cultural issue') is, for MacDiarmid, the ultimate goal for socialism and the human race.

Much of MacDiarmid's work focuses on the latent capacities of the masses and how art should be used to raise the consciousness of humanity (indeed, part of the point of the difficulty of MacDiarmid's Modernism is to act as catalyst to the transformation of public consciousness). For example, an early lyric such as 'The Bonnie Broukit Bairn' imagines the earth as minor in the

---

[112] Platt, 'Unfallable encyclicing', 107.   [113] *IMJJ*, 36.

[114] Lyall, *Hugh MacDiarmid*, 184–5.

[115] *RT III*, 365. MacDiarmid continues, 'But, you say, Joyce is very difficult. Isn't life today very difficult? Isn't it becoming more and more complicated?…If the world is becoming one, shouldn't we open our hearts and our minds and take it all in, and isn't this exactly what Joyce above all achieved?' (*RT III*, 367).

grand scheme of the cosmos as well as small and prosaic in comparison to Mars and Venus. However, the earth is the only site of potential and emotion: '*but greet an' in your tears you'll droun / The haill clanjamfrie!*'[116] *In Memoriam James Joyce* also expresses an anxiety regarding the possibility of human devolution: 'The ancestors of oysters and barnacles had heads. / Snakes have lost their limbs / And ostriches and penguins their power of flight. / Man may just as easily lose his intelligence.'[117] The unspoken implication here is that the power of language—and of works like *In Memoriam James Joyce*—can help humanity avoid such a scenario. This faith in the capacity of language to transform people is made explicit elsewhere in the poem: 'There lie hidden in language elements that effectively combined / Can utterly change the nature of man.'[118] For Joyce, as was mentioned in Chapter 2, humanity is basically unchanging. In one way, MacDiarmid is closer to Walter Scott than to Joyce, since MacDiarmid and Scott, despite their vast and obvious political and artistic differences, share a belief in the ability of societies, including Scotland, to drastically change and improve.

In Memoriam James Joyce is part of a thematically linked corpus of Irish-influenced or Irish-associated Scottish Modernist writing. One of the ways to understand the importance of Ireland and Irish culture for Scottish Modernism is to consider the relatively small but highly revealing tradition of Scottish Modernist elegies for deceased modern Irishmen. This mini-genre includes *In Memoriam James Joyce* and two Sorley MacLean texts, 'Àrd Mhusaeum na hÈireann' ('The National Museum of Ireland') and 'Aig Uaigh Yeats' ('At Yeats' Grave').[119] There is a minor collection of mid-twentieth century Scottish poetry dedicated to dead Irishmen; Joyce, Connolly, and, to a lesser extent, Yeats. MacDiarmid and MacLean write types of elegies for Joyce and Connolly, respectively, yet the Irishmen remain alive for the Scottish writers. This body of work—in which, to paraphrase MacDiarmid, Scottish

---

[116] *CP*, 17.

[117] *IMJJ*, 104. MacDiarmid adapted this from a section in J.B.S. Haldane's *The Inequality of Man: And Other Essays*. See Benstead, 290. For further analysis of MacDiarmid's use of Haldane see Riach, 115–16.

[118] *IMJJ*, 55. However, in 'Second Hymn to Lenin' MacDiarmid suggests that figures such as Joyce have 'affected nocht but a fringe / O' mankind in ony way' (*CP*, 324).

[119] 'Aig Uaigh Yeats' displays slightly less of a sense of Irish-Scottish solidarity than 'Àrd-Mhusaeum na h-Èireann' and is not concerned with the Gaelic world. After praising Yeats' poetic powers and describing Yeats' grave 'eadar a' mhuir is Beinn Ghulbain, / eadar an Sligeach 's Lios an Daill (between the sea and Ben Bulben, / between Sligo and Lissadell)', the speaker seems to admonish the Irishman for being a poet rather than a man of action like James Connolly, who is also mentioned in the text. In the final stanza, the speaker says 'tha leisgeul air do bhilean (there is an excuse on your lips)' (MacLean, 272–3).

Modernists look at the shamrock—searches modern Irish history and contemporary Irish culture for examples and exemplars of sacrifice, dedication,
and forms of artistic, personal, and political heroism. However, in these texts
MacDiarmid and MacLean distance themselves from the poetry of the Celtic
Revival, a phenomenon that both poets were heavily critical of.[120]

Aside from the actual contents of the poems, the naming and dedication
of these poems are significant symbolic acts in themselves. The gesture of
Scottish artists publicly recognizing specific Irish politicians and artists is a
way of signalling approval and admiration for the named individuals but it
is also a way for MacDiarmid and MacLean to place themselves within a
kind of preferred imagined community or lineage (similar to the way Joyce
thought of his work as being descended from a school of Celtic philosophy
including Hume and Berkeley). There is also the implicit sense in these texts
that Scottish writers should follow Irish artistic innovations and that
Scotland should follow Ireland's lead in terms of its struggle for independence. For MacDiarmid, 'In addressing Joyce, who died in 1941, on the subject of world language, MacDiarmid is speaking to a dead man who was
once gloriously alive to all the creative possibilities of language and who
attempted to create his own linguistic universe in *Finnegans Wake*.'[121] For
MacLean, James Connolly also remains a living presence: 'tha an curaidh
mòr fhathast…a' glanadh shràidean an Dùn Èideann (the great hero is
still…cleaning streets in Edinburgh)'. While not exactly a text of late
Celticism, MacLean's 'Àrd-Mhusaeum na h-Èireann' is based on Scottish-
Irish connections. And while Ireland and Irish culture were not as important to MacLean as they were to MacDiarmid, they were still considerable
influences on his work.

MacLean discussed his interest in Ireland and his view of the history of the
north in an interview with *Innti* in 1986. In this section, MacLean begins by
discussing the similarities between Scottish Gaelic and Irish:

[120] According to Peter Mackay, 'For MacDiarmid and MacLean the question is one of inauthentic
sentimentality (limp vagueness rather than limpid "virility"). But for MacLean it is also one of cultural
survival: the Twilight had infected or castrated Gaelic poetry' (Mackay, 'Optik to Haptik', 276).

[121] Bold, *Terrible Crystal*, 223. MacDiarmid never met Joyce, but he still claimed that the Irish
writer was his friend. In a letter to Sorley MacLean, MacDiarmid discusses an autobiography project
and mentions a supposed friendship with Joyce. See MacDiarmid's letter to MacLean, 3 December
1940, in Wilson, 190. Joyce was living in Paris at the time of MacDiarmid's first visit to Ireland in 1928
and MacDiarmid never visited Joyce's grave in Zürich. So, MacDiarmid's poem involves imagined
meetings with Joyce in his 'death chamber'. On the other hand, Sorley MacLean was able to visit Yeats'
grave in Drumcliffe. Yeats' remains were moved there from France in 1948. Recently there has been
some speculation as to whether they are actually Yeats' bones. See Marlowe.

Basically, they are the same language...I have little trouble reading prose in Irish, but I need translations to read the poetry. Ireland has more of my heart than any other country except Scotland. But the tragedy of events in the North breaks my heart. I am surprised by the viciousness and the violence of the reaction by Protestants to the Anglo-Irish Agreement. And one of the many things that bothers me is that many of the ancestors of the Protestants in Northern Ireland were forced to go there. It's a terrible thing trying to correct a great historical injustice. I find the story of the Six Counties of Ireland very depressing. But I have a great love for Ireland....[122]

As with Seamus Heaney's *Sweeney Astray* (his version of *Buile Suibhne*),[123] 'Àrd-Mhusaeum na h-Èireann' is influenced by events in the north of Ireland and combines modern and pre-modern settings. MacLean's brief but substantial poem is worth quoting in full:

> Anns na làithean dona seo
> is seann leòn Uladh 'na ghaoid
> lionnrachaidh 'n cridhe na h-Eòrpa
> agus an cridhe gach Gàidheil
> dhan aithne gur h-e th' ann an Gàidheal,
> cha d' rinn mise ach gum facas
> ann an Àrd-Mhusaeum na h-Èireann
> spot mheirgeach ruadh na fala
> 's i caran salach air an lèinidh
> a bha aon uair air a' churaidh
> as docha leamsa dhiubh uile
> a sheas ri peilear no ri bèigneid
> no ri tancan no ri eachraidh
> no ri spreaghadh nam bom èitigh:
> an lèine bh' air Ó Conghaile
> anns an Àrd-Phost-Oifis Èirinn
> 's e 'g ullachadh na h-ìobairt
> a chuir suas e fhèin air sèithear
> as naoimhe na 'n Lia Fàil
> th' air Cnoc na Teamhrach an Èirinn.

---

[122] MacLean, qtd in Wilson, 289.   [123] Discussed in Chapter 5.

Tha an curaidh mòr fhathast
'na shuidhe air an t-sèithear,
a' cur a' chatha sa Phost-Oifis
's a' glanadh shràidean an Dùn Èideann.[124]

'Àrd-Mhusaeum na h-Èireann' brings together contrasts of presence and absence, past and present, nationalism and socialism, bardic utterance and private reflection together with Modernist precision. MacLean's poem was written in 1971—at the height of the conflict in the north of Ireland—a year in which MacLean took part in the first Cuairt nam Bàrd ('poets' tour'), travelled around Ireland with Colonel Eoghan Ó Néill, and spoke at Trinity College Dublin.[125] MacLean's visit, combined with the 'evil days' of the Troubles in the North, leads to a contemplation in the poem of earlier Irish history, and the festering laceration MacLean sees in Ulster is connected with Connolly's wounding in the Dublin General Post Office (GPO) in 1916.[126] But how can the 'old wound of Ulster / seann leòn Uladh' be in the 'heart of Europe / cridhe

[124]
In these evil days
when the old wound of Ulster is a disease
suppurating in the heart of Europe
and in the heart of every Gael
who knows he is a Gael,
I have done nothing but see
in the National Museum of Ireland
the rusty red spot of blood,
rather dirty, on the shirt
that was once on the hero
who is dearest to me of them all
who stood against bullet or bayonet,
or tanks or cavalry,
or the bursting of frightful bombs:
the shirt that was on Connolly
in the General Post Office of Ireland
while he was preparing the sacrifice
that put himself up on a chair
that is holier than the Lia Fail
that is on the Hill of Tara in Ireland.

The great hero is still
sitting on the chair,
fighting the battle in the Post Office
and cleaning streets in Edinburgh.

(MacLean, 270–1)

There is a recording of MacLean reading this poem at a ceilidh. See the opening of the 1974 short film *Sorley MacLean's Island*. 'Àrd-Mhusaeum na h-Èireann' is not the only poem in which MacLean venerates James Connolly. In 'An Cuilithionn', as Niall O'Gallagher has noted, 'MacLean's veneration of Connolly is taken further. He becomes, in Christian terms, an icon, at once more and less than human, whose martyrdom allows him to "rise" ("èirigh"), escaping Earthly limits' (O'Gallagher, 445).

[125] See MacLean, xlix.

[126] See also: 'tràighte, faoin-lag, cràidhte, fo chreuchdaibh (weak and dazed, with tormenting wounds)' in the poem 'Séamas Ó Conghaile' (Ibid., 442–3).

na h-Eòrpa'? Despite its north-western position in Europe, Ulster is the 'heart' of the continent for MacLean because the fate of the Gaels is central to MacLean's concerns.[127]

As is well known, Connolly was seriously wounded during the British assault on the GPO, a location where he was commanding military operations during the Rising (MacLean's attention to wartime bodily injury may have a biographical connection—he was badly hurt by a mine at the Second Battle of El Alamein in 1942).[128] However, the bloodstain on Connolly's shirt exhibited in 'Àrd-Mhusaeum na h-Èireann' contrasts with the strange imagery of order and cleanliness at the poem's close: 'tha an curaidh mòr fhathast...a' glanadh shràidean an Dùn Èideann (the great hero is still...cleaning streets in Edinburgh)'.[129] Furthermore, the sacred terms used in the poem such as 'ìobairt' (sacrifice) effectively frame the Rising as a noble, sanctifying ritual. Perhaps this should not be that surprising, since even the Marxist Connolly eventually began to conceive of the Rising in these terms.[130] Connolly's shirt becomes, for MacLean, a quasi-religious icon and an object of veneration.[131]

'Àrd-Mhusaeum na h-Èireann' also demonstrates MacLean's heavy emotional investment in Irish-Scottish Gaeldom as a whole. The attention paid to Irish and Scottish connections here and elsewhere in his work comes from MacLean's sense of being a poetic spokesman of a specific people and community. The lines 'gach Gàidheal...dhan aithne gur h-e th' ann an Gàidheal

---

[127] 'It seems...likely that this refers to the seventeenth-century plantation of Ulster, largely with Scottish settlers, some of whom were Gaelic speakers themselves. The problem with MacLean's attempt to reconstruct a pan-Gaelic identity through Connolly – the Scottish son of Irish immigrants – is that the descendants of Scottish immigrants to Ulster stand in the way. The rejection of a Gaelic identity by Ulster's Protestants is itself dismissed, in Marxist terms, as an instance of false consciousness' (O'Gallagher, 449).

[128] The poem's slightly odd descriptions of 'tancan' and 'eachraidh' ('tanks' and 'cavalry') perhaps also point to MacLean's own experience of war creeping into the text here. However, reserve cavalry were transported to Dublin during the Rising and some improvised armoured trucks were used by the British Army.

[129] Connolly grew up in Edinburgh's Cowgate area, the son of Irish immigrants.

[130] See his comments in the 5 February 1916 issue of Worker's Republic: 'we recognise that of us, as of mankind before Calvary, it may truly be said: "Without the shedding of Blood there is no Redemption"' (Connolly, James, qtd in Foster, Modern Ireland, 479).

[131] As O'Gallagher has pointed out, 'While MacLean's vision is atheistic, his poetry is far from irreligious...Reprising a technique developed in his earlier poetry, MacLean deploys religious imagery for his atheistic political and poetic purposes. His diction is strikingly Biblical throughout. Words like 'gaoid'...and 'ìobairt'...recall the book of Leviticus when the God of the Old Testament instructs Moses on the prohibition on the unclean entering sacred places and the sacrifices necessary in atoning for sins. Connolly's shirt becomes the 'còta anairt naomha' of Leviticus, his chair the 'caithir-thròcair' on which God himself will appear, the Museum an 'ionad naomh' which only the pure may enter. The Province of Ulster is the 'stain...in the heart' which, implicitly, must be cleansed before approaching the sacred place. Repetition in the verse-paragraph gives it a liturgical quality, as does the obsessive, though not quite regular monorhyme on 'è' (O'Gallagher, 443–9). O'Gallagher also points out that "The rhetoric with which MacLean praises James Connolly bears a striking similarity to that deployed by Patrick Pearse in Gaelic poems like 'Fornocht do Chonac Thu' ('Annunciation')" (O'Gallagher, 450).

(every Gael...who knows he is a Gael)' and the shift from the Dublin GPO
to the streets of Edinburgh are part of this. Elsewhere, MacLean, like
MacDiarmid, 'envisages a kind of utopia, where the divisions between Scots
and Irish are negated'.[132] and his work has 'public, bardic strain'.[133] And yet, as
with MacLean's 'Hallaig', the ending of the poem 'suggests that the miracle it
embodies is dependent on the poem's individual consciousness'.[134] 'Àrd-
Mhusaeum na h-Èireann' is an unusual synthesis of a declarative public statement and a personal, lyrical epiphany. All of this is expressed with the
Modernist minimalism MacLean utilized in his *Dàin do Eimhir*.[135]

Of course, Connolly is a heroic figure to MacLean not simply because of
the Edinburgh/Scotland connection but also through the linkages of class-
consciousness and anti-colonial sentiment. The poem also suggests that
MacLean regards Connolly as a fellow Gael (although Pearse was the leading
Irish language advocate of the men of 1916, not Connolly). Mainly, MacLean's
admiration is a result of Connolly's Marxism and the action he took in the
April of 1916. As Raymond Ross notes, 'throughout MacLean's poetry...we
are confronted with images of, and references to, heroic figures whose moral
or political passion is evident through action'.[136] As MacLean himself stated,
'Names like Lenin, Connolly, John Maclean...are more to me than the names
of any poets'.[137]

Alongside the juxtapositions of nationalism and socialism and the personal
and the public, there is a tension in the poem 'Àrd-Mhusaeum na h-Èireann'
between absence and presence. The shade of James Connolly somehow
becomes more material despite his death, the haunting lack at the poem's
centre. Similarly, the Lia Fáil, a symbol of power and sovereignty, is still stand-
ing on the Hill of Tara.[138] Like the presentation of history in *Finnegans Wake*,
ancient and modern collide here and Connolly is supernaturally 'fighting the
battle' at the present moment ('a' cur a' chatha'). For many Irish writers, the

---

[132] Whyte, *Modern Scottish Poetry*, 73.   [133] Ibid., 157.   [134] Ibid., 74.
[135] *Dàin do Eimhir* also has important Irish connections, since one of the models for Eimhir was
the Irish scholar Nessa Ní Shéaghdha. MacLean met Ní Shéaghdha at a Celtic Congress in Edinburgh
in 1937. See Whyte, 'Introduction', 12.
[136] Ross, 97.
[137] MacLean, qtd in Ross, 94. MacLean's radicalism stemmed partly from the history of his island
and of his people: [h]is great-grandfather was the only one of his family who had not been evicted to
Canada or Australia during the Raasay clearance of 1852–4, and two of his paternal uncles had been
friends and fellow-workers of the revolutionary socialist John Maclean, who MacLean once described
as 'the last word in honesty and courage...a terrific man' (Black, Ronald, xxix).
[138] The chair is a recurring symbol in MacLean's work on Connolly: 'ceangailte gu dlùth ri cathair nam
pian dhut' (tightly bound to the chair you would be executed in)' (MacLean, 442–3). The seat in which
Connolly is executed becomes elevated to the position of a throne or ceremonial chair in 'Àrd-Mhusaeum
na h-Èireann' through a connection to the Lia Fáil. However, the actual Lia Fáil is not connected to a chair
and there seems to be a certain elision with the Stone of Scone. See O'Reilly and Ó Broin.

Easter Rising becomes subsumed into larger artistic preoccupations or themes: for Yeats it is linked to the issue of personal responsibility, and to his musings on the transformation of transient things into permanent forms. In Joyce's *Finnegans Wake*, the event is part of the cyclical histories of rising and falling peoples and societies in *Finnegans Wake*. For Sorley MacLean, Connolly is still with us and his bloodied shirt is a vivid relic linking together of some of the Scottish poet's great themes: heroism, violence, Marxism, and the fate of the Gaelic world.

The Gaelic world is a central subject within the poetry of MacLean and MacDiarmid. Within that world, Ireland was a particular source of inspiration for MacDiarmid's nationalist politics and Modernist poetics and for MacLean's contemplation of personal and political wounds. Although MacDiarmid wished to align himself with Irish culture his actual engagement with modern Irish literature is fairly superficial. Despite comparing himself to Joyce and dedicating a book to him, MacDiarmid's work is not Joycean in any substantial way. Aside from MacDiarmid's inability to work in a multi-lingual fashion beyond English and Scots (or 'Synthetic Scots'), Joyce and MacDiarmid have differing approaches to the relationship between text and reality, or between the word and the world. Immediately before 1916, Walter Scott was perhaps *the* major influence on modern Irish literature, at least in the novel form. Not long after Scotland ceased influencing Irish literature through Scott, the tide turns and the energies of Irish politics and culture become a major source of inspiration—if not instruction—for Scottish writers.

5

Heaney, the North, and Scotland

In the previous chapter, we studied the poetry of Hugh MacDiarmid and Sorley MacLean. Both of these poets were held in high regard by Seamus Heaney.[1] MacDiarmid and Heaney met on a number of occasions and Heaney heard MacLean recite his poetry in Dublin in 1971. As shown by his lectures, Heaney also had a keen interest in the works of the Scottish poets Robert Henryson, Robert Burns, Norman MacCaig, and Edwin Muir.[2] Heaney also travelled to places associated with Scottish texts and writers such as Alloway Kirk (one of the main settings of Burns' 'Tam O'Shanter'), Ettrick (the home of James Hogg), and Ecclefechan (Thomas Carlyle's birthplace).[3] Rather than discussing Heaney's appreciation for, or interpretations of, the work of these poets, this chapter will focus on the eco-Celticism and Irish-Scottish connections of *Sweeney Astray* (1983), his version of *Buile Suibhne*. So, after examining texts based on, or that engage with, the figures of Oisín, Deirdre, and Fionn Mac Cumhaill, we will end here with the figure of Sweeney.

As R.F. Foster has noted, 'Sweeney's function for Heaney is that of Aedh . . . for Yeats: a persona who articulates an inner voice which clarifies poetic thought'.[4] Heaney's use of the 'legendary' Sweeney roughly aligns with the much-discussed Modernist interest in myth or pre-modern literature (although there is no single, uniform Modernist application of these sources). Some Modernist texts include parallels between their characters and figures from ancient history, mythology, or older literature (for example, Odysseus and Bloom in *Ulysses* or the connections between Maud Gonne and figures such as Helen of Troy in Yeats' poetry), while others are set—for the most part—in a modern world that somehow repeats (often with high distortion) or resembles the mythic world (as in *Ulysses*) or is seen to be in need of the structures, certainties, or supposed purities of the mythic or pre-modern world (as in Eliot's *The Waste Land*). *Sweeney Astray* is set in the eighth century, not the modern world (a more Modernist approach can be found in the

---

[1] Although Heaney was well aware of the unevenness of MacDiarmid's work. See *FK*, 293.
[2] For a discussion on Heaney and Scottish poetry, see Patrick Crotty, 'Scotland'.
[3] See O'Hagan.   [4] Foster, *On Seamus Heaney*, 114.

Modern Irish and Scottish Literature: Connections, Contrasts, Celticisms. Richard Alan Barlow, Oxford University Press.
© Richard Alan Barlow 2023. DOI: 10.1093/oso/9780192859181.003.0006

'Sweeney Redivivus' poems, since Sweeney seems to be reborn into modernity in those pieces). However, the time-setting of *Sweeney Astray* is complicated by the use of modern English, quotations from Shakespeare and Heaney himself, and anachronistic terms such as 'mesmerized'.[5] The use of modern proverbial language like 'I wish we could fly away together, / be rolling stones, birds of a feather'[6] also ensures there is no sense for the reader that we are experiencing a fully ancient world through the text. Discussing Geoffrey Hill's *Mercian Hymns* in the piece 'Englands of the Mind', Heaney suggests that Hill 'does what Joyce did in *Ulysses*, confounding modern autobiographical material with literary and historical matter drawn from the past. Offa's story makes contemporary landscape and experience live in the rich shadows of a tradition.'[7] As Conor McCarthy has suggested, 'that last sentence might just as easily read "Sweeney" for "Offa" '.[8]

In his chapter on *Sweeney Astray*, McCarthy quotes Richard Kearney, who has written of 'the stereotype of Heaney as some latter-day Piers Ploughman from county Derry staving off the plague of modernity and guiding us back to a prelapsarian pastureland'[9] and, as an illustration of that kind of stereotype, he also quotes Antony Easthope's suggestion that 'again and again [Heaney's] political gestures, calling up ancient wrong, unconscious tradition and the living past, have invoked that old fantasy about premodernity, the organic community'.[10] However, *Sweeney Astray* is not using the 'mythic method' in the Eliotian sense of the term since the world of Sweeney is not some idealized pre-modern paradise—despite the descriptions of the beauties of nature—or some pre-Christian Celtic realm of peace and enchantment. Sweeney's world is a place of violence, suffering, confusion, displacement, loneliness, and madness. For McCarthy, 'Heaney's work, while expressing a desire for home, holds that desire in tension with a recognition that "at-homeness" is already pre-problematized' partly as a result of Heaney's 'second-class status as a Catholic in Ulster'.[11] In addition to this, there is no idealization of the pre-modern world—it is shown to be as chaotic as ours.

Sweeney Astray shares with Joyce's texts *Ulysses* and *Finnegans Wake* a sense that violence and disruption are eternal. Unlike Eliot, Heaney is not looking to the past or to religion or to literature for some experience of transcendence. Nor is Heaney attempting to set any lands in order in *Sweeney Astray*. However, Heaney's work frequently considers possible resemblances between the past and the present. In 'Earning a Rhyme' Heaney asks what connection

---

[5] See McCarthy, 19.   [6] *SA*, 28.   [7] *FK*, 87.   [8] McCarthy, 42.
[9] Kearney, 113.   [10] Easthope, 30.   [11] McCarthy, 35 and 34.

a 'Celtic wild man' has to 'the devastations of the new wild men of the Provisional IRA'[12] Of course, placing instances of violence in the modern world—such as acts carried out during the Troubles—into some larger pattern or structure, can leave writers open to accusations of a 'defeatist and even aestheticizing approach to the history of violence'.[13] Probably the most famous example of this danger arising in Heaney's career can be seen in the reaction to certain poems in his volume *North* (1975) in which, for example, a connection is drawn between the ancient and preserved body of a murdered young woman recovered from a bog in Scandinavia, and women tarred and feathered in the north of Ireland during the Troubles for associating with British soldiers. According to Ciaran Carson, when discussing the poem 'Punishment' in his review of *North* for *The Honest Ulsterman*, 'it is as if [Heaney] is saying, suffering like this is natural; these things have always happened; they happened then, they happened now, and that is sufficient ground for understanding and absolution. It is as if there never were and never will be any political consequences of such acts'.[14]

Heaney's *Sweeney Astray: A Version from the Irish*, his adaptation of the medieval *Buile Suibhne* story, is based on a 1913 translation by J.G. O'Keeffe.[15] The story is mainly concerned with the frenzied flights of king Sweeney after he has been cursed and driven insane by the cleric Ronan Finn. Heaney discusses the literary figure of Sweeney in his introduction to the text:

> What we have...is a literary creation; unlike Finn McCool or Cuchulain, Sweeney is not a given figure of myth or legend but an historically situated character, although the question of whether he is based upon an historical king called Sweeney has to remain an open one. But the literary imagination which fastened upon him as an image was clearly in the grip of a tension

[12] Heaney, 'Earning a Rhyme', 65. As Stephen Regan has noted, pivotal events of the Troubles have their echoes in Heaney's text. See Regan, 333–4. On the subject of Celticism and the Provisional IRA, it worth mentioning that the IRA chose not to bomb locations in Scotland during the Troubles, partly due to a sense of Celtic solidarity. See Carlin, 162 and Pittock, 111.

[13] Foster, *On Seamus Heaney*, 56.   [14] Carson, 'Escaped', 184.

[15] In his introduction to the text, Heaney writes, 'This version of *Buile Suibhne* is based on J. G. O'Keeffe's bilingual edition, which was published by the Irish texts society in 1913' (*SA*, i). O'Keeffe's 1913 version is based on three manuscripts, known as 'B', 'K', and 'L'. 'B' is 'one of the most valuable MSS. of the famous Stowe collection in the Royal Irish Academy. It is a paper folio, and was written between the years 1671 and 1674 at Sean Cua, Co. Sligo, by Daniel O'Duigenan' (O'Keeffe, xiii). 'K' is 'a quarto paper MS., also in the Royal Irish Academy...It was written in 1721–2 by Tomaltach Mac Muirghiosa for Seamas Tiriall' (O'Keeffe, xiv). 'L' is an 'MS...written by Michael O'Clery, one of the Four Masters, in 1629' (O'Keeffe, xiv). This manuscript is held at the Bibliothèque Royale de Belgique in Brussels.

between the newly dominant Christian ethos and the older, recalcitrant Celtic temperament.[16]

For the present study, the phrase 'Celtic recalcitrance', and, in particular, Heaney's use of the word 'Celtic', are worth dwelling on. Heaney's introduction suggests an association between a form of ancient Celtic recalcitrance and the 'free creative imagination' on the one hand, as opposed to societal constrictions on the other, in a neo-Yeatsian, 'Wanderings of Oisin' style conflict between an ancient freedom and the 'new' restraints of Christianity. Examples of this 'Celtic recalcitrance' are found at the beginning of Heaney's text where Sweeney indulges in a fit of anarchic nudity: 'She got the cloak all right but Sweeney had bolted, stark naked'[17] and when Sweeney launches Ronan Finn's 'beautiful illuminated' psalter into a lough and seizes its owner: 'Sweeney grabbed the book and flung it into the cold depths of a lake nearby, where it sank without trace. Then he took hold of Ronan and was dragging him out through the church when he heard a cry of alarm'.[18] Following these events, Ronan curses Sweeney, sentencing him to 'roam through Erin as a stark madman'.[19]

David Lloyd has claimed that Heaney's work forms a new addition to the development of Celticism, calling it 'a touchstone of contemporary taste within a discourse whose most canonical proponent [Matthew Arnold] argued for the study of Celtic literature as a means of the integration of Ireland with Anglo-Saxon industrial civilization'.[20] The single phrase 'Celtic temperament'[21] in Heaney's introduction is, on its own, scant evidence to claim that *Sweeney Astray* should be regarded as a late Celticist text. Furthermore, *Sweeney Astray* has important Anglo-Saxon and Early Modern English connections (links with the Old English poem *The Seafarer* and *King Lear*, as well

---

[16] *SA*, i-ii.   [17] *SA*, 3–4.

[18] Ibid., 4. Strangely, Heaney sticks to O'Keeffe's 'lake' here, rather than use 'lough' (O'Keeffe uses 'lough' elsewhere in his text). The use of 'lake' instead of 'lough' removes from the text something similar to what Heaney, in 'Broagh' from *Wintering Out*, calls 'that last / *gh* the strangers found / hard to manage' (Heaney, *Wintering Out*, 17). Indeed, Heaney himself pointed out that he was working, initially at least, with the English language, not with the Irish: 'my encounter first time round was more with the English language text on the right-hand page of O'Keeffe's edition than with the original on the left' (Heaney qtd in O'Driscoll, 153). Furthermore, Heaney was 'determined that his translation would avoid the kind of Hiberno-English associated with Douglas Hyde and the Irish Revival' (Regan, 324). As Heaney states in one interview, 'I didn't want it coloured with the picturesqueness of Irish idiom' (qtd in Druce, 36).

[19] O'Keeffe, 7.

[20] Lloyd, *Anomalous States*, 37. In 1989, Heaney took up the position of Oxford Professor of Poetry, a post once held by Matthew Arnold.

[21] *SA*, ii.

as the poetry of Ted Hughes and Geoffrey Hill).[22] However, in two later prose
pieces, 'The God in the Tree', originally a talk for RTÉ in 1978 reproduced in
Preoccupations: Selected Prose 1968–1978 (1980), and 'Earning a Rhyme', published in Rosanna Warren's edited collection *The Art of Translation: Voices
From the Field* (1989), Heaney places his version of the *Buile Suibhne* story
firmly into a wider Celtic context.

In 'The God in the Tree', in addition to discussing the Celtic languages,
Heaney mentions 'Celtic sensibility', 'the Celtic otherworld', 'the Celtic imagination', and 'the Celtic world'.[23] All of these are phrases we might expect to
appear in a text of the 1890s, rather than the 1980s. In his talk, Heaney also
refers to Ian Finlay's 1973 text *Introduction to Celtic Art* and P.H. Henry's 1966
volume *The Early English and Celtic Lyric*.[24] In the 'Earning a Rhyme' piece,
Heaney approvingly quotes the suggestion of Kenneth Hurlstone Jackson, the
English linguist and Celtic languages specialist, that 'in its earlier period
Celtic literature did not belong at all to the common culture of the rest of
Europe; nor did it ever become more than partly influenced by it'.[25] *Sweeney
Astray* is a late Celticist text partly because it has these connections while
appearing well after the heyday of early Celticism. The book also differs
starkly to the earlier strain of Celticism. For example, there is no sense that
the world of Sweeney is in any way doomed. Indeed, Heaney wrote of the
potential for the text to instill an encouraging sense of continuity and survival
in northern nationalists:

> I simply wanted to offer an indigenous text that would not threaten a
> Unionist (after all, this was just a translation of an old tale, situated for much
> of the time in what is now county Antrim and county Down) and that
> would fortify a Nationalist (after all, this old tale tells us we belonged here
> always and that we still remain unextirpated)...My hope was that that book
> might render a Unionist audience more pervious to the notion that Ulster
> was Irish, without coercing them out of their cherished conviction that it
> was British. Also, because it reached back into a pre-colonial Ulster of
> monastic Christianity and Celtic kingship, I hoped the book might compli
> cate the sense of entitlement to the land of Ulster which had developed so

[22] For an extensive discussion of these connections in relation to *Sweeney Astray*, see McCarthy.
On *Sweeney Astray* and 'British connections', McCarthy notes that 'if Heaney's translation of *Buile
Suibhne* is a reminder of the existence of a pre-British Ulster, it is nonetheless a translation that
includes points of comparison and influence from England, Scotland, and Wales' (McCarthy, 37).
[23] Heaney, 'The God in the Tree', 184, 186, 187, 188.   [24] Ibid., 186, 183.
[25] Heaney, quoting Jackson, Kenneth Hurlstone, 'The God in the Tree', 183.

overbearingly in the Protestant majority, as a result of various victories and acts of settlement over the centuries.[26]

Furthermore, there is no recycling of the feminine Celt idea in Heaney's text. As Denell Downum has discussed, Sweeney is 'distinctly masculine'.[27]

Heaney's construction of a Celtic context for his version of *Buile Suibhne* is partly due to his interest in ancient, pre-Christian Ireland and one of the primary meanings of the word 'Celtic' for Heaney seems to be 'the pre-Christian society and culture of Ireland'. However, the text—thanks to the flights of the figure Sweeney himself—takes place across a variety of locations within what Heaney (and Joyce) called 'the Celtic world',[28] both inside and outside Ireland. We are not told why Sweeney goes to these particular places and there is no obvious plan or logic to Sweeney's movements. Indeed, the restless, flitting nature of Sweeney's travels adds to the sense of frenzy in the text and Sweeney's journeys in the original sources are part of his madness (or 'geilt').[29] Sweeney's movements create a problem for approaching the text, as John Kerrigan has, as a specifically Irish 'national epic'.[30]

Heaney's interpretation of *Buile Suibhne* is a mixture of the personal and the political, and summons the ancient past as a model or ideal for modern Ireland. In his introduction to the text, Heaney writes:

> insofar as Sweeney is...a figure of the artist, displaced, guilty, assuaging himself by his utterance, it is possible to read the work as an aspect of the quarrel between free creative imagination and the constraints of religious, political, and domestic obligation. It is equally possible, in a more opportunistic spirit, to dwell upon Sweeney's easy sense of cultural affinity with both western Scotland and southern Ireland as exemplary for all men and women in contemporary Ulster....[31]

Heaney's introduction specifically refers to a zone of 'cultural affinity' that ought to appeal to everyone in contemporary Ulster—as though the tale

---

[26] Heaney, 'Earning a Rhyme', 16. There are examples of figures from indigenous culture being used by the 'Planter' and the 'Gael' during the Troubles. For example, Republican and Loyalist murals both made use of the figure of Cú Chulainn. However, Cú Chulainn is not used for 'inclusive' purposes in these designs. For photographs of these murals, see p. 58 of *Drawing Support: Murals in the North of Ireland*, pages 17 and 28 of *Drawing Support 2: Murals of War and Peace*, and pages 25 and 45 of *Drawing Support 3: Murals and Transition in the North of Ireland*, all by Bill Rolston.

[27] Downum, 77.   [28] Heaney, 'The God in the Tree', 188 and *OCPW*, 124.

[29] See Ó Riain, 193. Geilt also appears in Fenian sources. See Frykenberg, 51.

[30] Kerrigan, 243.   [31] *SA*, ii.

could offer an example of a time in which the inhabitants of the whole of Ireland and of western Scotland felt part of one society or culture.[32] Heaney seems to be suggesting, perhaps somewhat optimistically, that the text might encourage nationalists in the North to feel more of a connection with Protestant Scotland and that unionists in the North might start feeling a greater sense of kinship with Catholics in the south of Ireland. Heaney's thoughts on the matter are further revealed by an RTÉ interview from November 1983:

> Well, I was thinking primarily in that, I suppose, about the Planter as opposed to the Gael community in Ulster. And when I started on this eleven years ago and it was '72, a moment of tremendous excitement, there was still possibility in the air, even though there was violence in the air...Now, it seemed to me that, with this text set in County Antrim, north Country Down – I mean Sweeney is from Rasharkin – that the Irish tradition could be made inclusive as it were. I mean a lot of the impulse I suppose in late nineteenth century – the Gaelic League and the Irish Texts Society and so on – a lot of the impulse there was, in the best sense, exclusive, it said: 'We too have a tradition. We own this literature. We are a culture on our own and, thanks, we don't need altogether to ride the rails of the English trad- ition.' Now I would have thought of it slightly differently with this particular venture, as inclusive, saying to people who belong to the planter tradition, 'Look, you're on this ground – Moira, Dunseverick, Rasharkin'...everybody could feel at home.[33]

In his introduction to *Sweeney Astray*, Heaney writes 'My fundamental rela- tion with Sweeney...is topographical. His kingdom lay in what is now south County Antrim and north County Down, and for over thirty years I lived on the verges of that territory, in sight of some of Sweeney's places and in earshot

---

[32] Indeed, it has been suggested that the Sweeney story originated in Dál Riata, before traveling to Strathclyde then to Ireland. See Jackson, Kenneth, 549–50. However, this claim has been disputed. See Ní Dhonnchadha, 'The Cult of St Moling and the Making of *Buile Shuibne*'. See also: 'Suibhne...is called the son of Colmán Cúar, son of Cobhthach, king of Dál nAraidhe, but also occasionally identi- fied as one of the four sons of Eochaidh Buidhe, the king of Alba' (Bergholm, 101).

[33] Heaney, 'Folio' RTÉ interview with Patrick Gallagher. Heaney also discusses this period in *Stepping Stones*: 'unless I am greatly mistaken, there was even a sense in that pre-Bloody Sunday, pre- Bloody Friday period that the violence might be creative and a new order might emerge' (Heaney, qtd in O'Driscoll, 151).

of others.'[34] This attention to place is noticeable in Heaney's work but can also be found the early Irish texts themselves. According to O'Keeffe,

> Perhaps the outstanding feature of the composition is the extraordinary love of place which it reveals. I venture to say that this is one of the most distinctive features of early Irish literature…I believe it sprang from a very intimate knowledge of the actual place or of the spirit of the place; and I suggest that it will be found on investigation that the descriptions of places given in early Irish literature are in the main accurate.[35]

As a result of Sweeney's travels, the topography of *Sweeney Astray* extends beyond Ireland and into Scotland. Unlike O'Keeffe, Heaney generally opts for modern Irish and Scottish placenames such as Ailsa Craig, Kintyre, and Mourne in his poetic topos—rather than 'Carraig Alastair', 'Cenn Tire', and 'Boirche'. This creates a sense of grounded familiarity and immediacy for the reader rather than attempting to place Sweeney's misadventures in some dim, vague, or remote Ossianic location. However, in his 1978 radio programme 'Omphalos' (later published as part of a piece titled 'Mossbawn'), while discussing the places around Mossbawn, County Derry, Heaney suggests that the uttering of placenames has a transformative and distancing effect:

> In the names of its fields and townlands, in the mixture of Scots and Irish and English etymologies, this side of the country was redolent of the histories of its owners. Broagh, The Long Rigs, Bell's Hill; Brian's Field, the Round Meadow, the Demesne; each name was a kind of love made to each acre. And saying the names like this distances the places, turns them into what Wordsworth once called a prospect of the mind. They lie deep, like some script indelibly written into the nervous system.[36]

Elsewhere, Heaney writes that

> Irrespective of our creed or politics, irrespective of what culture or subculture may have coloured our individual sensibilities, our imaginations assent

---

[34] *SA*, iii–iv. Antrim is also the 'enchanted land' from 'whence Deirdrê and Naois fled from Concobar, and…sailed for Scotland'. Sharp, William qtd in Sharp, Elizabeth, 311. For a discussion of William Sharp's adaptations of the Deirdre story, see Chapter 2.

[35] O'Keeffe, xxxvii. As Oona Frawley has noted, 'Ireland's earliest literature demonstrates a marked preoccupation with place and the natural world, attested to by whole tracts dedicated to *dindshenchas* (a part of the larger *schenchas* of the Irish bard), or the lore of place' (Frawley, 2).

[36] *FK*, 6.

to the stimulus of the names, our sense of the place is enhanced, our sense of ourselves as inhabitants not just of a geographical country but of a country of the mind is cemented.[37]

Ireland and Scotland, as well as locations within Ireland and Scotland, are mentioned on a number of occasions in the text but not the words 'England' and 'Wales'.[38] Critics have rightly noted the 'vertical geometry' of Heaney's poetry, especially in downward-tending works such as 'Digging' and 'Personal Helicon' with its 'dark drop' of deep and shallow wells.[39] *Sweeney Astray* certainly has its vertical moments, especially in the flights of its central character (this is also evident in Heaney's return to the Sweeney persona in the 'Sweeney Redivivus' section of *Station Island*). However, *Sweeney Astray* is also marked by horizontal, western-eastern, Irish-Scottish coordinates. Of course, Heaney's version of *Buile Suibhne* is also about translation in the original sense: the act of moving across.

A western-eastern axis is common in Heaney's work, except that the western area involved is generally the west of Ireland rather than the counties of Antrim and Down. In the poem 'Postscript' from *The Spirit Level*, Heaney advises the reader to 'make the time to drive out west / Into County Clare, along the Flaggy Shore'.[40] The journey to the west of Ireland—or a longing to visit the west, or certain parts of the west[41]—is a common trope in modern Irish writing. W.B. Yeats's work was inspired by visits to the west, especially Coole Park in Galway and what is now 'Yeats Country' in Sligo. J.M. Synge is similarly synonymous with the Aran Islands and has his limestone Cathaoir Synge on the edge of Inis Meáin. Even Gabriel Conroy, supposedly 'sick' of his country, eventually has visions of the west at the end of Joyce's 'The Dead'.[42] For Tom Herron, the west of Ireland is the 'Irish poetic space par excellence'.[43] The Highlands and Islands have a similar power and allure in Scottish texts such as Scott's *Waverley*. As Ray Ryan has discussed, 'the creation of a mystique of Irishness and Scottishness' originates in 'depopulated zones'.[44]

---

[37] Heaney, 'The Sense of Place', 132.
[38] When Sweeney leaves Ailsa Craig he travels to 'the land of the Britons' (*SA*, 55). This is the same wording as in J.G. O'Keeffe's translation, the text Heaney based his version on. The phrase is 'Crioch Bhretan' in the Irish of O'Keefe's text.
[39] Heaney, 'Personal Helicon', *Death of a Naturalist*, 57.
[40] Heaney, 'Postscript', *The Spirit Level*, 70.
[41] As Tom Herron points out, the desire is seldom—perhaps unfairly—to visit western cities like Limerick or to stop by western towns like Ennis (see Herron, 75).
[42] *D*, 189.   [43] Herron, 76.   [44] Ryan, 10.

In the Revival period, the west of Ireland was seen as the site of an uncorrupted, primitive Celtic or Gaelic essence, one that survived in the language and folkways of the rural 'peasantry' hence, for example, the fieldwork undertaken by Synge in Inis Mór and Inis Meáin. In recent texts, poets such as Eavan Boland, Michael Longley, Louis MacNiece, Derek Mahon, Paul Muldoon, Tom Paulin, Justin Quinn, and Vincent Woods have all demonstrated a 'western vectorialism' in their work.[45] The coasts and islands of the west of Ireland, the places of 'Water and ground in their extremity',[46] have an obvious poetic magnetism. However, there were also important 'push' factors at work in the late twentieth century for poets from the north of Ireland.[47] As Herron has noted, 'it was...the period known as the "Troubles" that encouraged a new generation of poets to look to the West as a respite from the chaos on the streets around them'.[48] While there are many instances of the pull of the West in Heaney's work, Sweeney Astray—a translation composed during the Troubles—is striking in that it looks in the opposite direction, and his tale of 'Celtic recalcitrance' encompasses the west of Scotland rather than the west of Ireland. This Irish-Scottish setting exists in the source material but this aspect of the text is clearly one of the reasons Heaney chose to work with it.

This kind of 'eastern vectorialism' (or perhaps north-eastern vectorialism), to adapt Herron's phrase, can be found elsewhere in Heaney's work. For example, a surprising reference to Aberdeen appears in 'Granite chip', within the series 'Shelf Life', in relation to a meditation on Joyce. 'Granite chip' is a single line ('Houndstooth stone. Aberdeen of the mind') followed by three terse quatrains. The poem considers a piece of granite (hence the reference to Aberdeen—the 'granite city') 'hammered off Joyce's Martello / Tower', with 'Martello' and 'Tower' on separate lines as though the words 'Martello Tower' had also been hammered and chipped apart. The speaker (Heaney himself, for all intents and purposes) squeezes the igneous keepsake and it communicates something to him: 'it says' and 'it adds'. This possession, handling, and 'listening' to the chipped granite undermines somewhat the declaration that the speaker feels 'little in common with' it.

Despite this supposed lack of affinity, the speaker presses his hand almost masochistically around the piece of stone, suffering in the process: 'I have

---

[45] See Herron, 78.   [46] Heaney, 'The Peninsula', Door into the Dark, 9.

[47] See also: 'even a disenchanted critic, tired of exposing the mystifications of social and economic reality in that old Celtic Twilight of cottage and curragh, cannot fail to respond to vistas of stone-walled plains running to the horizon and shifting cloudscapes underlit from the Atlantic. For in spite of the west of Ireland's status as a country of myth, the actual place can still awaken an appetite for experience that is pristine and unconstrained' (Heaney, 'Introduction', 11).

[48] Herron, 79.

hurt my hand'. The stone is 'exacting' and jaggy' but also 'insoluble' and, due to its crystalline nature, 'brilliant'. The poem registers a confused mixture of interest and distrust towards the granite—and therefore towards Joyce's tough, towering artistic example ('Joyce's... Tower') and towards the harsh austerity of Scottish Protestantism ('Calvin edge').[49] Heaney's 'complaisant' nature here, in contrast to the granite-like toughness of Joyce, foreshadows the meeting in section XII of 'Station Island'. Unlike *In Memoriam James Joyce*, where Hugh MacDiarmid addresses, at length, the mute spirit of Joyce, Joyce speaks in 'Station Island', upbraiding Heaney: 'don't be so earnest / so ready for the sackcloth and ashes' and issuing a command: 'strike your note'.[50]

In his discussion of his identification with the poetic voice of Robert Burns, Heaney writes of a space 'north of a line drawn between Berwick and Bundoran' and this Irish-Scottish zone, with its eastern vectorialism, is essentially the setting of *Sweeney Astray*.[51] As mentioned above, Heaney composed his version of *Buile Suibhne* during the Troubles. He began work on his translation in 1972, the year of the Bloody Sunday massacre in Derry and the Bloody Friday bombings in Belfast. 1972 was also the year in which Heaney resigned his lectureship at Queen's University Belfast and moved to Glanmore Cottage in Wicklow. Heaney began revisions to the work in 1979—after years of it being 'in the drawer'—while living in New York.[52] The work was finally published in 1983. As Heaney seems to suggest in his introduction, seeing a

[49] The association of Joyce, an Irish Catholic unbeliever, with Scottish Protestantism—and Aberdeen—is a strange one, but not unprecedented. Ezra Pound once described Joyce as a 'dour Aberdeen minister' (*JJ*, 510). Aberdeen is also associated with Protestantism in Beckett's story 'Yellow' from *More Pricks than Kicks*: 'While he was still wasting his valuable time cursing himself for a fool the door burst open and the day-nurse came in with a mighty rushing sound of starched apron. She was to have charge of him by day. She just missed being beautiful, this Presbyterian from Aberdeen. Aberdeen!' (Beckett, *More Pricks than Kicks*, 178). When the riot over Synge's *The Playboy of the Western World* broke out at the Abbey Theatre in 1907, Yeats was in Aberdeen.
[50] Meditations on stone and stones feature prominently in twentieth century Scottish poetry. See MacDiarmid's 'Stony Limits' and 'On a Raised Beach'.
[51] Heaney, 'Burns's Art Speech (1)', 218. 'Burns's Art Speech' first appeared in Robert Crawford's edited volume *Robert Burns and Cultural Authority*. A revised version of the essay appears in Heaney's prose collection *Finders Keepers*. As there are differences between the texts—for example, the phrase 'the sullied political compost of Northern Ireland' becomes the slightly more neutral 'the political compost heap of Northern Ireland' in the later version—I have referred to the texts as 'Burns's Art Speech (1)' and 'Burns's Art Speech (2)', respectively. There is also an older, wider northern world in Heaney's work: 'For a while I found my needs satisfying themselves in images drawn from Anglo-Saxon kennings, Icelandic sagas, Viking excavations and Danish and Irish bogs, and the result is the bulk of the poems in the first section of *North*' (Heaney, qtd in Foster, *On Seamus Heaney*, 53). That northern world includes Scotland, or what is now Scotland: 'I faced the unmagical / invitations of Iceland, / the pathetic colonies / of Greenland, and suddenly / those fabulous raiders, / those lying in Orkney and Dublin / measured against / their long swords rusting' ('North' in Heaney, *North*, 19).
[52] Heaney, qtd in O'Driscoll, 153. See also O'Driscoll, xxv, xxvii. It should be mentioned that Heaney visited Scotland on a number of occasions during this period: St Andrews in 1973, Biggar in 1977 (to visit his friend Hugh MacDiarmid), and Orkney in 1982.

'cultural affinity' between Ireland and Scotland in the Sweeney story might be something of a 'reach', brought about by an 'opportunistic spirit' (although these connections also exist in O'Keeffe's translation). In any case, Heaney stresses the important Irish-Scottish connections of the story (as well as those between the north and south of Ireland) and highlights a zone of 'cultural affinity' as a response to events in the North. Of course, the Troubles were largely a conflict between what Heaney called elsewhere 'Planter and Gael', with many of the 'Planters' of the seventeenth century being non-Gaelic speakers from Lowland Scotland.[53] In *Sweeney Astray* we seem to return—to an extent—to an era before that epochal event, to a time of all-Gaelic affinity that is held up by Heaney as an exemplar. The ancient connections of Irish-Scottish history are made evident in the introduction to O'Keeffe's translation:

> The Irish state of Dal Riada comprised roughly the northern half of Antrim. At an early period in its history – possibly in the fourth century – some of its people passed over to the neighbouring shores of Scotland and established there in the course of the next two or three centuries the Scottish kingdom of Dal Riada, an event of great importance in the history of Scotland. Both the Irish and Scottish Dal Riada were under one ruler, who appears to have been subject to the High King of Ireland, at least as far as the Irish Dal Riada were concerned.[54]

If the 'pristine world' mentioned in 'The God in the Tree' is primarily meant in an ecological sense, it may also carry the meaning of a pre-Plantation Ireland, before the 'political compost of Northern Ireland' became 'sullied'.[55]

In *Sweeney Astray*, Sweeney can just as easily range within Ireland, from, say, 'the high peaks of Slieve Bloom, and from there to Inishmurray'[56] as he can fly from Ireland to Scotland and back: 'I went raving with grief / on the top of Slieve Patrick, / from Glen Bolcain to Islay, / from Kintyre to Mourne.'[57] Much of Heaney's translation—and the original Irish manuscripts that form the basis of O'Keeffe's version of *Buile Suibhne*—takes place north of that line

---

[53] Heaney, 'Burns's Art Speech (1)', 224.

[54] O'Keeffe, xx-xxi. This is very similar material to that used by Joyce in the composition to *Finnegans Wake*. Joyce took notes on the Picts and Scots from Stephen Gwynn's 1923 *The History of Ireland*, which includes material on Dal Riada. See Gwynn, 19. Joyce's notes from this text can be found in *Finnegans Wake* notebook VI.B.6.18. Joyce also took notes from J. M. Flood's *Ireland: Its Saints and Scholars* (1917) and Benedict Fitzpatrick's *Ireland and the Making of Great Britain* (1922) during his research on the strong Irish influence on ancient Scotland. Joyce, in the first part of the twentieth century and Heaney, in the second half, both stress the ancient links and affinities between Ireland and Scotland as a counterpoint to modern tensions and divisions.

[55] Heaney, 'Burns's Art Speech (1)', 221.   [56] *SA*, 50.   [57] Ibid., 18.

'between Berwick and Bundoran'.[58] A space immediately north of Heaney's imaginary line, beginning at a coastal town in the northwest of Ireland and ending at another coastal town right on the Scottish/English border (Berwick is now in England but passed between Scottish and English ownership on numerous occasions in the Middle Ages) would encompass some of the north of Ireland (including Derry) and most of Scotland. Allowing Heaney some latitude—and treating his phrase without any undue pedantry—the line demarcates an area that contains and joins together Ulster and Scotland.

In the Heaney text containing the 'Berwick and Bundoran' phrase— 'Burns's Art Speech'—this space is linked by a common language or dialect. Heaney writes of trips to the 'fair hill in Ballymena' where the farmers spoke 'a tongue that was as close to Ayrshire as to County Derry'.[59] Of course, the language and 'accent' in the north of Ireland that is close to the language of Burns' work, and therefore makes Heaney 'feel close' to the Ayrshire poet, is the 'trace elements of...Lowland Scots',[60] the linguistic legacy of the modern 'Planter', not the sister Celtic languages of Irish and Scottish Gaelic or anything to do with the ancient 'Celtic world'. So, there are two main strands linking Ireland and Scotland in Heaney's work as a whole (the poetry and the critical work): a linguistic strain concerned with modern plantation and modern poetry and the earlier, Celtic-related substrata of Sweeney and his frenzy.

The foregrounding of the proximity of Scotland to Ireland, or the sense that the west of Scotland is part of the same cultural area as Ireland, exists in Heaney's source text (O'Keeffe's translation): 'As trúagh mo nuallán choidhche / i mullach Cruachán Oighle, / do Ghlinn Bolcain for Íle, / do C[h]inn Tíre for Boirche' ('Sad forever is my cry / on the summit of Cruachan Aighle, / from Glen Bolcain to Islay, / from Cenn Tire to Boirche').[61] There is no differentiation between the places in the list above. Furthermore, there is hardly any sense in Heaney's text that travelling from Ireland to Scotland involves moving between fundamentally different spaces, even if they have different local rulers: 'I am upset that Congal's people are reduced to this, for he and I had strong ties before we faced the battle. But then, Sweeney was warned by Colmcille when he went over with Congal to ask the king of Scotland for an army to field against me'.[62] Scotland is so familiar to the Irish characters that it is used as a point of comparison: 'If my choice were given me / of the men of Erin and Alba, / I had liefer bide sinless with thee / on water and on

---

[58] Heaney, 'Burns's Art Speech (1)', 218. [59] Heaney, 'Burns's Art Speech (1)', 219.
[60] Heaney, 'Burns's Art Speech (2)', 348, 347, 348. [61] O'Keeffe, 30–1. [62] SA, 11.

watercress'.[63] The original text here reads 'Dá ttuchta mo rogha dhamh / d' feruibh Eirenn is Alban,/ferr lem it chom*air* gan chol/ar uisge *agus* ar bhiorar'.[64] In other words, Scotland is almost a part of Ireland in the text.

Sweeney's Irish-Scottish travels might seem slightly less impressive in the days of the Belfast to Cairnryan car ferry but they are still quite long trips.[65] One prominent Scottish location in Heaney's text is the small, distinctively shaped island of Ailsa Craig (a volcanic plug off the coast of Ayrshire), which is mentioned in both the prose and verse sections of the text. Ailsa Craig is first mentioned in a description of one of Sweeney's extensive journeys:

> He stayed in Roscommon that night and the next day he went on to Slieve Aught, from there to the pleasant slopes of Slemish, then on to the high peaks of Slieve Bloom, and from there to Inishmurray. After that, he stayed six weeks in a cave that belonged to Donnan on the island of Eig off the west of Scotland. From there he went on to Ailsa Craig, where he spent another six weeks, and when he finally left there he bade the place farewell and bewailed his state...[66]

Shortly after this, the tough conditions of Ailsa Craig are detailed in a section of free verse quatrains:

> I'll be overtaken
> by a stubborn band
> of Ulstermen
> faring through Scotland.
>
> But to have ended up
> lamenting here
> on Ailsa Craig.
> A hard station!

---

[63] O'Keeffe, 47. 'Liefer', meaning '*rather, prefer to*' is a Scots verb. See Crotty, 'Scotland', 16.

[64] O'Keeffe, 46.

[65] Mark Williams has mentioned the 'ferocious weirdness' of early Irish saga (Williams, Mark, 85) and perhaps the same could be said of *Buile Suibhne*, especially in moments such as the section where Sweeney laps milk out of a cup formed in cow-dung or where a 'hag...leaped quickly after [Sweeney] but fell off the cliff of Dunseverick, where she was smashed to pieces and scattered into the sea' (*SA*, 46). Of course, the oddest—or most puzzling—aspect of *Buile Suibhne* is the doubtful, quasi-avian status of Sweeney himself after he has been cursed by Ronan Finn. Does Sweeney actually become a bird, or is does he merely become bird-like? In Heaney's version, he is only '*like* a bird of the air' (*SA*, 9, my emphasis). However, Sweeney later says 'I have endured purgatories since the feathers grew on me' (*SA*, 66).

[66] *SA*, 50. As McCarthy has pointed out, 'From the late nineteenth century, Ailsa Craig was colloquially known as "Paddy's milestone," given its position as a conspicuous landmark for Irish immigrants sailing to Scotland' (McCarthy, 38).

Ailsa Craig,
the seagulls' home,
God knows it is
hard lodgings.

Ailsa Craig,
bell-shaped rock,
reaching sky-high,
snout in the sea—

it hard-beaked,
me seasoned and scraggy:
we mated like a couple
of hard-shanked cranes.[67]

Heaney's translation collapses the distance between Ireland and Scotland by removing the sense of distance present in O'Keeffe's version: 'There will over-take me / a warrior-band stubbornly, / far from Ulster, / faring in Alba'.[68] The original Irish lines are 'Béraitt oram-sa / fian co talchuraibh, /cían o Ultachaibh, / triall a nAlban*ch*aibh',[69] with O'Keeffe, unlike Heaney, opting for 'Alba' rather than 'Scotland'. Similarly, there is no corresponding version of the lines 'cían om eólas-sa, / crioch gusa ránag-sa' or 'far from home / is the country I have reached' in Heaney's text. Heaney's 'snout in the sea' keeps the original alliteration of 'srón re s*r*uthfairrge'—unlike O'Keefe's 'nose to the main'—while adding an animalistic element in keeping with the surrounding seagulls and cranes ('srón' is the Irish for the nose of a human or an animal).[70]

On one occasion, Heaney subtly adapts the language of *Sweeney Astray* to suit its Scottish location. Heaney introduces the Scottish tradition of 'first-footing' to describe Sweeney's lonely experience on Ailsa Craig: 'Haunting deer-paths, / enduring rain, / first-footing the grey / frosted grass'.[71] The use of 'first-footing' here is some distilled Heaney: a beautifully tactile and con-cise description of experiencing the natural world—in this case the sensation of stepping onto an undisturbed patch of frost (thus expressing Sweeney's utter loneliness). However, the phrase also suggests Sweeney is on Ailsa Craig at New Year, or Hogmanay, since that is when first-footing (the tradition of

---

[67]   *SA*, 53–4. This is an odd moment in Heaney's version: 'we mated like a couple / of hard-shanked cranes' O'Keeffe's text has only 'Sad our meeting; / a couple of cranes hard-shanked' (O'Keeffe, 97) at this point in the story, so Heaney seems to have substituted a mating for a meeting.
[68]   O'Keeffe, 95.   [69]   Ibid., 94.
[70]   See also: 'srón carraige'—'projecting part of rock' (Ó Dónaill, 1156).   [71]   *SA*, 51.

visiting a neighbour's house with gifts after midnight) is carried out in Scotland. Sweeney is certainly in Scotland during the desolation of winter—he braves 'frozen lairs', 'wind-driven snow', and a 'weak sun',[72] dreaming of 'Ulster in harvest' and 'a summer visit / to green Tyrone'.[73] The phrase 'first-footing' also carries a melancholic irony: first-footing is an act of celebration and hospitality, involving company and conviviality. Nothing could be further from Sweeney's plight on Ailsa Craig.

At this juncture the work is as much about Celtic temperatures as the 'Celtic temperament',[74] thus becoming what might be termed an eco-Celtic text. In 'Earning a Rhyme' Heaney discusses how he arranged the poem both to evoke cold weather and to adhere to the feel of the source material:

> I cannot remember when I got the idea that the stanzas should be recast in a more hard-edged, pointed way; that they should have the definition of hedges in a winter sunset; that they should be colder, more articulated; should be tuned to a bleaker note; should be more constricted and ascetic; more obedient to the metrical containments and battened-down verbal procedures of the Irish itself.[75]

Heaney's approach creates a tension between the constrictive format of the poetry and the ranging expansiveness of the texts and its locations, although this tension also exists in the broad geography and tight, compressed language and structure of the original Irish. Even so, Heaney's compact language does conjure a sense of Sweeney's solitude and penitence, by suggesting a repetitive existence of starkness and austerity. The sense of wintry bareness created by the neatness of the text is, as Stephen Regan has pointed out, partly a result of a progression from the volume *Wintering Out* (1972):

> What greatly eased the transition from *Wintering Out* to *Sweeney Astray* was Heaney's adeptness in handling the thin quatrain form he had developed for several poems, including 'The Tollund Man.' It was serendipitous that the principal verse form in *Buile Suibhne* was the rhymed quatrain. Heaney set about emulating this in free verse quatrains, initially disregarding the

---

[72] *SA*, 51.   [73] Ibid., 55.

[74] Ibid., ii. See also: 'It almost seems that since the Norman Conquest, the temperature of the English language has been subtly raised by a warm front coming up from the Mediterranean. But the Irish language did not undergo the same Romance influences and indeed early Irish nature poetry registers certain sensations and makes springwater music out of certain feelings in a way unmatched in any other European language' (Heaney, 'The God in the Tree', 182).

[75] Heaney, 'Earning a Rhyme', 63–4.

rhymed heptasyllabic lines of the Middle Irish, but later emulating the original with the smoother metrical basis, even introducing the Irish *deibidhe* rhymes (the rhyme of a monosyllabic word with a disyllabic word, stressing the non-rhyming syllable, as with 'wall / downfall').[76]

Heaney's English version consists of octosyllabic lines in the poetry sections of *Sweeney Astray*, rather than the heptasyllabic lines of the original Irish version.[77]

Since Heaney's *Sweeney Astray* is based on pre-Macpherson, pre-Romantic, and pre-Irish Revival literature, it is not surprising that nature is not romanticized or idealized. As Oona Frawley has suggested, nature in *Sweeney Astray* is, despite its beauty, 'too real – whether cold, wet or uncomfortable…to be styled into traditional, pastoral artifice'.[78] Yet nature in *Sweeney Astray* often corresponds—in a fairly Romantic fashion—to Sweeney's emotional or mental state: 'Descriptions literal in the Irish – Suibhne in a tree, buffeted by the storm – use rhyme, or alliteration, to hint at a psychological dimension; Heaney develops literal descriptions of the environment into metaphors (and similes) to convey Sweeney's mental state'.[79] The positions Sweeney rises to, and the places he goes to, offer no Yeatsian spiritual peace. Though he visits islands on his travels, these are not the isolated centres of racial or folk purity of Yeats, Synge, or Macleod—they are simply islands—places of rock, seabirds, and frequently bleak weather. In other words, by returning to older literature from before Romanticism and early Celticism, Heaney is able to depict a natural world stripped of some of the associations European culture has ascribed to it since the eighteenth century (the *Buile Suibhne* manuscripts date from the mid seventeenth and early eighteenth century, well before the advent of Macpherson's *Ossian*). Granted, O'Keeffe's translation dates from 1913, during the era of the Irish Revival. However, the translation is a sober scholarly work with very little in the way of late-nineteenth century Celticism. Heaney's attention to the environment itself—with Romantic associations filtered out—is in line with a linguistic approach that rejects late nineteenth century 'Hibernian' or 'Kiltartan' language in favour of a blanker, more

---

[76] Regan, 335. As Ciaran Carson has pointed out, 'Eleven different types of quatrain are in fact used in the original, each with its complex set of rules of metre, assonance (or rhyme) and alliteration. Clearly, to attempt an English equivalent is out of the question' (Carson, 'Escaping', 144).
[77] See McCarthy, 20.   [78] Frawley, 15.
[79] O'Donoghue, 459. See also: 'the original has a litanic, manic formality; but here, nature is not observed, it is addressed; in their personification, the trees become cyphers for Sweeney's state of mind; nature is internalized' (Carson, 'Escaping', 145).

neutral English. Thus, on the level of language, there is little local flavor in the text aside from the names of places.

As Heaney discusses in *Stepping Stones*, he returned to the figure of Sweeney in the 'Sweeney Redivivus' poems 'where "Sweeney" is rhymed with "Heaney", autobiographically as well as phonetically'.[80] In these poems, a reference to Scotland is set in fraught, tense lines that seem to link older connections between Ireland and Scotland (the ancient history mentioned previously but also the later Ulster Plantation) with the sectarian rituals of the north of Ireland and with events of the Troubles: 'so I mastered new rungs of the air / to survey out of reach / their bonfires on hills, their hosting / and fasting, the levies from Scotland'.[81] Indeed, the text is similar in some ways to Sorley MacLean's 1971 poem 'Àrd-Mhusaeum na h-Èireann' in that both texts were partly written in response to the Troubles—they both recall events of Irish history (though mainly fantastical and imaginative, *Sweeney Astray* also takes in events such as the Battle of Moira in 637 while 'Àrd-Mhusaeum na h-Èireann' looks back to the 1916 Easter Rising), and both texts shift between Ireland and Scotland.[82]

Sweeney Astray is part of a category of Heaney's work that engages with the links between northern European nations. His terse, 'neutral' language is distant from the kind of Revival style language of a work such as Gregory's *Cuchulain of Muirthemne* and his source text is, as Heaney notes in his introduction, more historically rooted than many of the products of the Revival. Heaney's text emphasizes Scottish-Irish connections—an eastern trajectory that contrasts with a western tendency in much modern Irish poetry—alongside an all-Ireland emphasis, as part of an attempt to create a work that could appeal to both 'Planter' and 'Gael' during the Troubles. The Scottish aspects of the text (modern Scottish placenames and the subtle inclusion of Scottish language) mean that *Sweeney Astray* creates greater emphasis on Irish-Scottish connections than comparable texts of the Revival era. The bare,

---

[80] Heaney qtd in O'Driscoll, 154.

[81] Heaney, 'The First Flight', *Station Island*, 103. The title 'Sweeney Redivivus' subtly recalls the title of Joyce's *Finnegans Wake*. The name *Finnegans Wake*—kept secret by Joyce for years as he worked on the project known initially as *Work in Progress*—derives from the Irish-American folk song 'Finnegan's Wake' in which a hod-carrier apparently dies after falling from a building. At his funeral, a fight breaks out and whiskey is accidentally splashed on the 'dead' man's face, miraculously 'reviving' him. So, Heaney and Joyce's titles both feature an Irish name alongside a word meaning (or suggestive of) rebirth or resurrection.

[82] MacLean's text mentions the Àrd-Phost-Oifis Èirinn (the General Post Office in Dublin where much of the fighting in 1916 took place) as well as Cnoc na Teamhrach (the Hill of Tara) and Dùn Èideann (Edinburgh).

wintry conditions Heaney evokes through his compact quatrains and cool, clean language creates a kind of contemporary eco-Celticism, where the realities of nature and the cold, wet, 'Celtic world' are represented clearly without Celtic Revival gloom or mystery but in keeping with the sense of desolation felt by mad king Sweeney.

Conclusion

Early Celticism/Late Celticism

James Macpherson's *Ossian* poems (1760–1763) are the foundational texts in the history of Scottish and Irish Celticisms. Macpherson's work had a profound effect on both scholarship and literature in Ireland. While *Ossian* was a significant influence on representations of the Celtic nature of Ireland, it was also the target of pointed criticism in Sydney Owenson's national tale *The Wild Irish Girl* (1806) at the beginning of the nineteenth century. Towards the end of the nineteenth century, *Ossian* was ignored in W.B. Yeats' 'The Wanderings of Oisin' (1889), despite Yeats working within an Ossianic discourse set up by Macpherson and theorists of Celtic literature such as Matthew Arnold. *The Wild Irish Girl* and 'The Wanderings of Oisin' are part of a broader Irish response—including a wave of hostility from scholars such as Charles O'Conor and Sylvester O'Halloran—to texts that had claimed Scotland as the 'original' Celtic nation and the real home of the Fenian ballads. The Celticism of *The Wild Irish Girl* functions as part of the text's presentation of a primitive, feminine, spiritual Ireland as a perfect political match for modern, masculine, industrialized England. In Scottish literature of the Celtic Revival period, the work of Fiona Macleod (William Sharp) owed a great deal to the vision of the Celtic world created by Macpherson, especially to Macpherson's presentation of the Celts as a beautifully fading, doomed race.

The *Ossian* controversy had largely died down by the arrival of Irish Modernism in the early twentieth century. However, Macpherson, and *Ossian* are referred to in a number of Irish Modernist texts as part of a larger trend in which Irish writing engages with Celtic matters and ancient literature, even as it transforms itself into new modernized forms. In Irish Modernism, *Ossian* is less associated with questions of literary or textual purity, and there is little concern with Macpherson's claims of authenticity or with his suggestion that Scotland is the oldest and purest Celtic nation. Instead, Macpherson's work is associated with schizoid voices in Samuel Beckett's *Murphy* (1938) and with textual recycling and hoaxes in James Joyce's *Finnegans Wake* (1939). In

Modern Irish and Scottish Literature: Connections, Contrasts, Celticisms. Richard Alan Barlow, Oxford University Press.
© Richard Alan Barlow 2023. DOI: 10.1093/oso/9780192859181.003.0007

Scottish Modernism, Macpherson is evoked in Hugh MacDiarmid's *To Circumjack Cencrastus* (1930), a text that imagines 'Gaeldom regained',[1] a Gaelic utopia where the divisions between Scotland and Ireland have been magically repaired and the anglicization of Scotland reversed through the restoration of 'Celtic genius'.[2]

MacDiarmid's Modernist late Celticism was written as part of a literary 'Celtic Front' and was partly a response to what he saw as the 'false Celticism' of the previous generation of Yeats, Gregory, and Macleod/Sharp. However, those earlier networks and forms of Celticism, with their centres in Dublin, Edinburgh, and London, was far from a unified, pan-Celtic, Irish-Scottish movement. Although these networks and activities overlapped with an actual pan-Celtic organization, there was little in the way of collaboration between Irish and Scottish Celticists aside from the activities of Yeats and Sharp and the publication of Irish writers such as Standish James O'Grady, Douglas Hyde, and Katharine Tynan in Patrick Geddes' Edinburgh-based journal *The Evergreen*. Indeed, Sharp was eventually tactfully ejected from Yeats and Gregory's network as their Celtic Theatre became the more nationalistic and Ireland-focused Irish Literary Theatre. Nor was there any sense of a MacDiarmidian 'Gaeldom regained' in that generation, at least not within Scottish Celticism. Indeed, the main figure of Scottish Celticism in that era, Fiona Macleod, was against Celticism being deployed as a nationalist force (at least in terms of Scottish or Irish nationalisms) and her work presents the Gaelic world as facing annihilation, rather than being on the cusp of renewal and regeneration as in MacDiarmid's work. Macleod's oeuvre contrasts markedly with the central texts of the Irish Revival, especially those of Augusta Gregory. While the work of both writers engages with issues of gender, Macleod associates femininity with weakness and death (though also with salvation). This is despite 'Fiona Macleod' being the female authorial persona of a male writer. Deirdre of the Sorrows—who kills herself at the end of the traditional story—is an ideal character for the death-obsessed Macleod to work with, and the tragic, doomed figure fits perfectly with Macleod's vision of the Celts as a 'passing' race on the verge of extinction. Macleod bases a number of works on the Deirdre tale. Perhaps the most revealing of these is her play *The House of Usna* (1900) which, although based on the story, is set after Deirdre's death. As such, a pervasive sense of gloom, grief, and despair suffuses the play, in keeping with Macleod's attitudes towards the Gaelic or Celtic world. Gregory's work, on the other hand, repeatedly foregrounds

---

[1] *CP*, 188.   [2] *CP*, 708.

active women of strength and conviction. For Gregory, Deirdre is too weak and passive a figure to be a central character of any of her plays and thus she appears only in her innovative Revivalist collection *Cuchulain of Muirthemne* (1902). Furthermore, Gregory's work displays little interest in Scotland, despite her use of Scottish source texts such as the work of the Lismore folk-lorist Alexander Carmichael, her reading of the *Transactions of the Gaelic Society*, and despite tales such as Deirdre and the Sons of Uisliu taking place to a significant extent in Scotland.

As with the personal links between the Irish and Scottish Celtic Revivals, Hugh MacDiarmid had a number of contacts in Ireland and visited the country in 1928 and 1978. Nevertheless, MacDiarmid never met James Joyce, perhaps his main Irish literary inspiration. Despite this, MacDiarmid felt a racial connection to the Irishman and was clearly inspired by the scale, complexity, and difficulty of Joyce's work. As MacDiarmid saw it, Joyce was not only the great literary-linguistic innovator of his day, he was also a fellow Celt. So, by naming a massive poem *In Memoriam James Joyce* (1955), MacDiarmid was signalling the artistic context he wished his work to be considered a part of— the context of massive, challenging, complicated modern artworks—but he was also attempting to link himself to Joyce through what he saw as a common Celtic background. Still, it is clear that the works of the two writers are vastly different in technique and outlook. MacDiarmid's art has little in common with Joyce's, despite MacDiarmid's attempts to align himself with Joyce's example. Indeed, *In Memoriam James Joyce*, a unique monument of material-ist Celticism written as an encyclopaedic 'poetry of facts' (a total inversion of Arnold's influential concept of the Celts as being inherently spiritual), stands in contrast to the idealism and scepticism of Joyce's work, particularly his final text, *Finnegans Wake*. In Scottish Celticism, there is a transition from spirituality to materialism as Marxism begins to influence Scottish culture. Arguably, it took World War I for (Scottish) nationalism to enter Scottish Celticism—since that was the point at which artists like MacDiarmid began to look to local, indigenous resources as an alternative to what they saw as an exhausted, 'mainstream' English-language culture. As a result of these devel-opments, there is a pronounced difference between the Celticisms of Macleod and MacDiarmid (or between Macleod's early Celticism and MacDiarmid's late Celticism). While Macleod looked forward to a future in which the Celtic spirit or genius is subsumed into the Teutonic or Germanic English race (and, by extension, the Celtic nations are permanently integrated into the British State), MacDiarmid looked to the Gaelic culture of Scotland as an antidote to English influence in Scotland and as a cultural link to Ireland.

MacDiarmid's work also differs greatly to Joyce's on the level of language. The warping, melding, and patterning of language Joyce achieved so spectacularly in *Finnegans Wake* is not at all matched by MacDiarmid's *In Memoriam James Joyce*, in which a selection of words and phrases from a range of world languages are merely inserted into the English language text.[3] MacDiarmid's poem certainly has an arresting style, but this is achieved through the unemotional application of intentionally sterile and unpoetic language, rather than through linguistic or structural virtuosity (MacDiarmid's later style also contrasts with his own earlier work with Scots vocabulary). However, both writers were interested in placing themselves within a Celtic tradition and in defining themselves partly through a distancing from 'Anglo-Saxon' culture, often through aesthetic innovation. These attempts at distancing from English culture may have been successful to some extent, since critics have detected a division between English Modernism and the Modernisms of Scotland and Ireland. Fredric Jameson has suggested that 'aesthetic modernism was less developed in England than in Scotland, let alone Britain's "other island" whose extraordinary modernisms mark a sharp contrast with the commonsense empirical intellectual life of London or Cambridge.'[4] So, perhaps we can employ the term 'Celtic Modernism' as a way to think about certain works by Joyce and MacDiarmid (and perhaps some of Yeats's drama). Indeed, such a development might be one logical conclusion of recent attempts to avoid thinking of the Irish Revival and Irish Modernism as totally separate and distinct cultural phenomena.[5] Future examinations of Celtic Modernism might consider how Modernism engages with early Celticism but could also examine the ways Modernism employs Celtic tropes in order to reject anglicization or particular aspects of modernity. The term 'Celtic Modernism' might seem slightly paradoxical, given that Celticism is very much bound up with images of the past and with 'marginal' and 'peripheral' cultures, whereas Modernism tends to be future-oriented (at least in formal or aesthetic terms) and is usually associated with the urban 'centre'. However, much of Modernism channelled its innovative energies from history or myth and, although it was a strongly urban phenomenon, it also sought to draw inspiration from 'marginal' places of 'primitive' vitality or purity.

---

[3] See Herbert, W.N., 195–6.   [4] Jameson, 103.
[5] For examples, see Kiberd, 'Joyce's Homer, Homer's Joyce,' 245 and Begam, 194. See also T.J. Boynton's discussion of 'Celticist Modernisms'. Boynton, 12–16.

James Joyce's own relationship with Celticism and Irish-Scottish connections is complex (similar to the complexity of his feelings and attitudes towards Ireland itself). Though he parodies the Celtic Twilight or '*cultic twalette*' in *Finnegans Wake*[6] (puncturing the explorations of Yeatsian mystical, otherwordly cult-like Celticism through an association with the bodily, everyday matters of the 'toilette') and had satirized '*The Celtic note*' in his *Dubliners* story 'A Little Cloud',[7] Joyce also demonstrated a fascination with Scottish literature, history, and philosophy, partly because of his interest in the links between Irish and Scottish histories. Joyce's work also expresses an anxiety towards the fate of the 'Celtic world' as it struggles against the domination of 'a stronger race'.[8] Furthermore, the atmosphere of doubt and uncertainty in *Finnegans Wake* is strongly influenced by Joyce's reading of Scottish literature and philosophy, especially the work of David Hume (according to Joyce, Hume is a Celtic philosopher like George Berkeley and, perhaps more eccentrically, Arthur Balfour and Henri Bergson). However, while *Finnegans Wake* does have a certain Humean quality of indeterminacy, Joyce's text differs greatly from the major philosophical concept of the Scottish Enlightenment in terms of history and society. The cycles and repetitions of *Finnegans Wake* contrast with the visions of capitalist development towards completion and stability offered by Adam Smith in his *Lectures on Jurisprudence* and in the historical novels and stories of Walter Scott. The sense of inevitable societal progress in Scott's texts is often linked to quasi-incestuous personal unions, forms of relationship Joyce associates with self-obsession and sterility.

Later in the twentieth century, Seamus Heaney also demonstrated a sustained interest in Irish-Scottish connections and in Celtic themes. Heaney lectured on and translated Scottish poetry, his unpretentious poetic voice was influenced by Robert Burns, and he was friends with Hugh MacDiarmid. In his 1983 book *Sweeney Astray*, Heaney revisits the ancient Sweeney story as a way of appealing to both sides of the political/religious divide in the north of Ireland and his version of *Buile Suibhne* demonstrates his interest in ancient, pre-Christian Ireland. However, the text takes place across a variety of locations within what Heaney (like Joyce) called 'the Celtic world',[9] both around Ireland and in several Scottish locations such as Ailsa Craig. The austere prose and verse of *Sweeney Astray* also subtly evokes the coldness and bareness of Irish and Scottish winters. Heaney's introduction to *Sweeney Astray* speaks of a 'cultural affinity' between Ireland and Scotland in Sweeney's era that might

---

[6] *FW*, 344.12.   [7] *D*, 74.   [8] *OCPW*, 124.
[9] Heaney, 'The God in the Tree', 188 and *OCPW*, 124.

appeal to everyone in the north of Ireland. His optimistic sense was that the text might encourage unionists in the North to feel a greater sense of kinship with their neighbours in the rest of the island and that nationalists in the North might start to feel more of a connection with Scotland (including Scottish Protestants). *Sweeney Astray* looks in the opposite direction to many texts of modern Irish poetry in that it surveys the west of Scotland rather than the west of Ireland. Much of Heaney's book—and the original manuscripts that form J.G. O'Keeffe's version of *Buile Suibhne*, Heaney's source text—takes place north of a line Heaney imagined 'between Berwick and Bundoran'[10] and, elsewhere in his work, Heaney notes the linguistic links between the north of Ireland and Scotland that formed following the seventeenth century plantation of Ulster.

This study has carried out a comparative analysis of modern Irish and Scottish writing through an examination of textual, historical, thematic, and personal links between Irish and Scottish literature, with a focus on the development of literary Celticism. The two main findings of this study are that, firstly, Celticism as a whole can be divided in two basic periods—the early romantic Celticism of Macpherson and the Irish and Scottish Revivals of the late nineteenth/early twentieth centuries, and the late Celticism displayed in twentieth century texts by Joyce, Beckett, MacDiarmid, and Heaney. Rather than ending around 1900, as has previously been suggested, Celticism—including forms of Celticism that stress Irish-Scottish connections—survives and evolves into new varieties in the work of a number of Irish and Scottish writers. The second conclusion of this text is that, of those two long periods of Celticism, pan-Celtic sentiment is much more conspicuous in the latter era (though it is not present in all of the texts studied here, Beckett's *Murphy* being a case in point). The scarcity of pan-Celtic sentiment in early, Romantic Celticism is mainly because of the divisive nature of James Macpherson's claims and practices in the eighteenth century and the negative reception of his work in Ireland. The lack of pan-Celtic sentiment in the Irish Revival can be explained by the generally nationalist (rather than pan-Celtic) aspirations of Celtic Revival figures such as Gregory and Yeats in Ireland, as well as by personal strains within the Celtic camp (partly caused, it seems, by the erratic behavior of William Sharp). Yeats discussed the cultivation of Celtic 'solidarity' in his letters,[11] but this was a short-lived interest that had little impact on his work. However, in late Celticism, Joyce looked how the 'sister'[12] nations

---

[10] Heaney, 'Burns's Art Speech (1)', 218.   [11] *CL II*, 73.
[12] Joyce, James, *Poems and Exiles*, 109.

Ireland and Scotland might be linked through similar philosophical cultures, MacDiarmid saw Irish political developments as a source of inspiration for Scotland and viewed Irish workers as a necessary means of restoring the partially lapsed Celtic nature of the Scottish nation, while Heaney turned to the *Buile Suibhne* story as a way of stressing cultural commonalities between the north and south of Ireland, as well as between Ireland and Scotland, and as a way of appealing to both communities in the north of Ireland.

As George Watson has pointed out, Celticism is 'frequently associated with the faintly ludicrous, the ersatz and the bogus'.[13] Watson mentions the faux-Celtic items on sale at tourist gift shops across Ireland and Scotland as an example of this kind of sham. With regards to literature, the artificial nature of Celticist texts has been there from the beginning, with the synthetic and misleading nature of Macpherson's *Ossian* (though, as mentioned earlier, his work did contain traces of genuine Gaelic poetry). The attempt to engage with Celtic matters, coupled with an awareness of the false or artificial nature of previous Celticism, are perhaps the defining characteristics that separates late Celticism from early Celticism. An understanding of Celticism's previous spuriousness—coupled with a lingering interest in the overall discourse and in questions of Celtic identity—leads to an attempt to look for alternatives in Celtic philosophy (as is the case with Joyce's *Finnegans Wake*), to the association of Celticism with schizoid voices (as in Beckett's work), to the 'Gaelic idea' and the rejection of the 'false' Celtic Revival in MacDiarmid's work, and an engagement with the materials of indigenous culture and 'the Celtic world' directly and in plain language, without the intervening misty Kiltartan idiom of the Celtic Revival (as is attempted in Heaney's *Sweeney Astray*). In all these cases there is a distancing from previous Celticism, together with a reclaiming or a rethinking of what the term 'Celtic' might mean or how it could be applied. Sometimes this process involves direct engagement or parodying of the texts of early Celticism, as can be seen in Joyce's *Finnegans Wake* and Beckett's *Murphy*.

The division between the two eras of Celticism can be attributed to a series of linked events: the decline of the British Empire, the slow fading of Romanticism, political developments on the island of Ireland, and the explosion of literary Modernism. In Irish and Scottish Modernisms, the impulse to renew culture often coincided with a search for 'original' or 'pure' cultural sources or places and an interest in race and nationality. P.J. Mathews has discussed the 'alternative modernity' of the Irish Revival, which considered

---

[13] Watson, George, 'Aspects', 129.

tradition 'as a stimulus towards innovation and change rather than a barrier to it'.[14] However, tradition and innovation also merged with the Modernist emphasis on scepticism, resulting in a new form of Celticism that was both fascinated by the Celtic world, keen to tap into possibilities of Celtic sources for technical or formal innovation, and yet sceptical towards the largely inauthentic culture and discourse surrounding or shrouding that world. Furthermore, there is a connection between the Celtic Revival and Modernism in that both cultural phenomena are driven in part by anxieties regarding modern society. With the Celtic Revival, this often takes the form of an Anglophobia that fears the approach of a soulless, encroaching materialism emanating outwards from England. This sentiment was also present in sections of Irish politics in the early twentieth century.[15] As this text has suggested, a major feature of Joyce's Modernism—his emphasis on consciousness—is compatible with the anti-materialist side of Celticism and is linked to his reading of 'Celtic' philosophy. In political terms, two of the most significant examples of late Celticism appear shortly after the foundation of the Free State and the partition of Ireland, and in the period of the Troubles, respectively. Joyce's *Finnegans Wake* 'registers and readjusts the experience of civil war, partition and state formation'[16] while *Sweeney Astray*, as Heaney himself discussed, was written partly as a response to the events in north of Ireland in the late twentieth century. Late Celticism in Scotland was linked to the rise of Scottish nationalism and was inspired by developments in Irish politics of the Revolutionary era, a sense of disillusionment and dissatisfaction with Scotland's place in the British state, and a negative attitude towards the supposedly 'false' and overly anglicized nature of contemporary Scottish culture.

In his introduction to the fourth volume of *The Cambridge History of Ireland*, Thomas Bartlett considers the conditions that made the accomplishments of modern Irish literature possible and compares these achievements to the absence of comparable feats in Scotland:

[14] Mathews, 2. See also: 'Traditional culture provides modernism with an adversary, but also lends it some of the terms in which to inflect itself' and 'The modernist sensibility...is not of course synonymous with *modernity*. On the contrary, it is in one sense its sworn enemy, hostile to that stately march of secular reason which was precisely, for many a nineteenth-century Irish nationalist, where a soulless Britain had washed up...Modernism is among other things a last-ditch resistance to mass commodity culture' (Eagleton, 297, 280).

[15] As James Fairhall writes, 'Pearse and his fellow rebels...felt a sense of moral superiority toward England, toward what they perceived as middle-class English materialism and hypocrisy' (Fairhall, 181).

[16] Allen, 34.

the poverty and squalor, alongside the pride and contentment, the misery and separation jostling warmth and conviviality, the galling failure and triumphant success, the generosity...the hypocrisy...Perhaps it was only in a petri dish occupied by these opposites that Irish literary talent could be incubated? Is it altogether accidental that Ireland during [the period 1880 to the present] produced four Nobel Prize winners in literature (William Butler Yeats 1865–1939), Samuel Beckett (1906–1989), George Bernard Shaw (1856–1950), and Seamus Heaney (1939–2013); five, if James Joyce (1882–1941) is accorded honorary status? By contrast, Scotland, with a similar population, though not with a similar violent recent history, had none.[17]

In fact, there has never been a Scottish winner of the Nobel Prize in Literature, although there have been numerous Scottish winners in other fields. In Scotland's defence, the prize only began in 1901 so the golden age of modern Scottish literature—the Enlightenment period of Robert Burns, James Hogg, and Walter Scott—was not covered. Perhaps there would have been a prize for Scott or Burns had the prize existed at that time. Alternate or fantasy literary history aside, it is difficult to avoid the conclusion that Ireland had a far more successful and influential late nineteenth/twentieth century in literature than Scotland. Bartlett suggests that this is partly due to the relative political stability in Scotland during the period, as opposed to the 'violent recent history' of Ireland.

The achievements of modern Irish culture cannot be fully explained by reductively pointing to the political tensions and upheavals of the times in which they were created. However, while the works of Yeats, Joyce, Beckett, and Heaney engage with an enormous range of issues in addition to modern Irish politics, their writing does emerge from a particularly volatile historical period of Irish life that stretches from the fall of Parnell to the era of the Troubles. That sense of instability does seem to have created a fertile and stimulating environment for genius, even taking into account the fact that all of the writers listed above spent significant periods of their lives outside of Ireland. Similarly perhaps, the greatest era of modern Scottish writing—including the emergence of the historical novel as well as crucially important developments in poetry, philosophy, and economics—developed partly as a response to the upheavals and cultural developments of the eighteenth century, including the loss of the Scottish Parliament as a result of the Union of

---

[17] Bartlett, 'Preface', xxxiv.

Scotland and England in 1707 and the 1745/46 Jacobite Rebellion. As is well known, Scottish literary culture of the Enlightenment era developed partly as a response to the manner in which philosophers such as Hume and Smith were conceptualizing Scotland's history as a movement from barbarism to refinement.

Without wishing to downplay the importance of events and phenomena such as 'Red Clydeside' unduly—the situation in Glasgow was considered serious enough to warrant the deployment of tanks in George Square in January 1919—Scotland did not go through the kind of rapid and violent transformations during the twentieth century that Ireland did. Having said that, the activities of Scottish writers such as Hugh MacDiarmid were aimed at such a transformation. There has been progress in Scotland in recent decades—for example, the devolution referendum in 1997 followed by the re-opening of the Scottish Parliament in 1999—but change in Scotland has been gradual and peaceful (rather like Scott's image of 'the stream of a deep and smooth river' in *Waverley* where 'we are not aware of the progress we have made until we fix our eye on the now-distant point from which we set out').[18] The late 1990s were a period of change, hope, and optimism in both Scotland and Ireland. The peace process in the north of Ireland—the final Provisional IRA ceasefire of 1997, the Good Friday Agreement of 1998, and the establishment of a power-sharing assembly at Stormont—overlapped with the events in Scotland mentioned above. Irish-Scottish connections also developed during this period with the appointment of an Irish consul-general to Scotland in 1999.

Some of the foundations for the progress in Scotland were cultural. As Margery Palmer McCulloch has pointed out, 'Scottish modernism of the post-1918 years...laid lasting foundations for the building of the confident, outward-looking culture Scotland takes for granted today'.[19] Cairns Craig has suggested that 'if politics and votes were the means of bringing the parliament into existence, they were not its direct cause' and that the Scottish parliament was built 'on the foundations of a revolution in the nation's culture'.[20] However, according to Scott Hames, 'Scottish devolution can be explained quite adequately without reference to artistic or intellectual developments, by attending to the (far from simple) governing interests and parliamentary pressures of the period'.[21] A Labour-Liberal Democrat coalition controlled

---

[18] Scott, *Waverley*, 340.   [19] McCulloch, 'Scottish Modernism', 781.
[20] Craig, 'Unsettled will', 12 and Craig, *Intending Scotland*, 73.
[21] Hames, 79.

the new Scottish Parliament until 2007, when a minority Scottish National Party (SNP) government took control at Holyrood. The rise of the left-of-centre civic nationalist SNP has coincided with the decline of the once-dominant Labour Party in Scotland and this development helped pave the way for the Independence Referendum of 2014.

There have been a number of important connections between Irish and Scottish literature in the contemporary period. Perhaps unsurprisingly, given the stunning achievements of modern Irish literature, this has mainly taken the form of Irish Modernism having an effect on Scottish literature. For example, Joyce's influence on the presentation of consciousness in James Kelman novels such as *The Busconductor Hines* (1984) and Flann O'Brien's influence on Alasdair Gray, as openly acknowledged in the 'List of Plagiarisms' section of *Lanark: A Life in Four Books* (1981).[22] Celtic matters and themes of the type studied in this text—the renewal of stories from traditional cultures—seem to have disappeared from mainstream or high-profile Irish and Scottish literature in the contemporary period (with the exception of books for children).

Despite the efforts of Joyce, MacDiarmid, and Heaney, the term 'Celtic' still has a slightly suspicious ring to it in the context of Anglophone literary culture. Furthermore, an additional meaning has been added to the word 'Celtic' in recent years, something that has been reflected in scholarship on contemporary Scottish and Irish literature. Tellingly, the only time the word 'Celtic' is used in Stefanie Lehner's recent study *Subaltern Ethics in Contemporary Scottish and Irish Literature* is in relation to the now extinct 'Celtic Tiger'.[23] Lehner mentions that 'on his visit to Dublin in February 2008, [former SNP leader Alex] Salmond outlined his vision of "Scotland's Future" as an emulation of Ireland's economic success; to create, in his words, "a Celtic Lion economy to match the Celtic Tiger on this side of the Irish Sea"'.[24] The growth of the SNP in Scotland in recent decades has had little to do with MacDiarmidian forms of ethno-nationalism or with Celticism. Indeed, as Murray Pittock has noted, from its inception the SNP 'rapidly distanced itself from Celtic Revivalism'.[25] Rather, the recent success of the party can be

[22] For an account of connections between Irish and Scottish fiction since the 1980s, see Lehner, 'Devolutionary States'.

[23] See Lehner, *Subaltern Ethics*, 2, 4–5, 28, 45, 46, 47–9.

[24] Ibid., 4. See also: 'What is the difference between Ireland and Scotland – the difference that makes the difference? I can tell you the answer – Ireland is doing so much with so little while Scotland is doing so little with so much' (Alex Salmond, Keynote Address, SNP conference, September 27, 1996).

[25] Pittock, *Celtic Identity*, 84. However, groups such as the Scots National League, founded in 1920, had links to Celtic Revivalism and advocated an 'unadulterated Celtic state'. See Pittock, 84.

attributed to an increasing sense of alienation in Scotland from Westminster and English politics. So, while the Celticism of the Celtic Revival was an important precursor to political change in early-twentieth century Ireland, Celticism never had the same political effect in Scotland. Celticism and pan-Celtic sentiment have had a minimal presence in modern Irish politics since the Revolutionary era.

The 'No' vote in the Scottish Independence referendum of 2014 looked to have settled constitutional matters in Scotland for the foreseeable future (although a 45% support for Scottish Independence would have been unthinkable until quite recently). However, in the 'Brexit' vote in 2016, Scotland and Northern Ireland voted to remain in the European Union while England and Wales voted to leave. As Colin Kidd has pointed out, 'The result of the vote undermine[d] Scottish unionists, one of whose central arguments in 2014 was that independence threatened Scotland's place in the EU.'[26] At the time of writing, the SNP have won every election in Scotland since 2014 (including the UK general election of May 2015, when they won fifty-six of the fifty-nine Scottish seats) and remain the dominant party in Scotland. The electoral success of Sinn Féin in the 2019 UK general election (with nationalists winning more seats than unionists in the North for the first time) and the 2022 Northern Ireland Assembly election (with Sinn Féin becoming the largest party in the North), along with the party's increasing popularity in the Republic of Ireland and an ongoing post-Brexit malaise within unionism in the North, has led to renewed discussions regarding the ending of partition and the reunification of Ireland. An Irish border poll and a second Scottish independence referendum are distinct possibilities.

Celticism has tended to trend at moments of political and constitutional tension or transformation in the Atlantic archipelago; the aftermath of Culloden in Scotland, the 1800 Union of Britain and Ireland, the post-Famine/pre-independence era in Ireland, the post-World War I period in Scotland, and the era of the Troubles in the north of Ireland. Whether any further political change in Ireland and Scotland leads to a revival of literary Celticism remains to be seen, but it is probable that literature stressing the deep connections between the two nations will continue to appear. And, given their longstanding and significant relationship, it is likely that Irish and Scottish literatures will continue to influence each other well into the future.

[26] Kidd, 12.

Bibliography

Ackerley, Chris, 'The Uncertainty of Self: Samuel Beckett and the Location of the Voice', *Samuel Beckett Today/Aujourd'hui* 14 (2004), 39–51.

Ackerley, C.J. and Gontarski, S.E., *The Faber Companion to Samuel Beckett: A Reader's Guide to His Works, Life, and Thought* (London: Faber & Faber, 2006).

Alaya, Flavia, *William Sharp—'Fiona Macleod'* (Cambridge, MA: Harvard University Press, 1970).

Allen, Nicholas, *Modernism, Ireland and Civil War* (Cambridge: Cambridge University Press, 2009).

Andrews, Elmer, 'Aesthetics, Politics and Identity: Lady Morgan's *The Wild Irish Girl*', *The Canadian Journal of Irish Studies* 13.2 (1987), 7–19.

Arnold, Matthew, *On the Study of Celtic Literature* (London: Smith Elder and Co., 1867).

Barlow, Richard Alan, 'The "united states of Scotia Picta": Scottish literature and history in *Finnegans Wake*', *James Joyce Quarterly* 48.2 (2011), 305–18.

——'"Hume Sweet Hume": Skepticism, Idealism, and Burial in *Finnegans Wake*', *Philosophy and Literature* 38.1 (2014), 266–75.

——'The Shirt that was on Connolly: Sorley MacLean and the Easter Rising', *Scotland and the Easter Rising*, eds. Willy Maley and Kirsty Lusk (Edinburgh: Luath Press, 2016), 31–6.

——*The Celtic Unconscious: Joyce and Scottish Culture* (Notre Dame, IN: Notre Dame University Press, 2017).

Baron, Scarlett, 'Joyce's "holiday wisdom": "Gustave Flaubert can rest having made me"', *Genetic Joyce Studies* 7 (2007), n.p.

Bartlett, Thomas, 'Preface', *The Cambridge History of Ireland Volume IV: 1800 to the Present*, ed. Thomas Bartlett (Cambridge: Cambridge University Press, 2018, xxxi–xxxvi).

Beckett, Samuel, *Disjecta: Miscellaneous Writings and a Dramatic Fragment*, ed. Ruby Cohn (New York: Grove Press, 1984).

——*More Pricks Than Kicks* (Paris, London, New York: John Calder, 1993).

——*Murphy*, ed. J.C.C. Mays (London: Faber and Faber, 2009).

Begam, Richard, 'Joyce's Trojan Horse: *Ulysses* and the Aesthetics of Decolonization', *Modernism and Colonialism: British and Irish Literature, 1899-1939*, eds. Richard Begam, and Michael Valdez Moses (Durham, NC and London: Duke University Press, 2007), 185–208.

Behrendt, Stephen, 'Mary Tighe in Life, Myth, and Literary Vicissitude', *A History of Irish Women's Poetry*, eds. Ailbhe Darcy and David Wheatley (Cambridge: Cambridge University Press, 2021), 127–41.

Bell, Eleanor, 'Into the Centre of Things: Poetic Travel Narratives in the Work of Kathleen Jamie and Nan Shepherd', *Kathleen Jamie: Essays and Poems on Her Work*, ed. Rachel Falconer (Edinburgh: Edinburgh University Press, 2015), 126–34.

Benstead, James, 'A Study of Hugh MacDiarmid's *In Memoriam James Joyce*', unpublished PhD thesis, University of Edinburgh, 2019.

Bergholm, Alexandra, 'The Authorship and Transmission of *Buile Shuibhne*: A Re-Appraisal', *Buile Suibhne: Perspectives and Reassessments*, ed. John Carey (London: Irish Texts Society/Cumann na Scríbheann nGaedhilge, Subsidiary Series 26, 2014), 93–110.

Black, Donald (MacGhilleDhuibh, Domhnall), 'Alexander Carmichael: The Influence of Lismore', *The Life and Legacy of Alexander Carmichael*, ed. Domhnall Uilleam Stiùbhart (Port of Ness: The Islands Book Trust, 2008), 40–3.

Black, Ronald (MacilleDhuibh, Raghnaill), 'Introduction', *An Tuil—Anthology of 20th Century Scottish Gaelic Verse/An Tuil: Duanaire Gàidhlig an 20mh Ceud*, ed. Ronald Black (Raghnaill MacilleDhuibh) (Edinburgh: Polygon, 1999), xxi–lxx.

Bold, Alan *MacDiarmid: The Terrible Crystal* (Boston, MA and London: Routledge and Kegan Paul, 1983).

——*Scots Steel Tempered Wi' Irish Fire: Hugh MacDiarmid and Ireland* (Edinburgh: Edinburgh College of Art, 1985).

Bowles, Noelle, 'Nationalism and Feminism in Lady Gregory's *Kincora, Dervorgilla*, and *Grania*', *New Hibernia Review/Iris Éireannach Nua* 3.3 (1999), 116–30.

Boynton, T. J., *Against the Despotism of Fact: Modernism, Capitalism, and the Irish Celt* (New York: SUNY Press, 2021).

Brannigan, John, *Archipelagic Modernism: Literature in the Irish and British Isles, 1890–1970* (Edinburgh: Edinburgh University Press, 2015).

Brown, Stephen J., *Ireland in Fiction: A Guide to Irish Novels, Tales, Romances, and Folklore* (Dublin and London: Maunsel, 1919).

Brown, Terence, ed. *Celticism* (Amsterdam and Atlanta, GA: Rodopi, 1996).

——'Cultural Nationalism, Celticism and the Occult', *Celticism*, ed. Terence Brown (Amsterdam and Atlanta, GA: Rodopi, 1996), 221–30.

Byrne, Michel, 'Tails o the Comet? MacLean, Hay, Young and MacDiarmid's Renaissance', *Scotlit* 26 (2002), 1–3.

Cairns, David and Richards, Shaun, *Writing Ireland: Colonialism, Nationalism and Culture* (Manchester: Manchester University Press, 1988).

Cameron, Alexander, *Reliquiæ Celticae: Texts, Papers, and Studies in Gaelic Literature and Philology Vol. II: Poetry, History, and Philology* (Inverness: The Northern Counties Newspaper and Printing and Publishing Company, 1894).

Carlin, Willie, *Thatcher's Spy: My Life as an MI5 Agent inside Sinn Féin* (Newbridge: Merrion Press, 2019).

Carmichael, Alexander, *Deirdire and the Lay of the Children of Uisne* (Edinburgh: Norman Macleod; London: David Nutt; Dublin: Gill and Son, 1905).

Carruthers, Gerard and McIlvanney, Liam, eds., *The Cambridge Companion to Scottish Literature* (Cambridge: Cambridge University Press, 2012).

Carruthers, Gerard, and Rawes, Alan, eds., *English Romanticism and the Celtic World* (Cambridge: Cambridge University Press, 2003).

Carson, Ciaran, 'Escaped from the Massacre', *Honest Ulsterman* 50 (1975), 184–6.

——'Sweeney Astray: Escaping from Limbo', *The Art of Seamus Heaney* ed. Tony Curtis (Ogmore-by-Sea: Poetry Wales Press, 1985), 139–48.

Castle, Gregory, *Modernism and the Celtic Revival* (Cambridge: Cambridge University Press, 2001).

Chapman, Malcolm, *The Gaelic Vision in Scottish Culture* (London: Croom Helm, 1978).

Cheape, Hugh, ' "Every Treasure You Chanced On": Alexander Carmichael and Material Culture', *The Life and Legacy of Alexander Carmichael*, ed. Domhnall Uilleam Stiùbhart (Port of Ness: The Islands Book Trust, 2008), 115–34.

Clancy, Thomas Owen, 'Gaelic Literature and Scottish Romanticism', *The Edinburgh Companion to Scottish Romanticism*, ed. Murray Pittock (Edinburgh: Edinburgh University Press, 2011), 49–60.

Colum, Mary, *Life and the Dream* (New York: Doubleday & Company, Inc., 1947).

Connolly, Claire, 'I accuse Miss Owenson: *The Wild Irish Girl* as Media Event', *Colby Quarterly*, 36.2 (2000), 98–115.

Connolly, S.J. *The Oxford Companion to Irish History* (Oxford: Oxford University Press, 1998).

Connor, Steven and Creasy, Matthew, *James Joyce* (second edition) (Tavistock: Liverpool University Press, 2012).

Cormack, Alistair, *Yeats and Joyce: Cyclical History and the Reprobate Tradition* (New York and London: Routledge, 2008).

Coxhead, Elizabeth, *Lady Gregory: A Literary Portrait* (London: Macmillan & Co Ltd, 1961).

Craig, Cairns, *Intending Scotland: Explorations in Scottish Culture since the Enlightenment* (Edinburgh: Edinburgh University Press, 2009).

——'Unsettled Will: Cultural Engagement and Scottish Independence', *Observatoire de la Société Britannique* 18 (2016), 15–36.

Crawford, Robert, 'Post-Cullodenism', *London Review of Books* 18.19 (1996), 18.

Crawford, Robert, ed., *Robert Burns and Cultural Authority* (Iowa City, IA: University of Iowa Press, 1997).

——*The Modern Poet: Poetry, Academia, and Knowledge since the 1750s* (Oxford: Oxford University Press, 2001).

Crotty, Patrick 'Swordsmen: W. B. Yeats and Hugh MacDiarmid', *Modern Irish and Scottish Poetry* eds. Peter Mackay, Edna Longley, and Fran Brearton (Cambridge: Cambridge University Press, 2011), 20–38.

——'Scotland', *Seamus Heaney in Context*, ed. Geraldine Higgins (Cambridge: Cambridge University Press, 2021), 15–27.

Cullen, L.M., and T.C. Smout, eds., *Comparative Aspects of Economic and Social History, 1600–1900* (Edinburgh: John Donald Publishers, 1977).

Cuming, G. F., 'Walter Scott in Ireland', *The Irish Monthly*, 50.584 (1922), 51–4.

Cunliffe, Barry, *The Ancient Celts* (second edition) (Oxford: Oxford University Press, 2018).

Davis, Leith, *Acts of Union: Scotland and the Literary Negotiation of the British Nation 1707–1830* (Stanford, CA: Stanford University Press, 1998).

Davison, Neil R., *James Joyce, Ulysses, and the Construction of Jewish Identity: Culture, Biography, and 'the Jew' in Modernist Europe* (Cambridge: Cambridge University Press, 1996).

Dawe, Gerald, ' "Pledged to Ireland": The Poets and Poems of Easter 1916', *The Oxford Handbook of Modern Irish Poetry* eds. Fran Brearton and Alan Gillis (Oxford: Oxford University Press, 2012), 79–94.

De Barra, Caoimhín, *The Coming of the Celts A D 1860: Celtic Nationalism in Ireland and Wales* (Notre Dame, IN: Notre Dame University Press, 2018).

Deane, Seamus, *A Short History of Irish Literature* (Notre Dame, IN: Notre Dame University Press, 1986).

——*Celtic Revivals 1880–1980* (Winston-Salem, NC: Wake Forest University Press, 1987).

——*Strange Country: Modernity and Nationhood in Irish Writing since 1790* (Oxford: Oxford University Press, 1997).

Degnan, James P., 'The Encounter in Joyce's "An Encounter" ', *Twentieth Century Literature* 35.1 (1989), 89–93.

Derrida, Jacques, '*Ulysses* Gramophone: Hear Say Yes in Joyce', in Derek Attridge, ed., *Acts of Literature* (New York and London: Routledge, 1992), 253–309.

Doloff, Steven, 'A Soporific Note on the Harp in Joyce's "Two Gallants"', *James Joyce Quarterly* 41.4 (2004), 823–5.

Donovan, Julie, 'Text and Textile in Sydney Owenson's *The Wild Irish Girl*', *Éire-Ireland* 43.3/4 (2008), 31–57.

Downum, Denell, 'Sweeney Astray: The Other in Oneself', *Éire-Ireland* 44 nos. 3/4 (2009), 75–93.

Doyle, Maria-Elena, 'A Spindle for the Battle: Feminism, Myth, and the Woman-Nation in Irish Revival Drama', *Theatre Journal* 51.1 (1999), 33–46.

Druce, Robert, 'A Raindrop on a Thorn: An Interview with Seamus Heaney', *Dutch Quarterly Review* 9 (1979), 24–37.

Duncan, Ian, *Modern Romance and the Transformations of the Novel: The Gothic, Scott, Dickens* (Cambridge: Cambridge University Press, 1992).

——*Scott's Shadow: The Novel in Romantic Edinburgh* (Princeton, NJ and Oxford: Princeton University Press, 2007).

——'"Upon the thistle they're impaled": Hugh MacDiarmid's Modernist Nationalism', *Modernism and Colonialism: British and Irish Literature, 1899–1939*, eds. Richard Begam and Michael Valdez Moses (Durham, NC and London: Duke University Press, 2007), 246–68.

——'Scott and the Historical Novel: A Scottish Rise of the Novel', *The Cambridge Companion to Scottish Literature*, eds. Gerard Carruthers and Liam McIlvanney (Cambridge: Cambridge University Press, 2012), 103–16.

Eadie, Douglas, *Sorley MacLean's Island* (Glasgow: Ogam Films, 1974).

Eagleton, Terry, *Heathcliff and the Great Hunger* (London and New York: Verso, 1995).

Easthope, Antony, 'How Good is Seamus Heaney?', *English* 46 (1997), 21–36.

Ellmann, Richard, *The Consciousness of Joyce* (New York: Oxford University Press, 1977).

——*Yeats: The Man and the Masks* (New York: Norton, 1978).

——*James Joyce* (revised edition) (New York: Oxford University Press, 1982).

Fahy, Catherine, ed., *The James Joyce-Paul Léon Papers in the National Library of Ireland: A Catalogue* (Dublin: National Library of Ireland, 1992).

Fairhall, James, *James Joyce and the Question of History* (Cambridge: Cambridge University Press, 1993).

Fergusson, John Duncan, 'A Note on the Decorations', in MacDiarmid, Hugh, *In Memoriam James Joyce* (Glasgow: William Maclellan, 1955), 10.

Ferris, Ina *The Achievement of Literary Authority: Gender, History, and the Waverley Novels* (Ithaca, NY and London: Cornell University Press, 1991).

——'The Historical Novel and the Problem of Beginning: The Model of Scott', *The Journal of Narrative Technique* 18.1 (1988), 73–82.

——'Narrating Cultural Encounter: Lady Morgan and the Irish National Tale', *Nineteenth-Century Literature* 51.3 (1996), 287–303.

——'Authorizing the Novel: Walter Scott's Historical Fiction', *The Oxford Handbook of the Eighteenth-Century Novel*, ed. Alan Downie (Oxford: Oxford University Press, 2016), 551–66.

Finneran, Richard J., ed., *The Yeats Reader: A Portable Compendium of Poetry, Drama, and Prose* (revised edition) (New York: Scribner, 2002).

Fitzpatrick, Benedict, *Ireland and the Making of Great Britain* (New York: Funk & Wagnalls, 1922).

Flanagan, Thomas, *The Irish Novelists, 1800–1850* (New York: Columbia University Press, 1959).

Flood, J.M., *Ireland: Its Saints and Scholars* (Dublin: The Talbot Press, 1917).

Fogarty, Anne, '"A Woman of the House": Gender and Nationalism in the Writings of Augusta Gregory', *Border Crossings: Irish Women Writers and National Identities*, ed. Kathryn Kirkpatrick (Tuscaloosa, AL and London: The University of Alabama Press, 2000), 100–22.

Foster, R.F., *Modern Ireland: 1600–1972* (London: Penguin, 1988).

——*W.B. Yeats: A Life. I: The Apprentice Mage 1865–1914* (Oxford: Oxford University Press, 1998).

——*The Irish Story: Telling Tales and Making It Up in Ireland* (London: Allen Lane, 2001).

——*On Seamus Heaney* (Princeton, NJ and Oxford: Princeton University Press, 2020).

Fowle, Frances, 'The Celtic Revival in Britain & Ireland: Reconstructing the Past, *c.* AD 1600–1920', *Celts: Art and Identity*, eds. Julia Farley and Fraser Hunter (London: The British Museum Press, 2015), 234–59.

Frawley, Oona, *Irish Pastoral: Nostalgia and Twentieth-Century Irish Literature* (Dublin and Portland, OR: Irish Academic Press, 2005).

Freedman, Carl, 'Beyond the Dialect of the Tribe: James Joyce, Hugh MacDiarmid, and World Language', *Hugh MacDiarmid: Man and Poet*, ed. Nancy K. Gish (Edinburgh: Edinburgh University Press/Orono, ME: National Poetry Foundation, 1992), 253–73.

Frykenberg, Brian, 'The "Death of the Wild-Man" in the Legend of Suibhne Geilt', *Buile Suibhne: Perspectives and Reassessments*, ed. John Carey (London: Irish Texts Society/ Cumann na Scríbheann nGaedhilge Subsidiary Series 26, 2014), 43–92.

Gairn, Louisa, 'MacDiarmid and Ecology', *The Edinburgh Companion to Hugh MacDiarmid*, eds. Scott Lyall and Margery Palmer McCulloch (Edinburgh: Edinburgh University Press, 2011), 82–96.

Garrigan Mattar, Sinéad, *Primitivism, Science, and the Irish Revival* (Oxford: Oxford University Press, 2004).

Gaskill, Howard, ed., *The Reception of Ossian in Europe* (London and New York: Thoemmes Continuum, 2004).

Geddes, Patrick, 'A Celtic Renascent. A Reply to the Celtic Revival', June 4, 1896, T-GED/5/2/2. Patrick Geddes Papers, University of Strathclyde Archives and Special Collections.

Gibb, Andrew Dewar, *Scotland in Eclipse* (London: Humphrey Toulmin, 1930).

Gibbons, Luke 'This Sympathetic Bond: Ossian, Celticism, and Colonialism', *Celticism*, ed. Terence Brown (Amsterdam and Atlanta, GA: Rodopi, 1996), 273–92.

——'From Ossian to O'Carolan: The Bard as Separatist Symbol', *From Gaelic to Romantic: Ossianic Translations*, eds. Fiona Stafford and Howard Gaskill (Amsterdam and Atlanta, GA: Rodopi, 1998), 226–51.

Gibson, Andrew, *Joyce's Revenge* (Oxford: Oxford University Press, 2002).

Gibson, George Cinclair, *Wake Rites: the Ancient Irish Rituals of Finnegans Wake* (Gainesville, FL: University Press of Florida, 2005).

Gillies, William, 'The Book of the Dean of Lismore: the Literary Perspective', *Fresche Fontanis: Studies in the Culture of Medieval and Early Modern Scotland*, eds. Janet Hadley Williams and J. Derrick McClure (Newcastle upon Tyne: Cambridge Scholars, 2013), 179–216.

Gish, Nancy, *Hugh MacDiarmid: The Man and His Work* (London and Basingstoke: The Macmillan Press Ltd, 1984).

Gish, Nancy and MacDiarmid, Hugh, 'An Interview with Hugh MacDiarmid', *Contemporary Literature* 20.2 (1979), 135–54.

Glen, Duncan, *Hugh MacDiarmid and the Scottish Renaissance* (Edinburgh and London: W. & R. Chambers, 1964).

Gogarty, Oliver St. John, 'Literature and Life: A Drunk Man Looks at the Thistle', *The Irish Statesman* 7.18, January 8 (1927), 432.

Gomes, Daniel, 'Reviving Oisin: Yeats and the Conflicted Appeal of Irish Mythology', *Texas Studies in Literature and Language* 56.4 (2014), 376–99.

Gontarski, S. E., *Beckett Matters: Essays on Beckett's Late Modernism* (Edinburgh: Edinburgh University Press, 2017).

Gregory, Lady, *Gods and Fighting Men* (London: John Murray, 1905).

——*Cuchulain of Muirthemne: The Story of the Men of the Red Branch of Ulster Arranged and Put into English by Lady Gregory with a Preface by W.B. Yeats* (London: John Murray, 1911).

——*Irish Folk-History Plays* (New York and London: G.P. Putnam's Sons, The Knickerbocker Press, 1912).

——*Our Irish Theatre: A Chapter of Autobiography by Lady Augusta Persse Gregory (1852–1932)* (New York and London: G.P. Putnam's Sons, The Knickerbocker Press, 1913).

——*Seventy Years: Being the Autobiography of Lady Gregory*, ed. Colin Smythe (New York: MacMillan, 1976).

——*Selected Plays* chosen and introduced by Mary FitzGerald (Gerrards Cross: Colin Smythe and Washington, D.C.: The Catholic University of America Press, 1983).

——*Lady Gregory's Diaries 1892–1902* ed. James Pethica (Gerrards Cross: Colin Smythe, 1996).

Grieve, C. M., *Albyn; Or Scotland and the Future* (London: K. Paul, Trench, Trubner & Co., Ltd.; New York: E. P. Dutton & Co., 1927).

Grieve, Dorian, 'MacDiarmid's Language', *The Edinburgh Companion to Hugh MacDiarmid*, eds. Scott Lyall and Margery Palmer McCulloch (Edinburgh: Edinburgh University Press, 2011), 23–35.

Gwynn, Stephen, *The History of Ireland* (London: Macmillan and Co., 1923).

Hague, Euan, Giordano, Benito, and Sebesta, Edward H., 'Whiteness, multiculturalism and nationalist appropriation of Celtic culture: the case of the League of the South and the Lega Nord', *Cultural Geographies* 12.2 (2005), 151–73.

Halloran, William F., 'W.B. Yeats, William Sharp, and Fiona Macleod: A Celtic Drama, 1897', *Yeats and the Nineties: Yeats Annual 14*, ed. Warwick Gould (Basingstoke and New York: Palgrave Macmillan, 2001), 159–208.

Halloran, William F., ed., *The Life and Letters of William Sharp and 'Fiona Macleod.' Vol. 2 1895–1899* (Cambridge: Open Book Publishers, 2020).

Hames, Scott, *The Literary Politics of Scottish Devolution: Voice, Class, Nation* (Edinburgh: Edinburgh University Press, 2019).

Harvie, Christopher, *A Floating Commonwealth: Politics, Culture, and Technology on Britain's Atlantic Coast, 1860–1930* (Oxford: Oxford University Press, 2008).

Heaney, Seamus *Death of a Naturalist* (London: Faber and Faber, 1966).

——*Door into the Dark* (London: Faber and Faber, 1969).

——*Wintering Out* (London: Faber and Faber, 1972).

——*North* (London and Boston, MA: Faber and Faber, 1975).

——'The God in the Tree', *Preoccupations: Selected Prose, 1968–1978* (London and Boston, MA: Faber and Faber, 1980), 181–9.

——'The Sense of Place', *Preoccupations: Selected Prose, 1968-1978* (London and Boston, MA: Faber and Faber, 1980), 131-49.

——Interview with Patrick Gallagher. 'Folio', RTÉ, November 22, 1983.

——*Sweeney Astray: A Version from the Irish* (Derry: Field Day, 1983).

——*Station Island* (London: Faber and Faber, 1984).

——'Seamus Heaney praises the Scottish poet Sorley MacLean', *London Review of Books* 8.19 (1986), n.p.

——'Earning a Rhyme', *The Art of Translation: Voices From the Field*, ed. Rosanna Warren (Boston, MA: Northeastern University Press, 1989), 13-19.

——'Introduction', *The Collected Poems of Padraic Fallon* (Oldcastle: Gallery Press, 1990), 11-20.

——*The Spirit Level* (London: Faber and Faber, 1996).

——'Burns's Art Speech', *Robert Burns and Cultural Authority*, ed. Robert Crawford (Iowa City, IA: University of Iowa Press, 1997), 216-33.

——*Finders Keepers: Selected Prose, 1971-2001* (London: Faber and Faber, 2002).

——'Burns's Art Speech', *Finders Keepers: Selected Prose, 1971-2001* (London: Faber and Faber, 2002), 347-63.

Hegglund, Jon, 'Hard Facts and Fluid Spaces', *Joyce, Imperialism, and Postcolonialism*, ed. Leonard Orr (Syracuse, NY: Syracuse University Press, 2008), 58-74.

Herbert, Máire, 'Celtic heroine? The archaeology of the Deirdre story', *Gender in Irish Writing*, eds. Toni O'Brien Johnson and David Cairns (Milton Keynes and Philadelphia: The Open University Press, 1991), 13-22.

Herbert, W. N., *To Circumjack MacDiarmid: The Poetry and Prose of Hugh MacDiarmid* (Oxford: Clarendon Press, 1992).

Herron, Tom, 'Mayo Littoral: Michael Longley's Eco-elegies', *New Hibernia Review/Iris Éireannach Nua* 14.4 (2010), 74-89.

Hewitt, John, *The Collected Poems of John Hewitt*, ed. Frank Ormsby (Belfast: Blackstaff Press, 1991).

Howes, Marjorie, *Yeats' Nations: Gender, Class, and Irishness* (Cambridge: Cambridge University Press, 1996).

——'Introduction', *Irish Literature in Transition, 1880-1940*, ed. Marjorie Howes (Cambridge: Cambridge University Press, 2020), 1-18.

Hutton, Clare, 'Joyce and the Institutions of Revivalism', *Irish University Review* 33.1 (2003), 117-32.

Hyde, Douglas, *A Literary History of Ireland from Earliest Times to the Present Day* (London: T. Fisher Unwin, 1899).

Innes, Sìm, and Mathis, Kate Louise, 'Gaelic tradition and the Celtic Revival in Children's Literature in Scottish Gaelic and English', *The Land of Story Books: Scottish Children's Literature in the Nineteenth Century*, eds. Sarah Dunnigan and Shu-Fang Lai (Glasgow: Scottish Literature International, 2019), 107-57.

Jackson, John Wyse and Costello, Peter, *John Stanislaus Joyce: The Voluminous Life and Genius of James Joyce's Father* (London: Harper Collins, 1997).

Jackson, Kenneth, 'The motive of the threefold death in the story of Suibhne Geilt', *Féilsgríbhinn Eóin Mhic Néill: Essays and studies presented to Professor Eoin MacNeill on the occasion of his seventieth birthday*, ed. John Ryan (Dublin: Three Candles, 1940), 535-50.

Jameson, Fredric, *A Singular Modernity* (London: Verso, 2002).

Johnston, Sheila Turner, *Alice: A Life of Alice Milligan* (Omagh: Colourpoint Press, 1994).

Jones, Catherine, 'History and Historiography', *The Edinburgh Companion to Walter Scott*, ed. Fiona Robertson (Edinburgh: Edinburgh University Press, 2012), 59-69.

Joyce, James *Finnegans Wake* (New York: Viking Press, 1939).

———*Letters of James Joyce Vol. I*, ed. Stuart Gilbert (New York: Viking Press, 1957).

———*A Portrait of the Artist as a Young Man* (New York: The Viking Press, 1964).

———*Dubliners* (New York: Viking Press, 1967).

———*Ulysses* (The Corrected Text), ed. Hans Walter Gabler (New York: Random House, 1986).

———*The Critical Writings of James Joyce* (Ithaca, NY: Cornell University Press, 1989).

———*Poems and Exiles*, ed. J.C.C. Mays (London: Penguin, 1992).

———*Occasional, Critical, and Political Writing* ed. Kevin Barry (Oxford: Oxford University Press, 2000).

———*The 'Finnegans Wake' Notebooks at Buffalo—VI.B.32*, eds., Vincent Deane, Daniel Ferrer, and Geert Lernout (Turnhout: Brepols, 2004).

Joyce, Stanislaus, *My Brother's Keeper* (London: Faber and Faber, 1958).

Jung, C. G., *The Collected Works, Volume Eighteen: The Symbolic Life*. Translated by R.F.C. Hull (London: Routledge and Kegan Paul, 1977).

Kearney, Richard, *Transitions: Narratives in Modern Irish Culture* (Dublin: Wolfhound, 1988).

Kerrigan, John, *Archipelagic English: Literature, History and Politics 1603-1707* (Oxford: Oxford University Press, 2008).

Kiberd, Declan, 'Joyce's Homer, Homer's Joyce', *A Companion to James Joyce*, ed. Richard Brown (Oxford: Blackwell, 2008), 241-53.

Kiberd, Declan and Mathews, P.J., *Handbook of the Irish Revival: An Anthology of Irish Cultural and Political Writings 1891-1922* (Notre Dame, IN: University of Notre Dame Press, 2016).

Kidd, Colin et al., 'Where Are We Now? Responses to the Referendum', *London Review of Books* 38.14 (2016), 8-15.

Kirkpatrick, Kathryn, 'Explanatory Notes', Owenson, Sydney (Lady Morgan), *The Wild Irish Girl*, ed. Kathryn Kirkpatrick (Oxford: Oxford University Press, 2008), 253-66.

Klein, Scott, 'National Histories, National Fictions: Joyce's *A Portrait of the Artist as a Young Man* and Scott's *The Bride of Lammermoor*', *ELH* 65.4 (1998), 1017-38.

Krielkamp, Vera, 'The Novel of the Big House', *The Cambridge Companion to the Irish Novel*, ed. John Wilson Foster (Cambridge: Cambridge University Press, 2006), 60-77.

Kristmannsson, Gauti, 'Ossian and the State of Translation', *The International Companion to James Macpherson and the Poems of Ossian*, ed. Dafydd Moore (Glasgow: Scottish Literature International, 2017), 39-51.

Kroeg, Susan M., ' "So near to us as a Sister": Incestuous Unions in Sydney Owenson's *The Wild Irish Girl* and Maria Edgeworth's *The Absentee*', *Anglo-Irish Identities 1571-1845*, eds. David A. Valone and Jill Marie Bradbury (Lewisburg, PA: Bucknell University Press, 2008), 220-37.

Larrissy, Ed., 'Introduction', In Yeats, W.B. *The First Yeats: Poems by W.B. Yeats, 1889-1899*, Unrevised texts, ed. Ed Larrissy (Manchester: Carcanet, 2010).

Lawrence, Karen, *The Odyssey of Style in Ulysses* (Princeton, NJ: Princeton University Press, 1981).

Leask, Nigel, 'Fingalian Topographies: *Ossian* and the Highland Tour, 1760-1805', *Journal for Eighteenth-Century Studies: Forum on Ossian in the Twenty-First Century* 39.2 (2016), 183-96.

———'Sir Walter Scott's *The Antiquary* and the *Ossian* Controversy', *Yearbook of English Studies* 47 (2017), 189-202.

Leeney, Cathy, *Irish Women Playwrights 1900-1939: Gender and Violence on Stage* (New York: Peter Lang, 2010).

Leerssen, Joep, 'Celticism', *Celticism*, ed. Terence Brown (Amsterdam and Atlanta, GA: Rodopi, 1996), 1–20.

——*Remembrance and Imagination: Patterns in the Historical and Literary Representation of Ireland in the Nineteenth Century* (Notre Dame, IN: Notre Dame University Press, 1997).

——'Ossian and the Rise of Literary Historicism', *The Reception of Ossian in Europe*, ed. Howard Gaskill (London and New York: Thoemmes, 2004), 109–25.

Lehner, Stefanie, *Subaltern Ethics in Contemporary Scottish and Irish Literature* (London: Palgrave, 2011).

——'Devolutionary States: Crosscurrents in Contemporary Irish and Scottish Fiction', *The Oxford Handbook of Modern Irish Fiction*, ed. Liam Harte (Oxford: Oxford University Press, 2020), 479–96.

Lennon, Joseph, *Irish Orientalism: A Literary and Intellectual History* (Syracuse, NY: Syracuse University Press, 2004).

Levitas, Ben, *The Theatre of Nation: Irish Drama and Cultural Nationalism* (Oxford: Oxford University Press, 2002).

Lincoln, Andrew. *Walter Scott and Modernity* (Edinburgh: Edinburgh University Press, 2007).

Lloyd, David, *Nationalism and Minor Literature: James Clarence Mangan and the Emergence of Irish Cultural Nationalism* (Berkeley, CA: University of California Press, 1987).

——*Anomalous States: Irish Writing and the Post-Colonial Moment* (Dublin: Lilliput Press, 1993).

Longley, Edna, 'Introduction', *Modern Irish and Scottish Poetry*, eds. Peter Mackay, Edna Longley, and Fran Brearton (Cambridge: Cambridge University Press, 2011), 1–19.

Lukács, Georg, *The Historical Novel* (London: Merlin, 1962).

Lyall, Scott, *Hugh MacDiarmid's Poetry and Politics of Place: Imagining a Scottish Republic* (Edinburgh: Edinburgh University Press, 2006).

——'Hugh MacDiarmid and the Scottish Renaissance', *The Cambridge Companion to Scottish Literature*, eds. Gerard Carruthers and Liam McIlvanney (Cambridge: Cambridge University Press, 2012), 173–87.

Lyall, Scott and McCulloch, Margery Palmer, eds., *The Edinburgh Companion to Hugh MacDiarmid* (Edinburgh: Edinburgh University Press, 2011).

Mac Craith, Mícheál, ' "We Know All These Poems": the Irish Response to *Ossian*', *The Reception of Ossian in Europe*, ed. Howard Gaskill (London and New York: Thoemmes Continuum, 2004), 91–108.

MacDiarmid, Hugh (C. M. Grieve), *At the Sign of the Thistle: A Collection of Essays* (London: Stanley Nott, 1934).

——*The Islands of Scotland: Hebrides, Orkneys, and Shetlands*. London: B. T. Batsford Ltd., 1939.

——*Lucky Poet: A Self-Study in Literature and Political Ideas, Being the Autobiography of Hugh MacDiarmid* (London: Methuen & Company, Limited, 1943).

——*In Memoriam James Joyce* (Glasgow: William Maclellan, 1955).

——*The Uncanny Scot* (London: MacGibbon & Kee, 1968).

——*Selected Essays of Hugh MacDiarmid*, ed. Duncan Glen (London: Jonathan Cape, 1969).

——*The Letters of Hugh MacDiarmid*, ed. Alan Bold (London and Athens, GA: Hamish Hamilton/University of Georgia Press, 1984).

——*Selected Poetry*, ed. Alan Riach and Michael Grieve (Manchester: Carcanet, 1992).

——*Selected Prose*, ed. Alan Riach (Manchester: Carcanet, 1992).

———*Scottish Eccentrics*, ed. Alan Riach (Manchester: Carcanet, 1993).

———*The Raucle Tongue: Hitherto Uncollected Prose* (in three vols.), eds. Angus Calder, Glen Murray, and Alan Riach (Manchester: Carcanet, 1996, 1997, 1998).

———*Complete Poems Vol. I* eds. Michael Grieve and W. R. Aitken (Manchester: Carcanet, 2017).

MacDonagh, Thomas, *Literature in Ireland* (Dublin: Talbot Press, 1916).

Macdonald, Murdo, 'The visual dimension of *Carmina Gadelica*', *The Life and Legacy of Alexander Carmichael*, ed. Domhnall Uilleam Stiùbhart (Port of Ness: The Islands Book Trust, 2008), 135–45.

Mackay, Peter 'The Gaelic Tradition', *The Cambridge Companion to Scottish Literature*, eds. Gerard Carruthers and Liam McIlvanney (Cambridge: Cambridge University Press, 2012), 117–31.

———' "From Optik to Haptik": Celticism, Symbols and Stones in the 1930s', *British Literature in Transition, 1920–1940: Futility and Anarchy*, eds. Charles Ferrall and Dougal McNeill (Cambridge: Cambridge University Press, 2018), 275–90.

Mackenzie, Henry, ed., *Report of the Committee of the Highland Society of Scotland into the nature and authenticity of the Poems of Ossian* (Edinburgh: Archibald Constable & Co., 1805).

MacLean, Sorley (MacGill-Eain, Somhairle), *Caoir Gheal Leumraich/A White Leaping Flame: Collected Poems in Gaelic with English Translations* eds. Christopher Whyte and Emma Dymock (Edinburgh: Polygon, 2011).

Macleod, Fiona (William, Sharp), *The Sin-Eater and Other Tales* (Edinburgh: Patrick Geddes & Colleagues/Chicago: Stone & Kimball, 1895).

———*The Washer of the Ford: Legendary Moralities and Barbaric Tales* (Edinburgh: Patrick Geddes and Colleagues, 1896).

———*The Laughter of Peterkin: A Retelling of Old Tales of the Celtic Wonderland* (London: Archibald Constable & Co., 1897).

———'A Group of Celtic Writers', *Fortnightly Review* N.S. 65 (1899), 34–53.

———*The House of Usna: A Drama by Fiona Macleod* (Portland Maine: Thomas B Moshner, 1903).

———*From the Hills of Dream: Threnodies, Songs and Later Poems* (London: William Heinemann, 1907).

———*Pharais: A Romance of the Isles* (New York: Duffield & Company, 1907).

———*Winged Destiny: Studies in the Spiritual History of the Gael* (London: William Heinemann, 1910).

MacNeill, Eoin, 'The Re-Discovery of the Celts', *The Irish Review* 3.34 (1913), 522–32.

———*Phases of Irish History* (Dublin: M.H. Gill & Son, Ltd, 1920).

Macpherson, James, *The Poems of Ossian and Related Works*, ed. Howard Gaskill (Edinburgh: Edinburgh University Press, 1996).

Marlowe, Lara, 'WB Yeats: Papers confirm bones sent to Sligo were not poet's', *Irish Times* online, July 18, 2015.

Marzaroli, Oscar, *Hugh MacDiarmid: No Fellow Travellers* (Glasgow: Ogam Films, 1972).

Mathews, P.J., *Revival: The Abbey Theatre, Sinn Féin, The Gaelic League and the Co-Operative Movement* (Notre Dame, IN: Notre Dame University Press, 2003).

Mathis, Kate Louise, 'An Irish Poster Girl? Writing Deirdre during the Revival', *Romantic Ireland: From Tone to Gonne; Fresh Perspectives on Nineteenth-Century Ireland*, eds. Paddy Lyons, Willy Maley, and John Miller (Newcastle upon Tyne: Cambridge Scholars Publishing, 2013), 263–80.

——'Mourning the Maic Uislenn: Blood, Death & Grief in Longes Mac n-Uislenn & Oidheadh Chloinne hUisneach.' *Scottish Gaelic Studies* 29 (2013), 1–21.

McCarthy, Conor, *Seamus Heaney and Medieval Poetry* (Dublin: D.S. Brewer, 2008).

McCulloch, Margery Palmer, ed., *Modernism and Nationalism: Literature and Society in Scotland, 1918–1939; Source Documents for the Scottish Renaissance* (Glasgow: Association for Scottish Literary Studies, 2004).

McCulloch, Margery Palmer, 'Scottish Modernism', *The Oxford Handbook of Modernism*, eds. Peter Brooker, Andrzej Gąsiorek, Deborah Longworth, and Andrew Thacker (Oxford: Oxford University Press, 2010), 765–81.

McCulloch, Margery Palmer, and Matthews, Kirsten, 'Transcending the Thistle in *A Drunk Man* and *Cencrastus*', *The Edinburgh Companion to Hugh MacDiarmid*, eds. Scott Lyall and Margery Palmer McCulloch (Edinburgh: Edinburgh University Press, 2011), 48–67.

McDonald, Rónán, 'The Irish Revival and Modernism', *The Cambridge Companion to Irish Modernism*, ed. Joe Cleary (Cambridge: Cambridge University Press, 2014), 51–62.

McGrath, Anthony, 'An Agon with the Twilighters: Samuel Beckett and the Primacy of the Aesthetic', *Irish University Review* 42.1 (2012), 6–23.

McIlvanney, Liam and Ryan, Ray. 'Introduction', *Ireland and Scotland: Culture and Society, 1700–2000*, eds. Liam McIlvanney and Ray Ryan (Dublin: Four Courts, 2005), 1–22.

McNaughton, James, 'Beckett, German Fascism, and History: the Futility of Protest', *Samuel Beckett Today/Aujourd'hui* 15 (2005), 101–16.

Meek, Donald E., 'The Gaelic Ballads of Scotland: Creativity and Adaption', *Ossian Revisited*, ed. Howard Gaskill (Edinburgh: Edinburgh University Press, 1991), 19–48.

Mercier, Vivian, 'The Morals of Deirdre', *Yeats Annual No. 5*, ed. Warwick Gould (London: Macmillan, 1987), 224–31.

Miller, Cecilia, *Enlightenment and Political Fiction: The Everyday Intellectual* (New York and London: Routledge, 2016).

Miller, Julie Anne, 'Acts of Union: Family Violence and National Courtship in Maria Edgeworth's *The Absentee* and Sydney Owenson's *The Wild Irish Girl*', *Border Crossings: Irish Women Writers and National Identities*, ed. Kathryn Kirkpatrick (Tuscaloosa, AL and London: The University of Alabama Press, 2000), 13–37.

Milligan, Alice, *Hero Lays* (Dublin: Maunsel and Co., 1908).

——*Poems* selected and edited with an introduction by Henry Mangan (Dublin: M.H. Gill and Son Ltd., 1954).

Mitchell, Sebastian, 'Ossian: Past, Present and Future', *Journal for Eighteenth-Century Studies* 39.2 (2016), 159–70.

——'Landscape and the Sense of Place in Macpherson's Ossian', *The International Companion to James Macpherson and the Poems of Ossian*, ed. Dafydd Moore (Glasgow: Scottish Literature International, 2017), 65–75.

Mooney, Sinéad, 'Kicking against the Thermolaters: Beckett's "Recent Irish Poetry"', *Samuel Beckett Today/Aujourd'hui* 15 (2005), 29–42.

Moore, Dafydd, '"A Comparison Similar to This": Ossian and the Forms of Antiquity', *Journal for Eighteenth-Century Studies* 39.2 (2016), 171–82.

——'Introduction', *The International Companion to James Macpherson and the Poems of Ossian*, ed. Dafydd Moore (Glasgow: Scottish Literature International, 2017), 1–13.

Moran, D. P., *The Philosophy of Irish Ireland* (Dublin: James Duffy & Co., 1905).

Morris, Catherine. 'Alice Milligan: Republican Tableaux and the Revival', *Field Day Review* 10 (2010), 133–65.

Muir, Edwin, *Collected Poems 1921–1958* (London: Faber and Faber, 1960).

Muir, Willa, *Imagined Selves* (Edinburgh: Canongate, 1996).

Mullin, Katherine, 'Typhoid Turnips and Crooked Cucumbers: Theosophy in *Ulysses*', *Modernism/modernity* 8.1 (2001), 77–97.

Murray, Christopher, *Twentieth-Century Irish Drama: Mirror up to Nation* (Syracuse, NY: Syracuse University Press, 2000).

Nagai, Kaori, '"'Tis optophone which ontophanes": race, the modern and Irish revivalism', *Modernism and Race*, ed. Len Platt (Cambridge: Cambridge University Press, 2011), 58–76.

Nagle, Christopher, 'From Owenson to Morgan: History, Sensibility, and the Vagaries of Reception in *The Wild Irish Girl*', *Anglo-Irish Identities 1571–1845*, eds. David A. Valone and Jill Marie Bradbury (Lewisburg, PA: Bucknell University Press, 2008), 199–219.

Ní Dhonnchadha, Máirín, Introduction to 'Gormlaith and her Sisters, c. 750–1800', *The Field Day Anthology of Irish Writing Vol. IV: Irish Women's Writing and Traditions*, eds. Angela Bourke et al (Cork: Cork University Press in association with Field Day, 2002), 166–249.

——'The Cult of St Moling and the Making of *Buile Shuibne*', *Buile Suibhne: Perspectives and Reassessments*, ed. John Carey (London: Irish Texts Society/Cumann na Scríbheann nGaedhilge Subsidiary Series 26, 2014), 1–42.

Ní Mhunghaile, Lesa, '*Ossian* and the Gaelic World', *The International Companion to James Macpherson and the Poems of Ossian*, ed. Dafydd Moore (Glasgow: Scottish Literature International, 2017), 26–38.

Nic Eoin, Máirín, 'Secrets and Disguises? Caitlín Ní Uallacháin and other female personages in eighteenth-century Irish political poetry', *Eighteenth-Century Ireland/Iris an dá chultúr* 11 (1996), 7–45.

O Hehir, Brendan, *A Gaelic Lexicon for Finnegans Wake, and Glossary for Joyce's Other Works* (Berkeley, CA: University of California Press, 1967).

Ó Broin, Tomás, 'Lia Fail: Fact and Fiction in Tradition', *Celtica* 21 (1990), 393–401.

Ó Dónaill, Niall, *Foclóir Gaeilge-Béarla* (Baile Átha Cliatha: An Gúm, 1977).

Ó Fiannachta, Pádraig, 'The Development of the Debate between Pádraig and Oisín', *Béaloideas*, 54/55 (1986/1987), 183–205.

Ó Gallchoir, Cliona, 'Celtic Ireland and Celtic Scotland: Ossianism and the *Wild Irish Girl*', *Scotland, Ireland, and the Romantic Aesthetic*, eds. David Duff and Catherine Jones (Lewisburg, PA: Bucknell University Press, 2007), 114–30.

Ó Riain, Pádraig, 'A Study of the Irish Legend of the Wild Man', *Buile Suibhne: Perspectives and Reassessments*, ed. John Carey (London: Irish Texts Society/Cumann na Scríbheann nGaedhilge, Subsidiary Series 26, 2014), 172–201.

O'Conor, Charles, *Dissertations on the History of Ireland: to Which is Subjoined, a Dissertation on the Irish Colonies Established in Britain. With Some Remarks on Mr. Mac Pherson's Translation of Fingal and Temora* (Dublin: G Faulkner, 1766).

O'Curry, Eugene, ed. and tr., 'The "Tri Thruaighe na Scéalaigheachta" (i.e. the "Three Most Sorrowful Tales",) of Erinn. – I. "The Exile of the Children of Uisnech"', *The Atlantis* 3:4 (1862), 377–422.

O'Donoghue, Josie, 'The Politics of Metaphor in Heaney's *Sweeney Astray*', *Irish University Review* 47 (2017), 450–69.

O'Driscoll, Dennis, *Stepping Stones: Interviews with Seamus Heaney* (London: Faber and Faber, 2009).

O'Flanagan, Theophilus, 'Derdri, or the Lamentable Fate of the Sons of Usnach; an Ancient and Dramatic Irish Tale, One of the Three Tragic Stories of Erin; Literally Translated into English from an Original Gaelic MS, with Notes and Observations; to Which Is

Annexed the Old Historic Account of the Facts on Which the Story Is Founded', *Transactions of the Gaelic Society of Dublin* 1 (1808), 1–236.

O'Gallagher, Niall, 'Ireland's eternal Easter: Sorley MacLean and 1916', *Irish Studies Review* 24.4 (2016), 441–54.

O'Hagan, Andrew, 'The Excursions: Andrew O'Hagan travels with Seamus Heaney and Karl Miller', *London Review of Books* 33.12 (2011), 23–8.

O'Halloran, Clare, 'Irish Re-Creations of the Gaelic Past: the Challenge of Macpherson's *Ossian*', *Past & Present* 124.1 (1989), 69–95.

——*Golden Ages and Barbarous Nations; Antiquarian Debate and Cultural Politics in Ireland, c.1750–1800* (Cork: Cork University Press in association with Field Day, 2004).

O'Keeffe, J.G. *Buile Shuibhne (The Frenzy of Suibhne): Being the Adventures of Suibhne Geilt. A Middle-Irish Romance edited with Translation, Introduction, Notes, and Glossary* (London: The Irish Texts Society/David Nutt, 1913).

O'Looney, Brian (ed.), 'Tir na nÓg: the land of youth', *Transactions of the Ossianic Society* 4 (1859), 227–79.

O'Reilly, J., 'Notes on the Coronation Stone at Westminster, and the "Lia Fail" at Tara', *The Journal of the Royal Society of Antiquaries of Ireland*. 32.1 (1902), 77–92.

Owenson, Sydney, *Twelve Original Hibernian Melodies with English Words, Imitated and Translated from the Works of Ancient Irish Bards* (London: Preston, 1805).

——*The Wild Irish Girl* edited with an introduction by Kathryn Kirkpatrick. (Oxford: Oxford University Press, 2008).

Parrinder, Patrick, *Nation and Novel: The English Novel from its Origins to the Present Day* (Oxford: Oxford University Press, 2006).

Perloff, Marjorie, *Unoriginal Genius: Poetry by Other Means in the New Century* (Chicago, IL and London: Chicago University Press, 2010).

Pethica, James, 'Yeats, Folklore, and Irish Legend', *The Cambridge Companion to W. B. Yeats*, eds. Marjorie Howes and John Kelly (Cambridge: Cambridge University Press, 2006), 129–43.

Pinkerton, John, *A Dissertation on the Origin and Progress of the Scythians or Goths: Being an Introduction to the Ancient and Modern History of Europe* (London: John Nichols, 1787).

——*An Enquiry Into the History of Scotland: Preceding the Reign of Malcolm III. Or the Year 1056. Including the Authentic History of that Period. In Two Volumes. Vol. I* (Edinburgh: James Ballantyne and Co., 1814).

Pittock, Murray, *Celtic Identity and the British Image* (Manchester and New York: Manchester University Press, 1999).

——*Scottish and Irish Romanticism* (Oxford: Oxford University Press, 2008).

Platt, Len, *Joyce, Race and Finnegans Wake* (Cambridge: Cambridge University Press, 2007).

——'"Unfallable encyclicing": *Finnegans Wake* and the *Encyclopedia Britannica*', *James Joyce Quarterly* 47.1 (2009), 107–18.

Pocock, J. G. A., *The Discovery of Islands: Essays in British History* (Cambridge: Cambridge University Press, 2005).

Pope, Rachel, 'Re-approaching Celts: Origins, Society, and Social Change', *Journal of Archaeological Research* (2021), 1–67.

Porter, James '"Bring Me the Head of James Macpherson": The Execution of *Ossian* and the Wellsprings of Folkloristic Discourse', *The Journal of American Folklore* 114.454 (2001), 396–435.

——*Beyond Fingal's Cave: Ossian in the Musical Imagination* (Rochester, NY: University of Rochester Press, 2019).

Power, Arthur, *Conversations with James Joyce* ed. Clive Hart (London: Millington, 1974).

Rabaté, Jean-Michel, *Joyce upon the Void: The Genesis of Doubt* (London: Macmillan, 1991).

Raleigh, John Henry, '*Ulysses* and Scott's *Ivanhoe*', *Studies in Romanticism* 22.4 (1983), 569–86.

Regan, Stephen, 'Seamus Heaney and the Making of *Sweeney Astray*', *Hungarian Journal of English and American Studies* 21.2 (2015), 317–39.

Renan, Ernest, *The Poetry of the Celtic Races and Other Studies* tr. William G. Hutchinson (Port Washington, NY: Kennikat, 1970).

Riach, Alan, *Hugh MacDiarmid's Epic Poetry* (Edinburgh: Edinburgh University Press, 1991).

Robertson, Fiona, *Legitimate Histories: Scott, Gothic, and the Authorities of Fiction* (Oxford: Clarendon Press, 1994).

Robichaud, Paul, 'MacDiarmid and Muir: Scottish Modernism and the Nation as Anthropological Site', *Journal of Modern Literature* 28.4 (2005), 135–51.

Roche, Anthony, 'The Irish "Translation" of Samuel Beckett's *En Attendant Godot*', *The Edinburgh Companion to Samuel Beckett and the Arts*, ed. S.E. Gontarski (Edinburgh: Edinburgh University Press, 2014), 199–208.

Rodgers, Vincentia, *Cluthan and Malvina; an Ancient Legend. With Other Poems* (Belfast: F.D. Finlay, 1823).

Rolston, Bill, *Drawing Support: Murals in the North of Ireland* (Belfast: Beyond the Pale, 1992).

——*Drawing Support 2: Murals of War and Peace* (Belfast: Beyond the Pale, 1995).

——*Drawing Support 3: Murals and Transition in the North of Ireland* (Belfast: Beyond the Pale, 2003).

Ross, Raymond J., 'Marx, MacDiarmid and MacLean', *Sorley MacLean—Critical Essays*, Raymond J. Ross and Joy Hendry (Edinburgh: Scottish Academic Press, 1986), 91–107.

Ryan, Ray, *Ireland and Scotland: Literature and Culture, State and Nation, 1966–2000* (Oxford: Oxford University Press, 2002).

Sassi, Carla, 'Hugh MacDiarmid's (Un)making of the Modern Scottish Nation', *The Edinburgh Companion to Hugh MacDiarmid*, eds. Scott Lyall and Margery Palmer McCulloch (Edinburgh: Edinburgh University Press, 2011), 111–24.

Scott, Walter, 'Laing's Edition of Macpherson / Report of the Highland Society upon Ossian', *Edinburgh Review* (July 6, 1805), 429–62.

——*The Miscellaneous Prose Work of Sir Walter Scott, Bart. Vol. VIII. Life of Napoleon Buonaparte, with a Preliminary View of the French Revolution, Vol. VI* (Edinburgh: Robert Cadell, 1835).

——*The Minstrelsy of the Scottish Border* in 4 vols (Edinburgh: Richard Cadell, 1849).

——*The Journal of Walter Scott*, ed. W. E. K. Anderson (Oxford: Clarendon Press, 1972).

——'General Preface', In Lamont, Claire, ed. *Waverley* (Oxford: Oxford University Press, 1981).

——*The Antiquary*, ed. Nicola Watson (Oxford: Oxford University Press, 2002).

——*Waverley; Or, 'Tis Sixty Years Since*, ed. Claire Lamont (Oxford: Oxford University Press, 2008).

Senn, Fritz, 'Ossianic Echoes', *A Wake Newslitter* 3.2 (1966), 25–36.

Sharp, Elizabeth A., *William Sharp (Fiona Macleod): A Memoir* (New York: Duffield and Company, 1910).

Sharp E. A. and Matthay, J. eds., *Lyra Celtica: An Anthology of Representative Celtic Poetry* (Edinburgh: John Grant, 1924).

Sharp, William, *The Human Inheritance, The New Hope, Motherhood* (London: Elliot Stock, 1882).

——*The Gipsy Christ and Other Tales* (Chicago, IL: Stone and Kimball, 1895).

——'Introductory Note', Macpherson, James, *The Poems of Ossian translated by James Macpherson, with notes, and with an introduction by William Sharp* (Edinburgh: Patrick Geddes and Colleagues, 1896), ix–xxiv.

——'Introduction', *Lyra Celtica: An Anthology of Representative Celtic Poetry*, eds. E. A. Sharp and J. Matthay (Edinburgh: John Grant, 1924), xix–li.

Shaw, Michael, *The Fin-de-Siècle Scottish Revival: Romance, Decadence and Celtic Identity* (Edinburgh: Edinburgh University Press, 2019).

Simon, Fabrizio, 'Adam Smith and Gaetano Filangieri: Two Alternative Faces of the Enlightenment Science of the Legislator', *The Adam Smith Review*, 10 (2017), 41–72.

Smith, Adam, *Lectures on Jurisprudence*, eds. R.L. Meek, D.D. Raphael, and P.G. Stein. Vol. V of the Glasgow Edition of the Works and Correspondence of Adam Smith (Indianapolis, IN: Liberty Fund, 1982).

Smith, Craig, *Adam Smith's Political Philosophy: The Invisible Hand and Spontaneous Order* (New York and London: Routledge, 2006).

St Clair, William, *The Reading Nation in the Romantic Period* (Cambridge: Cambridge University Press, 2004).

Stafford, Fiona, *The Sublime Savage: A Study of James Macpherson and the Poems of Ossian* (Edinburgh: Edinburgh University Press, 1988).

——'Introduction: The Ossianic Poems of James Macpherson', Macpherson, James. *The Poems of Ossian and Related Works*, ed. Howard Gaskill (Edinburgh: Edinburgh University Press, 1996), v–xviii.

——'Romantic Macpherson', in Murray Pittock, ed., *The Edinburgh Companion to Scottish Romanticism* (Edinburgh: Edinburgh University Press, 2011), 27–38.

Stiùbhart, Domhnall Uilleam, 'Alexander Carmichael and *Carmina Gadelica*', *The Life and Legacy of Alexander Carmichael*, ed. Domhnall Uilleam Stiùbhart (Port of Ness: The Islands Book Trust, 2008), 1–39.

Stokes, W.H. and Windisch, E., eds., *Irische Texte mit Übersetzungen und Wörterbuch* (Leipzig: Verlag Von. S. Hirzel, 1887).

Stone, Harry, ' "Araby" and the Writings of James Joyce', *The Antioch Review* 25.3 (1965), 375–410.

Stroh, Silke, *Gaelic Scotland in the Colonial Imagination: Anglophone Writing from 1600 to 1900* (Evanston, IL: Northwestern University Press, 2017).

Sturgeon, Sinéad, 'Night Singer: Mangan among the Birds', in Sinéad Sturgeon, ed., *Essays on James Clarence Mangan* (Basingstoke: Palgrave Macmillan, 2014), 102–23.

Sutherland, Kathryn, 'Fictional Economies: Adam Smith, Walter Scott and the Nineteenth-Century Novel', *ELH* 54.1 (1987), 97–127.

Swinson, Ward, 'Macpherson in *Finnegans Wake*', *A Wake Newslitter* 9.5 (1972), 89–95.

Synge, J. M., *Collected Works, Vol. II, Prose*, ed. Alan Price (London: Oxford University Press, 1966).

——*Collected Works Vol. III, Plays, Book I*, ed. Ann Saddlemyer (Gerrards Cross: Colin Smythe, 1982).

——*The Aran Islands* (London: Penguin, 1992).

Thomson, George Malcolm, *Caledonia: Or the Future of the Scots* (London: Kegan Paul, 1927).

Thuente, Mary Helen, *The Harp Re-strung: The United Irishmen and the Rise of Irish Literary Nationalism* (Syracuse, NY: Syracuse University Press, 1994).

Torchiana, Donald T., 'Joyce's "Two Gallants": A Walk through the Ascendancy', *James Joyce Quarterly* 6.2 (1969), 115–27.

Trumpener, Katie, 'National Character, Nationalist Plots: National Tale and Historical Novel in the Age of *Waverley*, 1806-1830', *ELH* 60.3 (1993), 685–731.

——*Bardic Nationalism: The Romantic Novel and the British Empire* (Princeton, NJ: Princeton University Press, 1997).

——'Ireland, Scotland, and the politics of form', *Ireland and Scotland: Culture and Society, 1700-2000*, eds. Liam McIlvanney and Ray Ryan (Dublin: Four Courts, 2005), 164–82.

Tynan, Katharine, *Peeps at Many Lands: Ireland* (London: Adam and Charles Black, 1911).

——*The Middle Years* (Boston, MA and New York: Houghton Mifflin Company, 1917).

Watson, George, 'Celticism and the Annulment of History', *Celticism*, ed. Terence Brown (Amsterdam and Atlanta, GA: Rodopi, 1996), 207–20.

——'Aspects of Celticism', *Ireland and Scotland: Culture and Society, 1700-2000*, eds. Liam McIlvanney and Ray Ryan (Dublin: Four Courts, 2005), 129–43.

——'Yeats, Victorianism, and the 1890s', *The Cambridge Companion to W. B. Yeats*, eds. Marjorie Howes and John Kelly (Cambridge: Cambridge University Press, 2006), 36–58.

Watson, Roderick, 'MacDiarmid and International Modernism', *The Edinburgh Companion to Hugh MacDiarmid*, eds. Scott Lyall and Margery Palmer McCulloch (Edinburgh: Edinburgh University Press, 2011), 6–22.

Welch, Robert, 'Lady Gregory: Talking with the Dead', *The Princeton University Library Chronicle* 68.1/2 (2007), 125–41.

Weller, Shane, ' "Some Experience of the Schizoid Voice." Samuel Beckett and the Language of Derangement', *Forum for Modern Language Studies* 45.1 (2008), 32–50.

Whyte, Christopher, *Modern Scottish Poetry* (Edinburgh: Edinburgh University Press, 2004).

——'Introduction', Sorley MacLean (Somhairle MacGill-Eain), *Dàin do Eimhir/Poems to Eimhir* ed. Christopher Whyte (Edinburgh: Polygon, 2007), 1–41.

Williams, Daniel G., *Ethnicity and Cultural Authority: From Arnold to Du Bois* (Edinburgh: Edinburgh University Press, 2006).

Williams, Mark, *Ireland's Immortals: A History of the Gods of Irish Myth* (Princeton, NJ and Oxford: Princeton University Press, 2016).

Wilson, Susan R, ed., *The Correspondence Between Hugh MacDiarmid and Sorley MacLean: An Annotated Edition* (Edinburgh: Edinburgh University Press, 2010).

Wright, William, *The Comical History of the Marriage-Union Betwixt Fergusia and Heptarchus* (Edinburgh: Robert Brown, 1717).

Yeats, W.B., 'The Literary Movement in Ireland', *The North American Review* 169.517 (1899), 855–67.

——*The Celtic Twilight* (London: A. H. Bullen, 1902).

——*Essays and Introductions* (New York: Macmillan, 1961).

——*Uncollected Prose Vol. I: First Reviews and Articles, 1886-1896* ed. John P. Frayne (London: Macmillan, 1970).

——*Uncollected Prose Vol. II: Reviews, Articles, and Other Miscellaneous Prose, 1897-1939* eds. John P. Frayne & Colton Johnson (London: Macmillan, 1975).

——Preface to the First Edition of *The Well of the Saints*, J. M. Synge, *Collected Works Vol. 3: Plays Book 1*, ed. Ann Saddlemyer (Gerrards Cross: Colin Smythe, 1982).

——*The Collected Letters of W.B. Yeats Volume I: 1865-1895* ed. John Kelly (Oxford: Clarendon Press, 1986).

——*The Poems*. ed. Daniel Albright (London: Everyman, 1994).

——*Selected Plays* ed. Richard Allen Cave (London: Penguin, 1997).

——*The Collected Letters of W.B. Yeats Volume II: 1896-1900* eds. Warwick Gould, John Kelly, and Deirdre Toomey (Oxford: Clarendon Press, 1997).

——*The Collected Works of W.B. Yeats Vol. III: Autobiographies*, eds. William H. O'Donnell and Douglas N. Archibald (New York: Scribner, 1999).

——*The Collected Works of W.B. Yeats Vol. IX: Early Art: Uncollected Articles and Reviews Written Between 1886 and 1900*, eds. John P. Frayne and Madelaine Marcheterre (New York: Scribner, 2004).

——*The First Yeats: Poems by W.B. Yeats, 1889–1899*. Unrevised texts, ed. Ed Larrissy (Manchester: Carcanet, 2010).

Young, Ella, *Poems* (Dublin: Maunsel & Co., 1906).

——*The Wonder Smith and His Sons: A Tale from the Golden Childhood of the World* (New York, London, and Toronto: Longmans, Green and Co, 1927).

——*The Tangle-Coated Horse and Other Tales: Episodes from the Fionn Saga* (New York and Toronto: Longmans, Green and Co, 1929).

Index

For the benefit of digital users, indexed terms that span two pages (e.g., 52–53) may, on occasion, appear on only one of those pages.

Abbey Theatre 54n.61, 130n.49
Aberdeen 129–30, 130n.49
Act of Union, 1703 147–8
Act of Union, 1800 22, 150
Aengus Óg 47n.28
Ailsa Craig 127, 128n.38, 133–5, 143–4
Anglican Church 13
Anglocentrism 2
Anglophilia 106–7
Anglophobia 106–7, 107n.90
Antrim, Co. 58, 60, 124–8, 127n.34, 131
Aran Islands 30–1, 51, 51n.44, 128
Armagh, Co. 58–9
Arnold, Matthew 10–13, 15, 19, 27–30, 34,
    42, 47–8, 55, 104–6, 123–4, 123n.20,
    139, 141
Atlantic archipelago 2, 3n.8, 5–10, 5n.18,
    32–3, 33n.70
Ayrshire 132–3

Balfour, Arthur 34–5, 83n.38, 143
Balfour, Mary 17–18
Barra 67n.124, 68n.132
'Bàs Chonlaoich' 36–7
Beckett, Samuel 22, 31–2, 38–42
    'Censorship in the Saorstat' 40
    En Attendant Godot 40
    'Fingal' 40
    More Pricks than Kicks 40, 130n.49
    Murphy 31–2, 38–42
    'Recent Irish Poetry' 39–40
Belfast 18, 18n.80, 75–6, 130–1, 133
Bergson, Henri 34–5, 83n.38, 143
Berkeley, George 34–5, 83n.38, 143
Berwick 130–2, 143–4
Blackie, John Stuart 14, 14n.63
    *Scottish Highlanders and the Land
    Laws, The* 14

Blair, Hugh 25–6, 25n.23
Blarney Castle 75–6
Bloody Friday, 1972 126n.33, 130–1
Bloody Sunday, 1972 126n.33, 130–1
Breton/Bretons 7–8, 7n.30, 8n.31, 12–13,
    34n.80, 47–8, 71n.142
British Army 107n.90, 117n.128
British Empire 31, 89–90, 95, 106–7, 145–6
British State 3, 30–1, 31n.60, 38, 141,
    145–6
Britons 6–7, 8n.31, 128n.38
Brooke, Charlotte 21
    Reliques of Irish Poetry 21
Bruce, Robert the 3n.10
Buchanan, George 7
Buile Suibhne 115, 120–38
Bundoran 130–2, 143–4
Bunting, Edward 21
    *General Collection of the Ancient Music
    of Ireland* 21
Burns, Robert 5, 25n.20, 34n.81

Caledonians 22n.7
Calvinism 50n.40, 66–7, 67n.124, 129–30
Cameron, Alexander/Cameron of Brodick
    49, 62n.106, 69, 69nn.134,138
Campbell, John Francis/Campbell of
    Islay 49
Carlyle, Thomas 5, 13n.58, 44n.6,
    96–7, 120
Carmichael, Alexander 44n.6, 49, 62n.106,
    68–70, 140–1
Carmichael, Ella 73n.149
Carson, Ciaran 121–2, 136nn.76,79
Catholicism 3, 13n.58, 15, 15n.72, 27, 46,
    50, 50n.40, 53–4, 67n.124, 94–5, 94n.6,
    97–9, 97n.26, 121, 125–6, 130n.49
Celtae 6n.27, 7–8

Celtic 'fringe' 5–6, 5n.18
Celtic Football Club 13n.58, 94n.6
Celtic languages 3–4, 7–11, 10n.42, 34–5, 124, 132
Celtic Revival(s) 1–2, 2n.4, 14–19, 22, 27–8, 30–1, 33, 40, 45–6, 46n.15, 49–50, 51n.41, 52–5, 57, 60n.91, 70–4, 93, 95, 100–2, 113–14, 129, 137–8, 141, 144–6, 149–50, 149n.25
Celtic/Saxon binary 10–13, 25–8, 30–1, 33–5, 42, 104–7, 105n.75, 123–4, 142
Celticism, early 8–9, 8n.32, 16–17, 22, 30–1, 37–8, 73–4, 124, 136–7, 139–50
Celticism, late 107–8, 139–50
Celts (ancient) 6–8, 6n.27, 88–9
Christianity 7, 10, 49–50, 97n.26, 123–5
Church of Scotland 94–5
    Menace of the Irish Race to Our Scottish Nationality, The 94–5
Clann Albain 95n.12
Coimín, Mícheál/Comyn, Micheal 22, 28, 28n.43, 97n.23
    Laoi Oisin i dTír na nÓg 22
Colmcille/Colm Cille/Columba 21n.1, 132–3
Colum, Mary 15
Communism 98–9
Comunn Gàidhealach, An 14, 98n.33
Concobar/Conchobar/Conchubar 58–9, 60n.91, 68, 127n.34
Connolly, James 15, 15n.70, 66, 66n.121, 94, 94n.5, 107n.90, 113–19
Conradh na Gaeilge 14
Coole Park 52, 52n.46, 128
Cork, Co. 75–6
Corkery, Daniel 95
    Hidden Ireland 95
Cornish 71n.142
Crofters' Party 13
Cromwell, Oliver 27n.30, 47n.28
Cúchulainn/Cú Chulainn/Cuchulainn/ Cuchulain 40, 68n.132, 122–3, 125n.26
Culloden, Battle of 8–9, 22–3, 38, 84, 150
Cymri/Cymric 7n.30, 12–13, 47–9

D'Annunzio, Gabriele 61
Dál Riata/Dal Riada 126n.32, 131, 131n.54
de Blácan, Aodh 95
    Gaelic Literature Surveyed 95

de Jubainville, Marie Henri d'Arbois 6n.27, 12–13, 12n.52
de Valera, Éamon 94, 100–1
Deirdre/Deirdrê/Derdri 55n.66, 57–74, 140–1
Dervorgilla 67
Diarmuid/Dermid 62n.106, 93n.3
Down, Co. 124–8
Drogheda 75–6
Dublin 23–4, 40, 43, 50n.38, 70–1, 71n.142, 75–6, 81–2, 91, 93, 108, 116–18, 117n.128, 120, 130n.51, 137n.82, 140–1, 149–50
Duncan, John 60n.91
Dundee 3–4
Dunseverick 126, 133n.65

Easter Rising, 1916. 93, 107n.90, 117–19, 137
Edgeworth, Maria 5, 75–7, 79, 82–3
Edinburgh 3–4, 17–18, 45–6, 47n.21, 69n.134, 70–1, 80n.23
Edinburgh, University of 14, 25n.23, 83–4
Eliot. T. S. 38, 106, 120–2
    Waste Land, The 38, 120–1
England 2–6, 3nn.9,10, 8–9, 11–13, 13n.58, 14n.65, 22, 24, 27, 28n.38, 30–3, 31n.60, 34n.81, 43, 47–8, 51, 54n.63, 56n.70, 71, 82–3, 105–7, 124n.22, 128, 131–2, 139, 142, 145–8, 146n.15, 150
Evergreen, The 14, 45, 101n.49, 140–1

Fenian Brotherhood/Fenianism 13n.59, 28, 28nn.38,42, 75
Fenian literature/an Fhiannaíocht 3–5, 5n.17, 21, 21n.1, 25n.25, 93n.3, 125n.29, 139
Ferguson, Adam 83–4, 84n.40
Ferguson, Samuel 12–13, 55n.66
    Congal 12–13
Fergusson, John Duncan 99–100
Ferris, William 95
    Gaelic Commonwealth, The 95
Finlay, Ian 124
    Introduction to Celtic Art 124
Fionn mac Cumhaill/Finn McCool 21, 32–3, 40, 53–4, 85–7, 120, 122–3
FitzPatrick, Bernard 70–1
Fournier d'Albe, Edmund Edward 70–1
Frazer, James 44n.6, 71

Gaelic Athletic Association 14
Gaelic League 49, 126
Gaelic Union 14
Gaidoz, Henri 12–13
Galatae/Galatai/Galli 6n.27
Galway, Co. 51, 58, 128
Gauls 6–8, 7n.30
Geddes, Patrick 14, 32n.62, 45, 45n.12,
    47n.21, 54n.57, 101–2, 101n.49, 140–1
Germanic/Teutonic 9, 9n.38, 55–7,
    88–9, 141
Gibb, Andrew Dewar 94–5
    Scotland in Eclipse 94–5
Gladstone, William 13, 13n.59
Glasgow 3–4, 13n.58, 80n.23, 148
Glenmasan/Glenn Masáinn
    manuscript 69, 69n.138
Gogarty, Oliver St. John 32n.65, 100–1,
    100n.44
Gonne, Maud 12n.52, 46, 51, 94, 120–1
Gore-Booth, Eva 60
    Buried Life of Deirdre, The 60
Gothic literature 79n.19
Goths 88–9
Grania/Grainne 67, 67n.126
Gregory, Augusta 1–2, 5n.18, 15, 17,
    19–20, 34–5, 43–74, 93–4, 137–8,
    140–1, 144–5
    Cuchulain of Muirthemne 59, 67–8,
    67nn.128,129, 73–4
    Irish Folk History Plays 67n.126
    Our Irish Theatre 43n.2, 44–5,
    54n.63, 60n.89
    Seventy Years 54n.62
Grieve, Christopher Murray (see also
    MacDiarmid, Hugh) 93, 93n.3,
    95n.15, 97n.26, 100n.45, 107n.90

Heaney, Seamus 1–2, 5n.18, 19–20, 47n.28,
    66, 70–1, 73–4, 93, 103–4, 110,
    110n.104, 115, 120–38, 143–50
    'Broagh' 123n.18
    'Digging' 128
    'Granite chip' 129–30
    'Mossbawn' 127
    North 121–2, 130n.51
    'North' 130n.51
    'Omphalos' 127
    'Personal Helicon' 128
    'Postscript' 128

Spirit Level, The 128
Station Island 128
'Station Island' 129–30
Sweeney Astray: A Version from the
    Irish 5n.18, 66, 73–4, 115, 120–38,
    143–6
'Sweeney Redivivus' 5n.18, 120–1, 128,
    137, 137n.81
Wintering Out 123n.18, 135–6
Hebrides 17–18, 30–1, 39, 41–2,
    41nn.125,126, 46
Hecataeus of Miletus 6
Henry, P.H. 124
    Early English and Celtic Lyric, The 124
Hewitt, John 15–16
Highland Land League 13
Hogg, James 83n.38, 120, 147
    Private Memoirs and Confessions of a
    Justified Sinner, The 83n.38
Hopper, Nora 45n.11, 46
Hubert, Henri 99n.38
    The Greatness and Decline of the
    Celts 99n.38
Hume, David 33n.70, 34–5, 34n.81, 83,
    83n.37, 84n.40, 108, 110, 110n.107,
    114, 143, 147–8
Hyde, Douglas 14–16, 45n.11, 49, 52,
    55n.66, 62n.106, 68, 69n.134,
    123n.18, 140–1

Ireland, North of 2–5, 14, 18–19, 58,
    114–17, 120–38, 143–6, 148, 150
Ireland, Partition of 38, 145–6, 150
Ireland, Republic of 3n.9, 150
Ireland, West of 24, 26–7, 51–2, 71,
    128–9, 143–4
Irish (language) 3–5, 7–8, 15n.72, 26,
    30–1, 34–5, 34n.80, 54n.62, 55n.66,
    64n.112, 98n.28, 99n.40, 111–12, 115,
    118, 123n.18, 132, 135–6, 135n.74
Irish Famine 3–4, 13, 30–1, 88, 150
Irish Free State/Saorstát Éireann 31n.60,
    40, 77, 145–6
Irish Literary Society 14, 49, 51n.41, 53–4
Irish Literary Theatre 15, 18n.80, 43–5,
    43n.3, 53–4, 140–1
Irish, Middle 135–6
Irish, Old 3–4
Irish Republican Army (Provisional) 121–2,
    122n.12, 148

Irish Revival 1–2, 2n.4, 5, 7–9, 12–14,
    12n.52, 15n.72, 16–21, 30–1, 33n.75,
    34–5, 39, 43n.1, 44n.6, 47–8, 57, 60,
    60n.87, 68, 72n.146, 73, 94n.5, 106–7,
    123n.18, 129, 136–8, 140–2, 144–6
Irish Texts Society 122n.15, 126

Jacobite Rebellion/Jacobites 5, 9n.38,
    30n.54, 40–1, 81–2, 84–5, 92, 147–8
Joyce, James 1–2, 5–6, 19–20, 22, 30–8,
    40–2, 41n.125, 66, 70–1, 72n.145,
    73–92, 98–114, 119–22, 125, 128–30,
    131n.54, 137n.81, 139–50
  'Aeolus' 29n.46, 108
  'An Encounter' 81
  'Anna Livia Plurabelle' 99n.40
  'Araby' 81–3
  'Cyclops' 32–3, 77, 80–1
  Dubliners 75, 81–3, 87, 110, 143
  'Eumaeus' 108–9
  Exiles 34–5
  Finnegans Wake 19–20, 31–8, 31n.61, 40,
    41n.125, 42, 60n.91, 73–5, 80–1, 83,
    85–9, 99n.40, 103–4, 104n.66, 107–8,
    110–12, 110n.107, 114, 118–19, 121–2,
    131n.54, 137n.81, 139–43, 145–6
  'Gas from a Burner' 79n.20
  'Holy Office, The' 80n.27
  'Ireland: Island of Saints and Sages' 79n.20
  'Little Cloud, A' 33, 143
  'Nestor' 85n.49
  Portrait of the Artist as a Young Man,
    A 75, 77–81, 87, 91n.77
  'Realism and Idealism in English
    Literature' 86
  'Scylla and Charybdis' 78
  Stephen Hero 80n.23
  'Two Gallants' 91–2
  Ulysses 29n.46, 32–3, 75, 77–8, 80,
    85n.49, 86–7, 86n.55, 100n.45, 102–4,
    104n.66, 108–9, 120–2
  Work in Progress 99n.40, 137n.81
Joyce, Stanislaus 77, 80–1, 91
  My Brother's Keeper 77, 80–1
Jung, Carl 39, 42

Keltoi 6n.27
Killiecrankie, Battle of 40–1
Kiltartan/Kiltartanese 67–8, 94n.5,
    136–7, 145

Kintyre 127, 131–2
Knox, Robert 13n.58

Laing, Malcolm 41n.125
Land Act, 1870 13
Leabhar Buide Leacain 58
Lebor Laignech 58
Lhuyd, Edward 7–8, 7n.30
  Archaeologia Britannica 7–8
Lia Fáil/Lia Fàil 36, 115, 116n.124, 118–19,
    118n.138
Loch Fyne 17–18, 61–2
Lockhart, John Gibson 75–6
London 1n.1, 10, 38–9, 47n.28,
    51n.41, 53–4, 60, 60n.92, 67–8,
    93n.1, 140–2
  Longes mac n-Uislenn 58, 64
Longford, Co. 75–6
Lowlanders (Scottish) 3–4, 9, 9n.38,
    13n.58, 84–5, 131
Lukács, Georg 88

Mac Diarmada, Seán 93
MacDiarmid, Hugh (Christopher Murray
    Grieve) 1–2, 4, 5n.18, 19–20, 30–2,
    50n.40, 66–7, 70–1, 73–4, 93–120,
    120n.1, 129–30, 130nn.49,52,
    139–45, 148–50
  'Bonnie Broukit Bairn, The' 112–13
  Circumjack Cencrastus, To 5n.18,
    50n.40, 95–9, 105, 139–40
  'Direadh I' 101
  'Direadh III' 98–9
  Drunk Man Looks at the Thistle, A
    100n.44, 103
  In Memoriam James Joyce 5n.18, 11,
    19–20, 73–4, 98n.29, 99–114,
    129–30, 141–2
  'Kind of Poetry I Want, The' 101n.46,
    104–5
  'Lament for the Great Music' 97n.21
  'On a Raised Beach' 102, 130n.50
  'Water Music' 99n.40
  'Watergaw, The' 109–10
MacDonagh, Thomas 15, 16n.73
Macdonald, Frances 46n.15
Macdonald, Margaret 46n.15
MacDonell, Alice 49–50
Mackintosh, Charles Rennie 46n.15
Maclean, John 105n.74, 118, 118n.137

MacLean, Sorley (MacGill-Eain, Somhairle) 19–20, 66, 97–8, 98n.28, 113–20, 137, 137n.82
  'Aig Uaigh Yeats' 113–14, 113n.119
  'Àrd Mhusaeum na hÈireann' 113–19
  Dàin do Eimhir 117–18, 118n.135
Macleod, Fiona (William Sharp) 1–2, 5n.18, 17, 19–20, 22n.5, 30–1, 43–74, 93, 136–7, 139–41
  'Cry on the Wind, A' 62n.109
  'Dan-nan-Ron, The' 51n.44
  'Deirdrê is Dead' 62–6
  From the Hills of Dream 62, 62n.109
  Gipsy Christ, The 65n.116
  Green Fire: A Romance 61–2
  House of Usna, The 60–2, 67–8, 140–1
  Laughter of Peterkin, The 61–2
  Washer of the Ford, The 51n.44
  Winged Destiny 54, 106–7
Macneil, John 68nn.132,133, 70n.139
MacNeill, Eoin 7, 8n.31
Macpherson, James 1–3, 5n.18, 8–9, 12, 17–19, 21–42, 44n.6, 45–6, 53–4, 55n.66, 59, 70–1, 80n.21, 89–90, 90n.74, 96–8, 96n.16, 102, 136–7, 139–40, 144–5
  'Battle of Lora, The' 35n.90
  'Carric-Thura' 35n.90
  'Cath-loda' 35n.90
  'Cathlin of Clutha' 35n.90
  'Colna-dona' 35n.90
  'Comala' 35n.90
  'Conlath and Cuthona' 35n.90
  'Croma' 35n.90
  'Death of Cuthullin, The' 35n.90
  Fingal 1n.2, 8–9, 23–4, 35–6, 35n.89, 41–2, 41n.126
  Fragments of Ancient Poetry 1–2, 1n.2, 8–9, 23
  'Lathmon' 35n.90
  'Oina-moral' 35n.90
  'Songs of Selma, The' 35n.90
  Temora 1n.2, 8–9, 22n.7, 23–4, 35–6, 35n.89, 41–2, 41n.126
  'War of Caros, The' 35n.90
  'War of Inis-thona, The' 35n.90
Martyn, Edward 43, 43n.3, 52–3
Marzaroli, Oscar 93n.3
  No Fellow Travellers 93n.3

Mathers, Moina 51
Mathers, Samuel Liddell MacGregor (Samuel Liddell) 1–2, 51, 93
Maturin, Charles 77, 90n.74
  The Milesian Chief 77, 90n.74
Meyer, Kuno 12–13, 49, 55n.66
Milligan, Alice 17–18, 18n.80
Moira, Co. Down 126
Moore, Thomas 25n.20
  Irish Melodies 25n.20
Moran, D.P. 15–16, 15n.72
  Philosophy of Irish Ireland, The 15–16
Mulholland, Rosa 45n.11

Naois/Naoise 58–60, 64, 65n.115, 68n.133, 69, 127n.34
National Mòd/Highland Mod 14, 49
National Party of Scotland 95n.12
Ní Shéaghdha, Nessa 118n.135
Ní Uallacháin, Caitlín/Ni Houlihan, Kathleen 47–8, 47n.28, 67
Nobel Prize in Literature 147

O'Brien, Flann (Brian O'Nolan) 40, 149
  At Swim-Two-Birds 40
O'Connell, Daniel 13, 30–1
O'Conor, Charles 23–4, 139
O'Curry, Eugene 59, 62n.106, 64, 64n.111, 69n.134
O'Flanagan, Theophilus 29, 59, 69n.134
  Deirdri 29
O'Grady, Standish James 44n.6, 45n.11, 49, 52, 140–1
O'Halloran, Sylvester 8–9, 21
  An Introduction to the Study of the History and Antiquities of Ireland 21
O'Keeffe, J.G. 122, 122n.15, 123n.18, 126–7, 128n.38, 130–4, 134n.67, 136–7, 143–4
O'Looney, Brian 22, 28, 28n.43
Ogham 99–100
Oireachtas na Gaeilge 14
Orange, William of 47n.28, 91, 91n.78
Orientalism 10n.41
Orkney 39, 41–2, 41nn.125,126, 130nn.51,52
Ossian/Oisín/Ussian 8–9, 14n.64, 18–19, 18n.84, 21–6, 21n.1, 25n.20, 32–3, 53–4, 80, 120
Ossianic Society of Dublin 29

Owenson, Sydney 1–2, 5n.18, 17, 19–20, 22, 24–8, 30–1, 37, 51, 53–4, 71, 77, 79, 83, 90–1, 90n.74, 139
  Wild Irish Girl, The 5n.19, 22, 24–7, 37–8, 42, 51, 70, 77, 90–1, 90n.74, 139

Pan-Celtic Congress 70–1, 71n.142
Pan-Celtic Society 14, 71
Pan-Celticism 8n.31, 16–17, 40–1, 45nn.7,11,14, 57, 70–2, 97n.23
Parnell, Charles Stewart/Parnellism 75, 77, 147–8
Pearse, Patrick 4, 15, 33, 34n.80, 47n.28, 117n.131, 118, 146n.15
  'Mise Éire' 47n.28
Pezron, Paul-Yves 7–8, 7n.30
  Antiquité de la nation et de la langue des Celtes 7–8
Picts 3–4, 88–9, 88n.67, 131n.54
Pinkerton, John 9, 88–9
  Dissertation on the Origins and Progress of the Scythians 88–9
Plaid Cymru 31n.60
Plunkett, Joseph Mary 15
Pocock, J.G.A. 2–4, 7–8
  Discovery of Islands, The 2–3
Polybius 6n.27
Poseidonius 6–7
Postcolonial theory 19–20
Postmodernism 42n.131
Pound, Ezra 38, 40, 106, 130n.49
Power, Arthur 81–2
Presbyterianism 45n.14, 50, 50n.40, 55n.67, 94–5, 130n.49
Protestant Action Society 94–5
Protestant Ascendancy 91
Protestant Reformation 9n.40, 50n.40, 97–8, 97n.26
Protestantism 3, 12–13, 27, 50n.40, 53–4, 66–7, 67n.124, 91, 94–5, 115, 117n.127, 124–6, 129–30, 130n.49, 143–4
Psychoanalysis 22, 31

Rangers Football Club 94n.6
Rasharkin 126
Renan, Ernest 10–13, 47–8
Revue Celtique 12–13, 69n.134
Rinder, Edith 48, 48n.31

Rodgers, Vincentia 17–18
Roman Empire 3–4, 3n.8
Romanticism 1–2, 17, 22–3, 22n.6, 30–1, 30n.54, 39, 81–3, 92, 136–7, 145–6
Royal Irish Academy 122n.15
RTÉ 123–6
Russell, George (Æ) 43n.3, 46–7, 49, 54, 60, 93–4
  Deirdre 60

Said, Edward 10n.41
Salmond, Alex 149–50, 149n.24
Saxon/Anglo-Saxon 10–11, 14, 25–8, 30–1, 33–4, 42, 56, 104–6, 105n.75, 123–4, 130n.51, 142
Scandinavia 15, 41n.126, 121–2
Scott, Anne 75–6
Scott, Walter 1–2, 4–5, 19–20, 26n.26, 27–8, 27n.31, 41n.125, 44n.6, 45n.14, 75–92, 96–7, 112–13, 119, 128, 143, 147–8
  Abbot, The 81–3
  Antiquary, The 26n.26, 88–9, 88n.67
  Bride of Lammermoor, The 77–8, 80–1, 80n.21, 91n.77
  Ivanhoe 44n.6, 78
  Kenilworth 78
  Lady of the Lake 80–1
  Lay of the Last Minstrel 44n.6
  Life of Napoleon Buonaparte 78
  Minstrelsy of the Scottish Border 88n.67
  Peveril of the Peak 78
  Rob Roy 84n.42
  Waverley 27n.31, 76, 81–4, 81n.30, 86–90, 128, 148
  Woodstock 78
Scottish Enlightenment 9n.38, 18n.81, 82–4, 89–90, 143, 147–8
Scottish Gaelic 3–5, 7–9, 8n.34, 18–20, 22, 30–1, 33n.70, 35n.89, 37, 49–50, 50n.40, 55n.66, 65–6, 68, 68n.133, 70, 72n.146, 94n.5, 95n.13, 97–8, 98nn.28,29, 100n.42, 111n.111, 114, 117n.127, 130–2
Scottish Highlanders 9, 16, 34n.81, 44n.6
Scottish Highlands/Highlands and Islands 1–4, 8–9, 14n.63, 49, 49n.32, 61–2, 68n.132, 81–2, 91, 128
Scottish Historical Society 14n.62
Scottish Liberal Association 13

Scottish National Party 148–50, 149n.24
Scottish National Portrait Gallery 14n.62
Scottish Protestant League 94–5
Scottish Revival/Renaissance 1–2, 2n.4,
    12–13, 16–17, 22n.5, 31n.60, 50n.40,
    73n.149, 93, 95n.15, 97–8, 101–2,
    141, 144–5
Scottish Text Society 14n.62
Scotus/Scoti 3–4
Sean Bhean Bhocht/Shan Van Vocht 47–8,
    47n.28
Shakespeare, William 60n.92, 61, 78,
    120–1
Sharp, Elizabeth 29n.46, 48n.31, 49–51,
    53–4, 55n.66, 71–2, 71n.142
    Lyra Celtica 29n.46, 53–6, 55n.66, 65
    Memoir, A 48n.31, 49, 71n.142, 72
Sharp, William (*see also* Macleod, Fiona)
    14n.62, 17, 22n.5, 29n.46, 43–74,
    127n.34, 139–41, 144–5
Shepherd, Nan 19
Shetland 39, 41–2, 41nn.125,126,
    101n.49, 102
Sigerson, George 49
'Silent, O Moyle' 91, 91n.77
Sinn Féin 95n.12, 150
Skene, W.F. 14
    Celtic Scotland 14
Sligo, Co. 113n.119, 122n.15, 128
Smith, Adam 75, 83–6, 88, 143, 147–8
    Lectures on Jurisprudence 84, 143
    Wealth of Nations 83–4
Socialism/Socialist 15, 95, 112, 116–19,
    118n.137
Society for the Preservation of the Irish
    Language 14
Stephens, James 60n.91
    Deirdre 60n.91
Stevenson, Robert Louis 83n.38, 97
    *Strange Case of Dr Jekyll and
    Mr Hyde* 83n.38
Stewart, Dugald 83–4
Stokes, Whitley 12–13, 49, 69,
    69nn.134,138
    Irische Texte 68–9, 69nn.134,138
Sweeney 66, 120–38, 143–4
Synge, J.M. 51n.44, 60, 60n.90, 71, 94,
    128–9, 130n.49, 136–7
    Aran Islands, The 51n.44

Deirdre of the Sorrows 60, 60n.90
*Playboy of the Western World,
    The* 130n.49

Tara, Hill of 36, 115, 116n.124, 118–19,
    137n.82
Thomson, George Malcolm 94–5, 95n.8
    Caledonia 94–5
Times Literary Supplement 103–4
Traquair, Phoebe 73n.149
Treaty of Limerick 91n.78
Troubles, The 116–17, 121–2, 122n.12,
    125n.26, 129–31, 137–8, 145–8, 150
Tuatha Dé Danann 50
Tulira Castle 51–3, 58
Tynan, Katharine 17–18, 45n.11,
    140–1

Ulster 9, 17–18, 40–1, 41n.126, 45n.14,
    58–9, 116–17, 116n.124,
    117nn.127,131, 121, 124–6, 124n.22,
    131–2, 134–5
Ulster Cycle 3–4, 17–18, 23, 57–8
Ulster Plantation 3–4, 88–9, 117n.127,
    131–2, 137, 143–4
Unionism 12–13, 50n.40, 54–7, 55n.66,
    71–2, 75, 91, 124–6, 143–4, 150
United Irishmen/United Irish Rebellion
    12–13, 22, 30n.54, 40–1

Vico, Giambattista 75, 86, 86n.53
    Scienza Nuova, La 86

Wales 3n.10, 5–6, 5n.18, 9, 10n.42, 13n.59,
    49, 55n.66, 56n.70, 66–7, 72, 95,
    101n.46, 105–6, 124n.22, 128, 150
Walker, Joseph Cooper 21
    Historical Memoirs of the Irish Bards 21
Welsh (language) 7–8, 8n.31, 10n.42,
    56n.70, 94n.5, 110–11
Wicklow, Co. 130–1
Wilde, Oscar 32–3, 32n.69
Windisch, Ernst 12–13, 49, 69,
    69nn.134,138
    Irische Texte 68–9, 69nn.134,138
World War I 148–9
World War II 98n.29, 117
Wright, William 47–8
    The Comical History 47–8

Yeats, J.B. 44n.6
Yeats, W.B. 1–2, 4, 12n.52, 14–16,
    19–20, 22, 28–35, 34n.81, 37,
    39–43, 43n.3, 44n.6, 45–9,
    45nn.7,11,14, 46n.20, 51–4,
    51nn.41,44, 54n.61, 55n.66, 56–7,
    59–62, 60nn.89,90, 67n.128, 68,
    71–4, 71n.142, 88–9, 93–5, 100–1,
    100n.44, 106–7, 112–14, 113n.119,
    119–21, 123, 128, 130n.49, 136–7,
    139–45, 147–8
  'Celtic Element in Literature, The' 29–30

Deirdre 60, 60n.89
  King's Threshold, The 60n.89
  On Baile's Strand 67n.128
  'Rose of Battle, The' 29
  Shadowy Waters, The 60–1
  Trembling of the Veil, The 1, 1n.1, 48
  'Wanderings of Oisin, The' 15, 28,
    28nn.42,43, 123, 139
Young, Ella 18–19
  The Tangle-Coated Horse 18
  The Wonder Smith and His Sons 18
Young Ireland 12–14